EVALUATION IN DISTANCE EDUCATION AND E-LEARNING

Evaluation in Distance Education and E-Learning

THE UNFOLDING MODEL

Valerie Ruhe
Bruno D. Zumbo

THE GUILFORD PRESS
New York   London

© 2009 The Guilford Press
A Division of Guilford Publications, Inc.
72 Spring Street, New York, NY 10012
www.guilford.com

Printed in the United States of America

This book is printed on acid-free paper.

Last digit is print number: 9   8   7   6   5   4   3   2   1

Library of Congress Cataloging-in-Publication Data
Ruhe, Valerie.
   Evaluation in distance education and e-learning : the unfolding model /
Valerie Ruhe, Bruno D. Zumbo.
      p. cm.
   Includes bibliographical references and index.
   ISBN 978-1-59385-872-8 (pbk.: alk. paper) — ISBN 978-1-59385-873-5
(hardcover: alk. paper)
   1. Distance education—Evaluation.   2. Computer-assisted instruction—
Evaluation.   3. Web-based instruction—Evaluation.   I. Zumbo, Bruno D.
II. Title.
   LC5800.R84 2009
   378.1′75—dc22
                                                            2008028535

Preface

This book is dedicated to the memory of Sam Messick and is an expression of our esteem for his remarkable contribution to our understanding of validity. A distinguished research scientist at the Educational Testing Service, Messick debated the merits of his four-faceted conception of validity with measurement scholars for more than 10 years. The consequential basis of validity seemed to be the area of greatest contention (Green, 1998; Reckase, 1998a), and there are not a great number of applications of Messick's (1989) framework in its original context: standardized testing. Empirical studies of consequential validity include Cizek's (2001) work on high-stakes tests and Jones, Jones, and Hargrove's (2003) work on achievement tests. Although Popham (1997) believed consequential validity was the "right concern" but the "wrong concept," his recent work gives an extensive list of the unintended consequences of mandated standardized testing under the No Child Left Behind legislation (Popham, 2004).

This book had its origins in a mixed-methods project at the University of British Columbia to evaluate distance courses. One day, it became clear that the themes that kept emerging from the data analysis were the same themes found in the four facets of Messick's (1989) framework. Although this insight seemed like a revelation, it is less surprising in hindsight because Messick's framework is a comprehensive conception of merit and worth or value, and "value" is the heart of evaluation (Wolf, 1987). We and other authors have found Messick's framework to be useful and appropriate as a model to guide studies in both program evaluation and test validity (Ruhe, 2002, 2003; Ruhe & Zumbo, 2006). Chapelle, Jamieson, and Hegelheimer (2003) have also used an adapted version of Messick's framework to guide evaluation studies of distance programs.

Finally, Bunderson's (2003) validity-centered design is an adaptation of Messick's framework into a model of cyclical course design and evaluation.

Why Do We Need Evaluation?

Program evaluation is an important component of successful distance education (Martinez, Liu, Watson, & Bichelmeyer, 2006) and e-learning instructional programs. We are living in a time of rapidly changing technology and course delivery structures, rising stakeholder expectations, and increasing competition as more providers enter these expanding markets. This context creates an ongoing need for continuous improvement, course updates, and blending of new technologies and pedagogies. This is where evaluation fits in. "Every time we try something new, it is important to consider its value" (Davidson, 2005). Evaluation is a systematic investigation to determine the merit and worth of a set of activities. The root of the word "evaluation" is *value*. Educational evaluation is "an enquiry which sets out to explore some educational program, system, project or event in order to focus on its worthiness" (Bassey, 1999, p. 63). There are many reasons to evaluate e-learning courses, including to determine whether course objectives are being achieved, to justify investments, to make better decisions, and "to buy, license or build particular courses" (Horton, 2001, p. 2). We believe that the best evaluation studies are *comprehensive*: that is, they provide insights into (1) the process or course implementation; (2) *all* effects, intended and unintended, positive and negative; and (3) underlying values. Armed with this information, course designers can then identify specific areas for course improvement, work the "bugs" out of their courses, tweak existing materials, and add more and better technologies and technological features. In this respect, the evaluation process may be "more important than the data it gathers if it strengthens efforts to apply knowledge" (Horton, 2001, p. 2).

Why Do We Need a Professional Approach to Evaluation?

Evaluation is highly political, and stakeholders can wield considerable influence in terms of what questions are asked, which data are collected, and how these data are interpreted. In distance education, evaluation theory and practice have, by and large, been done by distance educators, the very people responsible for the success of distance courses. To be more credible, evaluation practice should be based on a professional approach (i.e., an approach based on the literature of professional program evaluation) and the science of educational measurement and assessment. In the literature of distance education, there have been recurring calls for a professional approach to program evaluation but uncertainty as to what this approach would look like. In this book, we propose the unfolding model, a professional approach rooted in the history of evaluation theory in distance education and e-learning.

What Are the Special Features of This Book?

There are several unique features of this book. First, we explain why evaluation is so important for distance education and e-learning. In a time of rapid technological change, evaluation studies provide valuable information about how well a course is working and which areas are in need of improvement. Moreover, as we shift from distance education to e-learning, the pedagogical paradigm will shift dramatically, thereby creating even more need for professional evaluations of innovative e-learning courses or revisions of traditional courses for new technologies. Second, we offer a comprehensive evaluation model that can be adapted and tailored to local needs. Third, we offer practice tools and strategies for conducting evaluations. Fourth, we show results from test-driving this model in two authentic courses: a distance course and an e-learning course. Finally, readers should note that words in bold in the text indicate the first text discussion of words in the Glossary (see Appendix B).

What Is a Professional Approach to Evaluation?

This book responds to the recurring calls for a professional approach to program evaluation in distance education and spells out the features of this approach. First, a professional approach is based on contemporary theory from the field of professional program evaluation. We explain why evaluators need to understand the major theoretical paradigms that shape research methods and evaluation practice (Mertens, 2004).

   An evaluation model is a set of theoretical concepts that serve as a road map to guide evaluation practice. We would never think of driving across the country without a good map. Similarly, you need an evaluation model to guide you when you evaluate a course. Without a model, you risk getting lost, missing important information, and being unduly influenced by the conflicting demands of stakeholders (Stufflebeam & Shinkfield, 2007).

This book, then, compares evaluation models in distance education with those of program evaluation and shows that models in both fields differ in their relative emphasis on three recurring themes in professional program evaluation: scientific evidence, underlying values, and unintended consequences. We also show that Messick's (1989) framework of test validity is really an omnibus program evaluation model because it encompasses scientific evidence, values, and consequences.

The Unfolding Model
An Adaptive Approach

The real power of the unfolding model, an adaptation of Messick's (1989) framework, is that it is comprehensive, dynamic, and adaptive to diverse course designs and technologies. The unfolding model can be applied to all different kinds of technologies and delivery modes. Evaluators can pick and choose from among the tools presented to tailor the evaluation to their own local needs. This feature is important because technology is constantly evolving. The paradigm shift from Web 1.0 to 2.0, in particular, has huge implications for evaluation practice. Our framework is not only comprehensive but also adaptive, dynamic, and responsive to constantly evolving technologies and the new e-learning environments under "Web 2.0 and beyond" (Sinclair, McClaren, & Griffin, 2006).

Practical Guidelines and Tools

After an in-depth overview of the unfolding model, we then address the practical, providing step-by-step guidelines and tools for conducting evaluation studies. We discuss what evaluators need to do before they begin evaluation studies and provide strategies for dealing with stakeholders and tools for collecting data. We show how to use the model to write surveys and interview protocols, provide guidelines for high-quality surveys and protocols, collect data online, analyze and blend mixed-methods data, and provide a template for writing reports.

Two Authentic Case Studies

In Chapter 8, we take the unfolding model on a "test drive" with data from two authentic postsecondary courses. Computing Science 200 is a distance computer-based training course, whereas Professional Writing 110 is an e-learning course. These two case studies show that the unfolding model is practical and easy to use to guide "real" evaluation studies, and leads to rich and informative findings and specific recommendations for course improvement. Finally, in the last chapter, we encourage readers to adapt, add to, or change the elements of the unfolding model so that it continues to evolve in response to the paradigm shifts ushered in by Web 2.0 and Learning Environments 2.0.

This book is for those who want to learn how well distance education courses really work and for those who want to design the *very best* distance education courses. Our goal is to impact evaluation practice. After you read this book, you will be ready to use our model to guide a comprehensive evaluation study of *any* distance course.

Acknowledgments

We give our sincere thanks to C. Deborah Laughton at The Guilford Press for her constant patience and unflagging support. It is a joy to work with someone who has such a thorough understanding of both evaluation and academic writing. We would especially like to thank her for the book's title, *Evaluation in Distance Education and E-Learning: The Unfolding Model*. We experimented with many other titles, including *The Triple-E Approach: E-ffective E-valuation for E-Learning*, but finally caved in when C. Deborah made the astute point that her title would generate more "hits" from a web search. Without her many very helpful comments, this book would never have been written. Second, we would like to thank Dr. Tony Bates for conceptualizing an approach to mixed methods that proved to be rigorous, scientific, practical, and productive. Dr. Bates's extraordinary vision of evaluation preceded our approach to evaluation, just as his extensive publications have consistently provided rare and immensely valuable insights into distance education, e-learning, and professional program evaluation. We have found that equal and parallel mixed methods have consistently led to rich and textured findings about the merit and worth of distance and e-learning courses. Third, we thank Dr. Mark Bullen, associate dean of the Learning and Teaching Centre at the British

Columbia Institute of Technology in Vancouver for his extensive expertise on the constantly changing language and future directions of technology. Finally, we thank Michael Simonson, Instructional Technology
and Distance Education Program, Nova Southeastern University; Eleanor
L. Witta, Department of Educational Research, Technology and Leadership, University of Central Florida College of Education; Jennifer D.
Robins, Department of Library Science and Information Services Program, University of Central Missouri; and Dianna Newman, Evaluation
Consortium and Division of Educational Psychology and Methodology,
University at Albany, State University of New York School of Education,
whose rigorous feedback on two drafts led to major improvements in this
book. Thanks to these individuals, we made improvements that will vastly
increase this book's relevance and utility as we move into "Web 2.0 and
beyond" (Sinclair et al., 2006).

Contents

CHAPTER 1

■ ■ ■ ■ ■ ■ ■ ■

Why Do We Need a New Approach to Evaluation in Distance Education and E-Learning?

In this chapter, we discuss the need for a new approach to **evaluation** in **distance education**. This need arises from rapid and unrelenting technological change and the rapid expansion of distance and **e-learning** courses. In this new, global environment, course design is a complex problem-solving process. The right blend of course components is a "balancing act," and future iterations lead to greater effectiveness (Christensen, 2003, p. 242). Evaluation is a systematic investigation to determine the merit and worth of a set of activities. The comprehensive approach to evaluation reflected in our **unfolding model** is a professional approach that can be applied to both distance and e-learning. Our approach goes beyond **surveys** of learner satisfaction to include **relevance**, **cost–benefit**, underly-

1

ing values, and unintended consequences. Moreover, the unfolding nature allows evaluators to select from, and add to, the instruments and strategies, so that the **model** is responsive and adaptive to new technologies and pedagogies for distance education and e-learning in **Web 1.0**, **Web 2.0**, and beyond. In this book, we have distinguished distance education from e-learning because they are two different concepts, and, with respect to evaluation, many lessons from the past still apply.

Distance Education versus E-Learning

With distance learning, "students study at the time and place of their choice (home, work or learning centre) and without face-to-face contact with a teacher" (Bates, 1995, p. 5). With its origins in print distance delivery, distance education **delivery methods** include print distance, **videoteleconferencing**, and CD-ROM, and can serve either on- and off-campus learners. Distance education includes an array of **hybrid delivery** methods. "**Blended learning** environments often combine technology-driven resources with human interaction, whether local or remote, via telephone or video conferencing or computer mediation (Sinclair, McClaren, & Griffin, 2006). The added value provided by distance education is more access and flexibility than traditional on-campus courses. Distance programs offer a second chance at a postsecondary education, access to those bound by time or disabilities, skill upgrading for workers at their jobs (Willis, 1993), and new opportunities for senior citizens (Awalt, 2007).

DISTANCE EDUCATION VERSUS E-LEARNING

Distance education: "a generic, all-inclusive term used to refer to the physical separation of teachers and learners" (Schlosser & Simonson, 2006, p. 65).

E-learning: an instructional program delivered online or through the Internet. Includes tutorials delivered on campus, workshops, short courses, and worksite-based instruction.

In contrast, e-learning is training delivered over the Internet to support individual or organizational performance goals (Clark & Mayer, 2003). E-learning provides "in-process interactivity and cross student and even out of class communication" (Goldman-Segall, 2006, p. 231). **Asynchronous** environments, such as **podcasting** or online discussions allow for **self-paced learning** any time and anywhere. **Synchronous** e-learning environments are characterized by different types of interactions through chats, real-time audio, application sharing, whiteboards, **webcasting**, videoteleconferencing, and so on, which imposes additional considerations concerning usability and its evaluation. **Learning management systems (LMS)**, such as **Blackboard**, Desire2Learn, **personal digital assistants** (PDAs), and WebCT, have become a common resource at universities, colleges, and distance learning organizations (Malikowski, Thompson, & Theis, 2007). These systems can be used to create learning content, customize learning paths for individual students, facilitate student collaboration, and evaluate learning with a rich set of assessment tools (Blackboard, 2007).

E-learning is emerging as one of the fastest growing organizational uses of the Internet (Harun, 2002); therefore, **human–computer interaction** and usability standards based on the **web accessibility initiative** attributes are important areas for evaluation. The **worldwide web** is now more than ten years old, and Web 1.0 is based on an architecture of presentation similar to traditional distance education; that is, it is essentially a content transmission model (Sinclair et al., 2006). However, the paradigm shift currently underway from Web 1.0 to Web 2.0, and its implications for learning environments, is laid out by Sinclair et al. (2006). Learners can upload their own videos on YouTube and publish their own work on blogs, **Wikipedia**, or Amazon.com.

> The emergence of Web 2.0 will have profound implications for learners and for society. . . . Ordinary people can become capable of production, publishing, resource sharing and participating in one-to-many communication, and global dialogue. Some blogs currently have larger subscriber bases than many conventional, small town newspapers. . . . With learning applications such as Open Source code, course management systems allow teachers and learners to select, edit or extend learning components most appropriate to their purposes. (Sinclair et al., 2006, p. 7)

Moving from Web 1.0 to Web 2.0 also takes us from **Learning Environment 1.0** to **Learning Environment 2.0**. New information and communications technologies are generating "a fundamental shift from an **architecture of presentation** to an **architecture of participation**" (Sinclair et al., 2006, p. 8). We are moving "from closed linear models to those that are open and dynamic [and] . . . the learning game is being played on new fields" (Sinclair et al., 2006, p. 4). It is this paradigm shift from distance to e-learning that we wanted to capture in our title, *Evaluation in Distance Education and E-Learning: The Unfolding Model*. Finally, the title reflects Bates's belief that there is much to learn about e-learning from the history and practice of distance education.

The Rapid Expansion of Distance Education and E-Learning

Over the past 10 years, there has been explosive growth in the delivery of distance courses and a growing competition among colleges and universities to expand into this market. Universities have made "substantial financial investments in learning technologies and students expect that 'learning technology' will be a key component of their education" (Academic Committee for the Creative Use of Learning Technologies, 2000, p. 5). Schiffman, Vignare, and Geith (2007) found that there are nine reasons higher education institutions pursue online education, from contributing to extension efforts to returning a surplus. According to the 2006 *Keeping Pace with K–12 Online Learning* study (North American Council for Online Learning and the Partnership for 21st Century Skills, 2006), 38 states have state-led online learning programs or policies regulating online learning. Twenty-five states have statewide or state-led virtual schools. Finally, Michigan became the first state to require high school students to take at least one **online course** for graduation.

The Sloan Consortium (Allen & Seaman, 2006) found that nearly 3.2 million students in the United States were taking at least one online higher education course during fall 2005, a substantial increase from 2.3 million in 2004. Moreover, the additional 900,000 online students is more than double the increase in any previous year. More than 96% of the very largest institutions (more than 15,000 total enrollments) have some online offerings, which is more than twice the rate observed for the smallest institutions. The proportion of institutions with fully online programs rises steadily as institutional size increases, and about two-thirds of the very largest institutions have fully online programs compared with only about one-sixth of the smallest institutions. In 2005, 62% of academic leaders rated the learning outcomes in online education as the same as or superior to those in face-to-face education, compared with 57% in 2003. Despite these impressive numbers, however, they also found a lower percentage growth rate than in previous years. "Could this be an early indicator that online enrollment growth has finally begun to plateau?" (Allen & Seaman, 2006, p. 1).

Rapid Structural Change

Through distance education and e-learning, universities are offering **educational programs** across states and nations and around the world. Traditional universities, such as the University of Missouri, the University of Indiana, the University of Texas, and Brigham Young University, are increasingly committed to distance courses. Private universities such as Nova Southeastern and the University of Phoenix are dedicated to distance degrees, and the development of for-profit, **virtual schools** and distance and virtual learning is part of a multibillion-dollar education market (Clark, 2001). Technology is used to link all levels of education and share costs with industry and government through state-sponsored video networks such as the Alaska **Teleconferencing** Network and Oregon Ed-Net (Willis, 1994). There are also several virtual **consortia** at the national and multistate levels that offer postsecondary courses or act as brokers for external providers. Universitas 21 (2000), for example, is an international network of 21 leading research *universities* in 13 countries that offers a highly recognized brand name for educational products and **quality assurance**.

Virtual schools, colleges, and universities make hundreds of introductory college-level courses available. Both traditional and innovative institutions are also integrating postsecondary with online high school diploma programs. Virtual High School, for example, was the winner of the United States Distance Learning Association's 21st Century Best Practices Award for Distance Learning. The state-funded Florida Virtual School offers a full online curriculum and provides courses to school districts in Florida and other states. If we are serious about ensuring that all students master the skills they will need for life, work, and citizenship in the 21st century, the continued expansion of virtual schooling (blended and wholly online) will be required (Patrick & Levin, 2007).

Finally, online **degree or diploma mills** promise degrees or transcripts in a very short time, even as few as 5 days (Council for Higher Education Accreditation, 2006; Ezell & Bear, 2005). Degree mills not only undermine the value of learning and of educational standards by treating degrees as commodities, but they also offer credentials that may not be recognized for employment or for entry into higher educational programs (Council for Higher Education Accreditation, 2006).

Rapid Technological Change
and Rising Stakeholder Expectations

According to Gene Wilhoit (2007), executive director of the Council of Chief State School Officers, a leading organization of state superintendents, commissioners, and the heads of the state departments of education in the United States, online learning and virtual schools are solutions to the most important issues in American education today. Delivery methods tend not only to multiply but also to diversify. CMSs, such as Blackboard, Desire2Learn, and WebCT, have become a common resource at universities, colleges, and **distance learning** organizations (Malikowski et al., 2007). Through learning management systems, learners have remote access to web-based, "one-stop" shopping centers with audio- and video-based welcome messages, **online learning** and **individualized learning** plans, lesson viewers, virtual libraries, and help resolving technical glitches.

The web, for example, evolved from a text-only medium to **multimedia, interactive media**, and **learning objects** such as **applets**, animation, simulation, maps, and games, making their way into distance/e-learning courses (Educause Evolving Technologies Committee, 2004). There is a growing convergence between "libraries, **digital** repositories, and web content management" (p. 86), which provides more resources to learners at home.

With **interactive television** (iTV), learners can access the web with a TV, phone line, and **digital set-top box** "without the use of a separate computer" (Chen & Iris, 2004, p. 161). According to Interactive TV Alliance (2002), 20 million homes around the world have digital set-top boxes capable of some form of interactive television. Another new development is "**nomadicity**," that is, "multiple devices of mobile computing and communications" (p. 88), including "multi-function cell phones, voice-over IP, peer-to-peer file sharing, digital video capture and wireless data cards" (p. 88). "Teens use the Internet to multi-task—instant message, reserve books at the library, order online, participate in an online quiz or games" (Sener & Humbert, 2003). In sum, technological change is unrelenting; and the learning game is being played on new fields (Sinclair et al., 2006). As a result, teens and university students are increasingly Net-savvy, have high expectations of online student services, and "are frustrated that teachers don't use the web more effectively" (Sener & Humbert, 2003).

Postsecondary educational institutions are not limited to the public; some are also expanding to serve corporations. For example, WebCampus.Stevens, the online graduate education and corporate training unit of Stevens Institute of Technology, delivers one of the largest and most effective blended programs in New York City (Fisher, Esche, Ubell, & Chassapis, 2007). Under a Sloan Foundation grant, the school is extending its engineering and management programs to local corporations, supporting local telecommunications, pharmaceutical/life sciences, media, finance, and other key industries. The school provides companies with access to **online training**, preparing them for success anywhere in the world.

The Need for Continuous Course Improvement

With constantly evolving technologies, there is unrelenting pressure to redesign distance/e-learning courses. Simple e-mail-based courses are giving way to courses integrated within **portals** and CMSs. Broadband networks combine older technologies such as teleconferencing with newer digital networks, so that older and newer technologies are blended to form an "amalgam" (Willis, 1994). However, when new technologies are grafted on to existing courses, they often bring adaptations not only in course content and activities but also in underlying pedagogical theories. For example, control may shift from the developer to the user, challenges to network security may emerge, or new funding models may be required "to support a wide variety of legacy and next-generation technologies" (p. 89).

The key to effective online instruction is better course design (Simonson, 2006). The integration of new technologies involves critical decisions and trade-offs in the design phase. As course designers experiment with new hybrids, they adjust their instructional packages and redesign their products. In doing so, they need to balance the utility of new technologies against other aspects of value, such as instructional needs and benefits, the costs of new applications, and programming difficulty (Chou, 2003). With iTV, for example, each interactive function must be weighed against instructional necessity and programming difficulty (Chou, 2003). Capella University, for example, now takes online learning as the new norm and has turned face-to-face learning into a *supplement* of online learning (Offerman & Tassava, 2006). These kinds of dynamics are behind Sloan-C's (Lorenzo & Moore, 2002) five quality pillars or benchmarks of evaluation, which are based on continuous quality improvement.

What Is Evaluation?

Evaluation is "the process of determining the merit, worth and value of things and evaluations are the product of that process" (Scriven, 1993, p. 1). Evaluation is an attempt to judge the worth, value, or quality of something (Coldeway, 1988). "Every time we try something new, it is important to consider its value" (Davidson, 2005), and the "heart" of evaluation is a judgment of the overall value or worth of an endeavor (Wolf, 1987). "Evaluation is a process giving attestations on such matters as reliability, effectiveness, cost-effectiveness, efficiency, safety, ease of use and probity. Evaluation provides evidence and evaluative claims

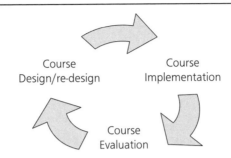

Course
Design/re-design

Course
Implementation

Course
Evaluation

FIGURE 1.1. The cycle of course implementation, evaluation, and redesign.

with respect to the worth, value and improvement of individuals, programs, projects, services, and organizations" (Stufflebeam & Shinkfield, 2007). Evaluation studies can be **formative evaluation** (used to improve a program) or **summative evaluation** (used to determine the success of a completed program). Evaluation is a distinct profession and is supportive of other professions (Stufflebeam & Shinkfield, 2007). In contrast, the term **research** refers to studies that determine cause and effect rather than value, merit, or worth.

The term **program**, as in "**program evaluation**," refers to "a set of resources and activities directed toward one or more common goals, typically under the direction of a single manager or a management team" (Wholey, 1987, p. 78). By this definition, a university course is a program, just as a set of courses leading to a degree such as a master's of educational technology is also a program. For this reason, professional program evaluation models can be applied to either a single course or to a complete educational program. In contrast, the term **assessment** refers to the measurement of individual students' knowledge, skills, and abilities (Popham, 1995). Course evaluation provides valuable information that informs course redesign in a continuous cycle of improvement (see Figure 1.1).

Why Do We Need
a Professional Approach to Evaluation?

Evaluation in distance education is often done by distance educators, that is, by those who are responsible for the success of distance courses.

Although there have been recurring calls for "proper evaluative studies" in distance education (Rumble, 1981; Academic Committee for the Creative Use of Learning Technologies, 2000, p. 20; Tallant-Runnels, 2006), these calls have gone largely unheeded.

It is true that e-learning systems "have not yet been caught up in the wave of results-based activity that has hit hard the schools, business and the military" (Baker & O'Neil, 2006). However, the need for a professional approach to evaluation is even greater today than in the past. With the expansion of distance education and e-learning, increasingly complex and blended course designs, increasing global competitiveness, and the need for continuous improvement, distance and e-learning course design is a complex, problem-solving process. Designers need to choose the best combination of components and future iterations that lead to higher quality instruction (Christensen, 2003, p. 242). Constant upgrades have increased **stakeholder** expectations (Baker & O'Neil, 1994), and students are becoming "sophisticated and informed consumers of education" (Academic Committee for the Creative Use of Learning Technologies, 2000, p. 20). Professional evaluation is needed because it provides valuable information about flaws in the course design and implementation system, which in turn generates specific directions for course improvement. To quote Bill Thomas, director of educational technology, Southern Regional Education Board (SREB), "The use of the Web (online learning) to provide academic courses is extremely important to students everywhere. For online learning to expand and grow, students, parents and policy- and decision-makers need assurance that the online courses are of quality. If [so], there is little doubt that online learning will grow rapidly" (North American Council for Online Learning [NACOL], 2007).

What Does a Professional Approach to Evaluation Look Like?

Evaluation is the systematic investigation of the merit and worth of programs, as well as a discipline in its own right (Scriven, n.d.). First, it has an "intelligible self-concept" (p. 4), with its own and mission, territory, and fields of application, such as education and international development. Second, it has a core methodology, major results, body of literature, and dedicated professional journals. Third, it has its own organizations and professional meetings. Fourth, there are established standards for professional and ethical practice (Joint Committee on Standards for Educational Evaluation, 1994). Finally, the field of evaluation requires "professional-level skills and knowledge" (Scriven, n.d., p. 5) and skills that are "specialized, difficult, time-consuming, and sophisticated" (p. 2).

In higher education, there has been reluctance to adopt a professional approach to evaluation (Scriven, n.d.) due, in part, to "a fear of evaluation that leads to a denial of its legitimacy" (p. 5). In distance education and e-learning, there may be some uncertainty about what a professional approach would look like or how evaluation should be conducted in a postmodern world, given the disappointments with experimental methods and their limited application to technology-based environments. In response, we have identified five characteristics of a contemporary, professional approach to the evaluation of distance and e-learning courses in the following box.

WHAT DOES A PROFESSIONAL APPROACH TO EVALUATION LOOK LIKE?

1. Based on a theoretical model from professional program evaluation.
2. Provides a comprehensive assessment of merit and worth.
3. Reports on scientific evidence, underlying values, and unintended consequences.
4. Uses mixed methods.
5. Uses systematic, thorough, and rigorous methods and procedures (Stufflebeam & Shinkfield, 2007).

Finally, our purpose in this book is to provide readers with some of the specialized skills and knowledge that they can immediately put to use in conducting evaluation studies of distance and e-learning courses. Although this book focuses on postsecondary courses, we believe the unfolding model could also be used to evaluate a broad range of educational products from workshops to programs (i.e., a series of courses leading to a credential such as a master's degree).

Professional Program Evaluation Models

An evaluation **model** is a set of beliefs about "the concepts and structure of evaluation work" (p. 19) that provides guidelines for arriving "at defensible descriptions, judgements and recommendations" (Madaus & Kellaghan, 2000, p. 20). Stufflebeam (2001) prefers the term **approach** because "the former is broad enough to cover illicit as well as laudatory practices" (p. 9). In their debate in *Social Indicators Research*, Moss (1998a), Messick (1998), and Markus (1998) seem to use the terms *model, framework,* and *approach* interchangeably. For the sake of consistency and to avoid confusion, we use the term *model* to refer to a set of concepts organized in a schematic diagram.

VIGNETTE

Your supervisor says that you can't use program evaluation theory to evaluate a distance education course because a course is not a program. How would you respond?

Scientific Evidence

A professional program evaluation approach is comprehensive; that is, it includes scientific evidence, values, and consequences. In this book, a **scientific approach** is defined broadly as a rigorous, evidence-based argument in support of evaluative claims. "With the influx of online courses and the prospect that [distance] courses will increase in number, it is imperative that researchers continue to inquire into . . . [evaluation] and use sound scientific methods" (Tallant-Runnels, 2006, p. 119). We do not define the term **scientific evidence** *narrowly* as experimental designs but *broadly* as empirical findings obtained from surveys, student grades, completion rates, interviews, **focus groups**, and cost–benefit analysis. Moreover, professional program evaluation models are distinguished by the relative emphasis they place on evidence, values, and consequences (Alkin & Christie, 2004a). This definition includes not only rigorous experimental designs (with respectable sample sizes determined by programs such as G★Power) but also rigorous qualitative and **mixed–methods** research. In our mind, what makes something "scientific" is the *rigor* of the methods and the *quality and defensibility* of the empirical evidence in support of the researcher's argument. Moreover, no matter how rigorous scientific studies are, they never *prove* anything. They only provide empirical evidence to support the researcher's theory. In other words, we think of scientific evidence the way lawyers do, as a preponderance of evidence to support one or more hypotheses or inferences. Moreover, qualitative methods are often the best way to bring forward the diverse perspectives of those who have been perceived as "other" and whose perspectives could not be anticipated, or captured, in a predesigned survey. These points fall out of Sam Messick's extraordinary insight that scientific evidence, values (e.g., rhetoric, theories, and ideologies), and unintended social consequences are *always* intertwined.

In Chapter 3, we also show that many distance education evaluation models are based on scientific evidence alone, whereas others include evidence, values, and consequences, but that the latter two aspects of value are merely implied. However, a comprehensive, professional model of evaluation for distance education would include all three aspects of value, which, moreover, would be given equal emphasis in the determination of merit and worth.

Underlying Values

The values underlying distance courses are an important aspect of the merit and worth of distance courses because new technologies have always brought new values with them. Moreover, we can only take advantage of the capabilities of new technologies if we transform our fundamental conceptions about learning and institutions. Technology has moved us away from philosophies of knowledge transmission toward "a culture of collaboration capable of engaging everyone in life-long educational attainments" (Sinclair et al., 2006). Therefore, a professional program evaluation study should include an analysis of the **underlying values** of distance courses. As in any academic field, there is often little conscious awareness of value-laden rhetoric and underlying values and ideologies. For this reason, it is important to bring forward the values, ideologies, and theories of pedagogy underlying distance and e-learning courses and to compare these aspects of value with the scientific evidence (Figure 1.2).

As a reminder, the term *underlying values* refers to the value labels, goals/objectives, theories, and ideologies underlying distance courses. The term *rhetoric/value labels* refers to rhetoric, such as "world class," "innovative," and "cutting-edge technology," in course outlines and grant proposals. The term *theory* refers to theories of teaching and learning, such as constructivism, whereas *ideology* refers to broader underlying values,

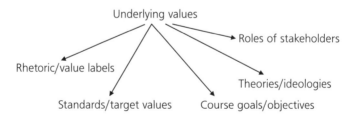

FIGURE 1.2. Aspects of values underlying distance and e-learning courses.

such as team-based learning, on which more narrow theories are based. These kinds of theories form the underlying theoretical foundations on which distance course designs, activities, and assessments are based. **Standards** refers to specific goals for distance and e-learning courses that can be found in the literature (e.g., Sloan-C's five pillars of quality). *Target values* refers to setting measurable goals based on standards for specific courses. *Course goals/objectives* refers to content mastery, access for learners in remote geographical areas, and schedule flexibility. *Roles of stakeholders* refers to persons with a vested interest in the evaluation findings and raises the question of what the roles of stakeholders will be in your study. It is important to know that not all of these need to apply in any particular evaluation study; instead, evaluators can pick and choose those categories that are most pertinent to their context.

Why Are Underlying Values Important?

We believe strongly that distance courses are based on different underlying theories, goals, and ideologies. As we demonstrate in later chapters, distance/e-learning courses reflect a plethora of different underlying goals, values, theories, and ideologies. Should a distance course be designed for flexibility or geographical reach? On what pedagogical theory is the course based? Is geographical reach more important than richness and depth? Is the technology **seamless**? Is the course being redesign to increase enrollment and generate more revenue to pay off the investment in technology? What values must be traded off to ensure that low costs, another important value, will be maintained? Can different values be compatible in the same course, or do they sometimes work at cross-purposes? These underlying theories and ideologies need to be identified.

Another aspect of underlying values is how evaluators in distance education should deal with stakeholders. It is important to note that evaluation is distinct from research in that it involves politics and stakeholders, which are subsumed under values, and carry important implications for evaluators (Fitzpatrick, Sanders, & Worthen, 2004). Different stakeholders may feel differently, and quite strongly, about the goals, design, and activities of distance/e-learning courses. How should evaluators handle disagreements among stakeholders? Should evaluators disclose their own values in their evaluation studies? In our review of evaluation models in distance education, we found almost no models that focus on bringing forward underlying values into the foreground. We believe that an **evaluation model** is needed that brings into the foreground all of these elements of underlying value.

```
1.  Bugs
2.  Productivity paradoxes
3.  Side effects
4.  Revenge effects
    a.  Rearranging
    b.  Repeat
    c.  Recomplicating
    d.  Regenerating
    e.  Recongesting effects
```

FIGURE 1.3. The four kinds of unintended consequences of technology (Tenner, 1996).

Unintended Consequences

According to Tenner (1996), there are four kinds of **unintended consequences**: bugs, *productivity paradoxes, side effects,* and *revenge effects* (Figure 1.3). A *bug* is a small mechanical glitch often experienced by users. A *productivity paradox* is a situation in which huge investments in technology produce little, no, or even negative gains in productivity, even though costs tend to be high, stable, or increasing (Fahy, 1999). One example is the unrealized dream that computers would lead to the paperless office (Tenner, 1996). A *side effect* is an unanticipated consequence that is less central to the desired effects. A *revenge effect* is some negative outcome of technology that counters the predicted benefits (e.g., carpel tunnel syndrome). A revenge effect is not produced by technology alone. Only when technology is anchored "in laws, regulations, customs and habits does the irony reach its full potential" (p. 7). Finally, there are five kinds of revenge effects: *rearranging, repeat, recomplicating, regenerating,* and *recongesting effects* (Tenner, 1996), which we discuss in Chapter 7.

Why Are Unintended Consequences Important?

Unintended consequences are important because they provide valuable insights and specific directions for course improvement. With constantly evolving technologies and increasingly innovative, complex, and blended systems, unintended consequences will continue to emerge in new and unanticipated ways despite the best efforts to control them (Davis, 2002). From their surveys of learner satisfaction, for example, Zhang, Sun, Wang, and Wu (2003) found that there was an unbalanced development of course packages and the provision of learning support services. "It is one of the most urgent tasks to establish a more powerful, flexible, and effective learning support and services system in order to assure quality distance learning" (p. 1). In Chapter 8, we provide authentic examples, such as mismatches among the course components or between the goals and the **course implementation**. In sum, an analysis of unintended consequences can lead to specific directions for course improvement. After these improvements are made, courses can be "scaled up" and best practices diffused to a wider, global audience (Dede, Honan, & Peters, 2005).

Responding to the Call for a Professional Evaluation Approach: The Unfolding Model

To answer the call for a professional model in distance education, we offer our unfolding model, based on **Messick's (1989) framework** of validity (Figure 1.4). As shown in Figure 1.4, the merit, worth, or value of any distance course can be evaluated in terms of two rows—the **scientific basis** and the **consequential basis**—crossed with two columns—*interpretation* and *use*. The *scientific basis* consists of scientific evidence and relevance and cost–benefit. The two upper boxes comprise the scientific evidence (both **quantitative** and **qualitative**) that has traditionally been used to evaluate both educational programs in general and distance education courses in particular. The upper left box includes scientific measures and the context of their application, whereas the upper right box includes additional aspects of value or constructs that are scientifically measured (i.e., relevance and cost–benefit). Relevance can be measured with all of the tools in the upper

	Interpretation	Use
Scientific basis	**Scientific evidence (SE)** (surveys/interviews)	**Relevance/cost–benefit (RC)** (SE) + (RC)
Consequential basis	**Underlying values (UV)** (SE) + (RC) + (UV)	**Unintended consequences (UC)** (SE) + (RC) + (UV) + (UC)

FIGURE 1.4. The unfolding model.

left box, whereas cost–benefit is measured with its own unique set of tools, strategies, and techniques.

The consequential basis comprises *underlying values* and *unintended consequences*. Because unintended consequences can be either positive or negative, values and unintended consequences are intertwined. In fact, all four aspects of the unfolding model are intertwined, an insight with important implications to which we keep returning in this book.

As shown in Figure 1.5, scientific evidence unfolds to include (1) *surveys/interviews*, (2) **outcomes**, (3) *checklists and rubrics*, and (4) data/statistics to track learner progress. Surveys and interviews with learners are vital for measuring learner satisfaction with the **course components** and should also be conducted with course designers and instructors. They are included in the first layer of our framework (Figure 1.5) because they are essential to our approach to evaluation. In contrast, all other categories in Figure 1.5 (i.e., outcomes, checklists, and data/statistics) are not essential to our approach but depend on the type of course you are evaluating and reporting needs. *Outcomes* refers to grades, enrollment numbers, completion and retention rates, quality control measures, and performance indica-

---

Scientific evidence
Surveys/interviews/focus groups/online ethnographies
to measure learner satisfaction with course components
- Tutor
- Online discussion group
- Course package
- Textbook
- Course webpages

Outcomes
- Grades
- Completion and retention rates
- Student assessment and feedback

Checklists and rubrics to measure environmental quality
- Course management systems
- Webpage quality
- Learning objects quality
- Accessibility for learners with disabilities
- Instructor competencies

Data/statistics to track learner progress
- Course management data

FIGURE 1.5. The unfolding model: Scientific evidence unfolded.

Relevance
- Alignment between the course and needs of society
- Meaningfulness of course to learners
- Transfer of learning to authentic contexts

Cost–Benefit
- Costs to the university
- Costs to learners

FIGURE 1.6. The unfolding model: Relevance/cost–benefit unfolded.

tors. **Checklists** can be used to measure student assessment and instructor **feedback** on student assignments and to evaluate webpages and learning objects, accessibility for learners with disabilities, and instructor competencies. Finally, *course management data* refers to progress-tracking statistics and any other data relevant to your study. Of this evidence, surveys and interviews with learners, course designers, and instructors are essential to our approach, and you may choose from the other **data sources** depending on your delivery method and the needs of your study. It is important to note that these are exemplars and do not provide all of the measures and approaches available.

The upper right box of our framework is relevance and cost–benefit (Figure 1.6). As shown in Figure 1.6, relevance unfolds to include (1) alignment between the course and needs of society, (2) meaningfulness of course to learners, and (3) transfer of learning to authentic contexts. Cost–benefit unfolds to include (1) costs to the university and (2) costs to learners.

Underlying Values and Consequences

The two lower boxes of the unfolding model—*underlying values* and *unintended consequences*—make up the *consequential basis*. Figure 1.7 shows the unfolded cells. There are five kinds of *underlying values*: (1) course goals and objectives, (2) rhetoric or value labels, (3) theory, (4) ideology, and (5) stakeholder roles and influence. There are several kinds of *unintended consequences*: instructional and social as well as *course implementation* (i.e., how the course as delivered on a daily basis). These implementation effects emerge from analyzing the data in the other three cells and the fit among the four facets, which are unfolded into additional categories further in the book.

> **Underlying values**
> - Course goals and objectives
> - Rhetoric/value labels (e.g., "world class," "innovative")
> - Theory (e.g., schema theory, e-learning cognition)
> - Ideology (e.g., open access, learner centeredness)
> - Stakeholder roles and influence
> - Standards/target values
>
> **Unintended consequences (negative and positive)**
> - Instructional
> - Social
> - Course implementation
> - "Fit" across the four facets

FIGURE 1.7. The unfolding model: The consequential basis unfolded.

Overlap in the Unfolding Model

It is important to note that, as well as being adaptive to diverse contexts, the unfolding model is also **dynamic**. This means that the four facets of the framework are not distinct or clear-cut but rather overlap and cut across each other. Thus, the analysis of your data will not really "fit" into just one of the boxes but will overlap and cut across other boxes. When analyzing your data, you will discover the overlap of the various aspects of value. This overlap will provide you with insights into the fit between the intended and the actual course implementation as well as with specific directions for course improvement. For example, an analysis of cost–benefit brings into the foreground a hidden aspect of the value of e-learning. Contrary to an ideology that e-learning is "an approach that favors the advantaged" (p. 15), a cost–benefit analysis may demonstrate that e-learning can be distributed "to the masses" (p. 15) precisely because of its low cost (Graham, 2006). This example shows that underlying values (ideology) and unintended social consequences overlap. You will encounter this overlap in the analysis of your data, and we provide more examples from two authentic case reports in Chapter 8.

The Unfolding Nature of the Model

The reason our model is called the unfolding model is that each cell expands to show further information needed for your evaluation study.

Our model is not, therefore, a closed, linear model but, like contemporary technology, is "open and dynamic" (Sinclair et al., 2006, p. 4). This open and dynamic quality provides the flexibility to evaluate courses in diverse subject areas and delivery methods from print distance to e-learning. For example, scientific evidence unfolds to include all types of scientific evidence (e.g., survey and interview data, outcomes, and checklists [see Figure 1.5]).

Conclusions: Our Approach to Evaluation

We began this chapter with definitions of the terms *distance education* and *e-learning* and an overview of the contemporary context. We have discussed how this context is behind the call for a professional approach to evaluation. We have shown that this professional approach looks like Messick's (1989) framework, which is comprehensive because it is based on three recurring program evaluation themes: scientific evidence, values, and consequences. This theoretically rich and highly sophisticated framework is really an omnibus model for professional program evaluation. The unfolding model is a "road map" to practice and can be used to guide evaluation studies. The unfolding model is both adaptive and dynamic and can be applied to both distance and e-learning. The versatility of the model means that it can be used for both contemporary and leading-edge delivery methods, regardless of the role of the instructor, physical location of learners, and the types of technologies used. Although the courses used as examples in Chapter 8 are based on Web 1.0, we are confident that the unfolding model could also be used for Web 2.0, with a shift toward an architecture of participation and "interactive tools such as blogs, wikis, interactive discussion threads, chat and virtual meetings (Sinclair et al., 2006, p. 5).

Where Do We Go from Here?

In this book, we (1) explain Messick's (1989) framework, (2) give an in-depth overview of the unfolding model, and (3) provide practical, step-by-step guidelines for conducting evaluation studies. An overview of this book is given in Figure 1.8.

In this chapter, we discussed the contemporary context of distance education and e-learning, argued for a new approach to evaluation, and introduced the unfolding model. In Chapter 2, we review the theory and practice of professional program evaluation, while in Chapter 3, we review

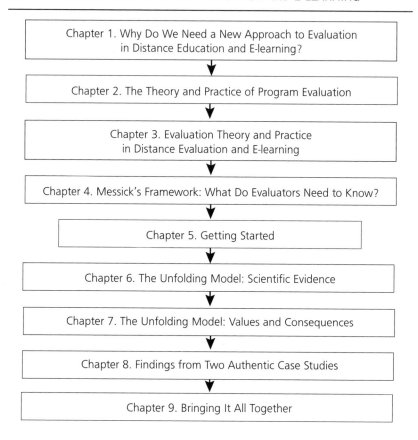

FIGURE 1.8. Overview of the book's approach to evaluation.

evaluation theory and practice in distance education and e-learning. We show that *any* evaluation model can be classified according to the relative emphasis on evidence, values, and consequences. Messick's (1989) framework, which encompasses these three recurring themes, can be adapted into the unfolding model to guide evaluation studies in distance education and e-learning.

In Chapter 4, we discuss Messick's (1989) framework in detail. Then, in Chapter 5, we show readers how to get started with an evaluation study. In Chapter 6, we show how to use the upper two boxes of the unfolding model to guide **evaluation practice**, and in Chapter 7, we show how to use the lower two boxes of the model. In Chapter 8, we present our findings from applying the unfolding model to two authentic, postsecondary courses: Computing Science 200 and Professional Writing 110. In Chapter 9, we bring everything together with a summary of our main points and an assertion that our approach will continue to be relevant and useful in the new environments of "Web 2.0 and beyond" (Sinclair et al., 2006, p. 1). Finally, the appendices include a summary of the 1994 Program Evaluation Standards (Appendix A), a glossary of definitions of key terms (Appendix B), as well as a list of professional associations (Appendix C).

CHAPTER 2

■ ■ ■ ■ ■ ■ ■ ■

The Theory and Practice
of Program Evaluation

*P*rogram *evaluation* is the systematic investigation of the merit and worth of social or educational services. Modern program evaluation grew out of applied social science research, which began to help train military personnel in World War II, and expanded into job training, family planning, and community development in the next decade (Fitzpatrick et al., 2004). Program evaluation is applied research that takes place in complex and diverse social contexts such as health, education, and social work and has been strongly influenced by them. These multiple contexts require different evaluation approaches, raise diverse issues, and yield different types of scientific evidence (Davidson, 2000). Program evaluation is a transdiscipline and does not have a permanent "disciplinary house" (Christie, 2001, p. 59). However, program evaluation transforms evaluation theory and practice in other disciplines and is, in turn, is transformed by them. Today, program evaluation is an emerging profession in its own right (Fitzpatrick et al., 2004; Stufflebeam, 2001), with a rich and diverse history of professional evaluation *paradigms*, theories, values, methods, practices, and use (Caracelli, 2000; Stufflebeam, 2001). Finally, because education is a predominant social service that affects almost everyone, educational evaluation is one of the pillars of the evaluation field (Kellaghan, Stufflebeam, & Wingate, 2003).

Why Are Program Evaluation Models Important?

Program evaluation studies tend to be practical activities, focused on producing studies for clients, not on testing or validating theory (King, 2003). These studies are highly contextual, varying widely from hurricane disaster relief to English language training to teenage leadership skills. In general, therefore, evaluation theorists do not specify the *contexts* in which their models should apply, nor do they often say where their models have been applied (King, 2003). In the research literature, some evaluation models have been empirically tested and validated, whereas others have not. In practice, then, evaluators often start out with questions or methods, and not theory, when doing evaluation studies. However, there is a general consensus among both scholars and the former presidents of the American Evaluation Association (AEA) that theory *should* be used to guide practice (King, 2003; Mertens, 2004). Several scholarly articles and presentations at the 2006 AEA conference reported on how various program evaluation models were used to guide program evaluation practice: "What could be more practical than a well-formulated theory that is consistently useful for solving real-world problems?" (King, 2003, p. 60).

> Program evaluation models serve as "road maps" to guide evaluation practice. Therefore, to plan and conduct evaluation projects, evaluators must understand the major theories that have shaped research and evaluation methods (Mertens, 2004).

Models not only guide you to your destination, but they can also include important aspects of value, steps in the evaluation process, and strategies for success that may not be readily apparent. The Key Evaluation Checklist, for example, is a list of key aspects of value designed by Scriven (2004) to fill in the "recurring holes" and "missing elements" in the evaluation plans for educational products of American research and development labs. Good theories, well validated and supported with empirical evidence, have direct implications for evaluation practice, which is why students of program evaluation should be taught to understand both theory and practice (Christie, 2001).

A Classification Framework for Program Evaluation Models

Classification schemes are sets of characteristics for grouping evaluation models (Alkin & Christie, 2004a). Over the past 50 years, there have been many classification schemes for program evaluation models (e.g., Baker & Niemi, 1996; Guba & Lincoln, 1985) but little consensus on their characteristics, merits, or weaknesses. Fitzpatrick et al. (2004) for example, categorizes program evaluation models into (1) objectives-oriented, (2) management-oriented, (3) consumer-oriented, (4) expertise-oriented, and (5) participant-oriented approaches. Stufflebeam (2001) classified models into (1) pseudoevaluations, (2) questions- and methods-oriented approaches, (3) improvement/accountability-oriented approaches, and (4) social advocacy models. Finally, Greene (2007) classifies models by whose interests are being served and which values are being promoted.

Alkin and Christie's (2004a) Evaluation Tree

Alkin and Christie (2004a) designed a program evaluation classification tree consisting of two roots—accountability and social inquiry—and three branches—method, valuing, and use. Evaluation theorists were then classified according to whether their predominant focus, or greatest emphasis, was on (1) method, (2) valuing, and (3) use. Alkin and Christie (2004a) did not classify all scholars who contributed to program evaluation theory, only those with new approaches, models, or theories. Their approach was historical, with the base of the tree consisting of the two historical roots of accountability and social inquiry, the earlier theorists near the trunk, and the most recent theorists placed on the upper branches. Their classification tree was validated by the theorists themselves, who mostly agreed with their placement on the tree. Finally, Alkin and Christie's (2004a) tree was revised into a second version (Alkin & Christie, 2004b).

A Comparison of Alkin and Christie's (2004b) and Messick's (1989) Classification

Messick's (1989) framework consists of three categories: (1) scientific evidence, (2) values, and (3) consequences. Alkin and Christie (2004a, 2004b) conceptualize evaluation as a tree with three branches: (1) methods, (2) valuing, and (3) use. Both approaches are conceptually almost identical (Table 2.1).

As shown in Table 2.1, *methods* is the means by which data or research results are obtained. Methods is the process, and evidence is the product. Similarly, *valuing* is the judgment or interpretation placed on the evidence, which Messick refers to as the meanings attributed to outcomes. *Use* refers to how evaluation is used, whereas Messick's *consequences* refers to both actual and potential use of information or data. As these definitions show, Alkin and Christie's (2004a) methods, valuing, and use maps nicely onto Messick's scientific evidence, values, and consequences. Because of this shared conceptual overlap with Alkin and Christie's (2004b) classification tree, Messick's (1989) framework can be used for program evaluation. In addition, Messick's (1989) model is a comprehensive, omnibus model that embraces the major themes in program evaluation theory over the past 50 years. We now classify program evaluation models according to their relative emphasis on Messick's three themes: (1) scientific evidence, (2) values, and (3) consequences. We rely heavily on Alkin and Christie's (2004b) classification and, like them, take a historical approach.

TABLE 2.1. A Comparison of Alkin and Christie (2004b) and Messick (1989)

Alkin & Christie (2004b)	Messick (1989)

Methods
  Research methods
  Knowledge construction
	Scientific evidence
	  Data
	  Research results

Valuing
  Placing value on data
  The manner in which the data
    are judged
	Value implications
	  The meanings attached to attributes,
	    actions, and outcomes (p. 59)

Use
  Concern for how evaluation
    information is used
	Consequences
	  The actual and potential effects
	    of test use

The categories of method, values, and use (Alkin & Christie, 2004b) are the same categories as scientific evidence, value implications, and social consequences (Messick, 1989). For this reason, Messick's (1989) framework can be used as a comprehensive program evaluation model.

Alkin and Christie's Evaluation Tree: The Roots and Branches

As mentioned, Alkin and Christie's (2004a) classification tree consists of two roots—accountability and social inquiry—and three branches—method, valuing, and use. The roots reflect the origins of program evaluation in Johnson's War on Poverty and Great Society programs and the Elementary and Secondary School Act of 1965, when an unprecedented amount of federal funding was given to schools, states, and regions to implement a wide range of educational programs (Fitzpatrick et al., 2004). To demonstrate the wisdom of these policies, huge sums were poured into program evaluation. In their classification tree, accountability is designed to "improve and better programs and society," and social inquiry represents "a systematic and justifiable set of methods for determining accountability" (Alkin & Christie, 2004a, p. 12). Accountability provides the rationale, but evaluation models have been derived primarily from the social inquiry root.

Types of Evaluation Methods

Methods-driven evaluations center on an appropriate research design and methodology; the emphasis is on technical quality, not a comprehensive assessment of merit and worth (Stufflebeam, 2001). This category includes experimental studies, **case studies**, mixed-method studies, cost–benefit analysis, and others (Figure 2.1; Stufflebeam, 2001). The primary limitation of questions- and methods-oriented approaches is their narrow focus, often a research question, which is tangential to a comprehensive assessment of the overall merit and worth of programs (Stufflebeam, 2001). In distance education, for example, the equivalence studies are question-oriented approaches because they answered the question of whether the distance and face-to-face sections of the same course were equivalent. Research questions commonly involve cause and effect, such as "Did this technology-based intervention result in higher student performance, as

• Objectives-driven approaches	• Mixed methods
• Experimental methods	• Cost–benefit
• Qualitative methods	• Accreditation
• Case studies	

FIGURE 2.1. Types of evaluation methods.

measured by mean course grades?" A question may involve multiple variables of cause and effect, such as "What are the various factors that contribute to student retention?" or "What is the relative importance of each variable?"

Objectives-Driven Approaches

In the early days, the focus of educational evaluation was to determine whether educational objectives were being achieved (Worthen, Sanders, & Fitzpatrick, 1997). This approach originated with the work of Tyler (1942) and is referred to as the objectives-driven approach. Educational goals are defined, translated into performance-based objectives, and measured with various kinds of tests (Tyler, 1942). Tyler's distinction between measurement and evaluation had a huge influence on educational evaluation, which for years consisted of student achievement tests and psychometrics (Kellaghan et al., 2003). Although still very influential today, this early approach provided the foundation for the method-oriented approaches (Stufflebeam, 2001), all of which emphasize the design, procedures, and controls for obtaining hard scientific evidence.

Experimental Methods

Experimental methods were adopted from the applied sciences (e.g., Campbell & Stanley, 1963). In an experimental design, learners are randomly assigned to an experimental or a control group, and a treatment is given to the experimental group but not to the control group. When random assignment to groups is not possible, as is often the case in educational research, quasi-evaluation designs, such as an interrupted time series or a nonequivalent group design, are often used (Fitzpatrick et al., 2004). Campbell and Stanley's (1963) *Experimental and Quasi-Experimental Designs for Research* was instrumental in laying the foundations of scientific methodology in program evaluation.

The problem with experimental methods is that it is difficult to control for intervening variables, or task conditions, which are decided by state governments, school boards, or teachers (Chatterji, 2005). In addition, experimental studies focus on outcomes, not on processes, side effects, or unanticipated complexities (Parlett & Hamilton, 1977). Experimental findings are often too narrow to provide an assessment of overall merit and worth (Stufflebeam, 2001) or to explain why a particular outcome occurred for one group and not another. Finally, there are concerns about **ethics**: No one who needs a treatment should be deprived because they are randomly assigned to a control group.

Qualitative Methods

With qualitative paradigms, findings "emerge" and are not the result of "some pre-ordinate, inquiry plan projected before the evaluation is conducted" (p. 133). Findings are ethnographic, detailed, and naturalistic (based on program activity not intent). Hammond (1973), for example, recommended a detailed analysis of the impact of contextual (i.e., institutional and instructional) factors relevant to the attainment of program objectives. Similarly, with their illuminative approach, for example, Parlett and Hamilton (1977) recommended qualitative methodologies to describe and interpret programs as holistic entities, identify intended outcomes, compare them to actual outcomes, analyze program implementation, and uncover side effects. The problem with qualitative methods is researcher bias, which needs to be controlled by **triangulation**, preferably by an independent evaluator. The second problem is that, because sample sizes are smaller than with surveys, generalizability is more suspect.

Case Studies

The purpose of a case study is to "delineate and illuminate a program, not necessarily to guide its development or to assess and judge its merit and worth" (Stufflebeam, 2001, p. 34). A single case can provide an in-depth, stand-alone picture of a specific program, or several cases can be sampled from a range of scenarios to enhance generalizability (Reigeluth, 1999). In case research, the evaluator uses coding categories to make the conceptual connections that constitute theory building (Miles & Huberman, 1994) or, in the case of program evaluation, an in-depth understanding of the workings of the program. The problems with case studies are researcher bias and generalizability.

> With mixed methods, quantitative and qualitative data are blended to provide an analysis of both outcomes and process. Mixed-methods studies result in greater validity, generalizability, and usefulness than qualitative or qualitative methods alone (Stufflebeam, 2001).

Mixed Methods

Strategies for blending the epistemologies and underlying value systems of the two paradigms are provided by Tashakkori and Teddlie (1998, 2003). According to Stufflebeam (2001), qualitative and quantitative methods "can complement each other in ways that are important to the evaluation's audience" and the consideration of mixed methods is "almost always appropriate" (p. 41). Chatterji (2005) recommends "extended-term" mixed-method designs, which track the development of a program over time. Chatterji's (2005) mixed-method, time-series design includes a systemic, contextually based study in the early phase, a more analytical experimental or quasi-experimental design in the later phase, and causal explanations based on both types of evidence. Mixed methods are more time consuming than qualitative or qualitative methods alone, but the multiple data sources provide more information than is obtained by either method alone.

Cost–Benefit

Cost–benefit studies consist of sets of quantitative procedures to determine the ratio of investments to social benefit. Cost-effectiveness compares the costs and outcomes of alternative programs and does not require monetary units; therefore, it is more appropriate than cost–benefit analysis for educational programs (Levin, 2001). Costs can be determined by summing various components of total costs, including facilities, equipment, and client input (Levin, 2001). Benefits are often operationalized quantitatively, such as the number of graduates in different programs. Benefits can be intangible or difficult to measure, such as the acquisition of "basic transferable skills" or the "appreciation of cultural diversity," but intangible benefits are no less important than tangible ones (Simpson, 1991, p. 25). The major problem with cost–benefit studies is that they are difficult to quantify in terms of educational benefits; with distance education, future estimates of costs are also important, and these estimates need to reflect rapidly changing technologies and market conditions.

Accreditation studies address questions of whether programs are meeting established standards of quality, whether programs should be certified, and whether institutions should be approved to deliver these programs.

Accreditation

The accreditation of schools and colleges is a major stand that began in the 1800s and continues today (Kellaghan et al., 2003). **Accreditation** is "the process by which an organization grants approval of institutions such as schools, universities and hospitals" (Fitzpatrick et al., 2004, p. 214). This process is based on information-gathering tools and concepts adopted from industrial models of evaluation (Forsyth, Jolliffe, & Stevens, 1995). In an accreditation study, evaluators rate aspects of the program using lists of objective, predetermined criteria and guidelines in a formal professional review system developed by a professional accrediting body (Stufflebeam, 2001). In the past, quantitative measures of facilities (e.g., buildings, classrooms, lightbulbs, and staff qualifications) were used to analyze how inputs and processes are related to outcomes (Worthen et al., 1997). Today, however, physical indicators such as numbers of classrooms are less important, and the focus is usually on outcomes and qualitative indicators such as the purpose of schooling (Fitzpatrick et al., 2004).

One example of an accreditation study is the National Accreditation of Teachers of Education, which is implemented by American public universities every 5 years. Accreditation models emphasize the merits of programs from competing institutions (Stufflebeam, 2001) but usually stop short of being candid consumer reports. With the exception of a few accreditation mills (bogus accrediting organizations that attempt to provide diploma mills with legitimacy), in general, accreditation is critical to ensuring effectiveness and high-quality educational services (MacDonald, Breithaupt, Stodel, Farres, & Gabriel, 2002, p. 36). Finally, because accreditation is associated with quality assurance and control procedures, it "has played an important role in institutional change" (Fitzpatrick et al., 2004, p. 117).

Accreditation studies can help individuals make informed judgments about the quality of educational services from competing providers. Guides (e.g., Deane's, 2005, guide to choosing online courses) provide some assistance in navigating a bewildering array of choices.

The Limitations of Using Methods without Models

There are several limitations and constraints of using methods without models to guide program evaluation studies. First, the focus of methods is narrow, and evaluation studies guided only by methods do not lead to a comprehensive picture of merit and worth. Second, the program goals, the values underlying the program, and the role of stakeholders are not considered. It was precisely to address these kinds of concerns that Cronbach (1980) took the field of program evaluation in a new direction with his 95 theses, which challenged the attribution of causes to outcomes, given the complexities of educational environments, and called for a better understanding of contextual factors and stronger social programming. Cronbach called for program evaluation to broaden out from measurable outcomes to "process and judgment based on multiple data sources" (Ross & Morrison, 1997, p. 335), thereby leading the way to more comprehensive approaches based on models and not on methods alone.

Models with Values in the Foreground

When we refer to evaluation models based on values, we are referring to models that bring values to the foreground in any of a number of ways. Values underlie the collection and use of scientific evidence and are reflected in diverse epistemologies, purposes, goals, and uses of program evaluation studies (Popham, 1993). Evaluators also need to think about the values underlying educational programs and devise strategies for negotiating the interpretation and use of evaluation findings with stakeholders (Ross & Morrison, 1997). By rejecting an "unquestioned, singular value base" (p. 91), evaluators are less interested in finding the "right answer" than in gathering the multiple perspectives of stakeholders, all of which may be equally valid. Evaluators are sensitive and responsive to stakeholders' diverse values and shift the locus of judgment to the participants (Hamilton, 1977, p. 339).

MODELS WITH VALUES IN THE FOREGROUND

- Consumer orientation
- Responsive evaluation
- Deliberative democratic evaluation
- Constructivism
- Theory-based evaluation

Consumer Orientation

With the consumer approach, evaluators produce independent, consumer-like assessments where the consumer's welfare is the ultimate value. They take on the role of the "enlightened consumer" (Stufflebeam, 2001, p. 58) and make judgments about the merit and worth of products and services. This approach is "hard-hitting, independent assessment intended to protect consumers from shoddy programs, services or products" (Stufflebeam, 2001, p. 60). With Scriven's (1972) goal-free evaluation, for example, evaluators are encouraged to ignore statements of intended effects and focus only on actual effects. The reason is that statements of intent constitute a "rhetoric of intent," often couched in the fashionable jargon of current trends, which is often used "as a substitute for evidence of success" (p. 7). The Key Evaluation Checklist provides a comprehensive assessment of merit and worth and emphasizes independent assessment, thereby earning "high credibility with consumer groups" (Stufflebeam, 2001, p. 60).

Responsive Evaluation

Stake's (1967) countenance approach has had a major impact on later theoretical developments in evaluation (Fitzpatrick et al., 2004). Stake's (1967) two countenances to evaluation are description and judgment. Each program is a complex case to be investigated qualitatively and comprehensively in its unique context. The approach is responsive to the complexity and diversity of contemporary social realities, and, by involving stakeholders, they enhance the credibility of findings obtained in political environments. According to Stake, the role of the evaluator is to document the multiple realities of all program participants, including teachers, administrators, and taxpayers.

Deliberative Democratic Evaluation

With the deliberative democratic model, the focus is obtaining the equitable participation of all stakeholders, documenting their views, and negotiating a credible assessment of overall worth (House & Howe, 2000). Multiple methods such as discussions, surveys, debates, and negotiation are often used. Because the equitable participation of stakeholders at all stages is critical, power imbalances are unacceptable (Stufflebeam, 2001). It is up to the evaluator to reject input that appears to be invalid or unethical, and it is the evaluator who is responsible for reaching a final judgment on the worth of a program (Stufflebeam, 2001). The approach is "democratic, transactional, collaborative, participatory, empowerment and emancipatory evaluation" (Fitzpatrick et al., 2004, p. 133) and "adds a political element inasmuch as they foster and facilitate the activism of recipients of program services" (p. 147).

> Constructivism is based on the assumptions that there is no "objective" truth and, ultimately, no best answers or clearly preferable values. Evaluations are iterative processes grounded in communities of practice, with stakeholders playing an important role in determining the questions and variables (Guba & Lincoln, 1985).

Constructivism

Constructivism is based on the beliefs that science is never value free and that knowledge is problematic, subjective, and changing and is constructed from diverse perspectives (Stufflebeam, 2001). "[These approaches] favour . . . the use of qualitative methods . . . eschew the possibility of finding right or best answers and reflect the philosophy of postmodernism, with its attendant stress on cultural pluralism, moral relativity, and multiple realities. They provide for democratic engagement of stakeholders in obtaining and interpreting findings" (Guba & Lincoln, 1985, p. 62). The values underlying the evaluation design are to empower disenfranchised stakeholders and improve society (Fitzpatrick et al., 2004).

Constructivist evaluations are iterative processes grounded in communities of practice, with stakeholders playing an important role in determining the questions and variables (Guba & Lincoln, 1985). Evaluators document the multiple realities of all participants with first-hand experience of the program, including teachers, administrators, and taxpayers; facilitate the reconciliation of different perspectives; and may even give stakeholders control over the study and let them decide how to handle differences in values and goals. "Clients must also be receptive to ambiguous findings, multiple interpretations, the employment of competing value perspectives, and the heavy involvement of stakeholders in interpreting and using findings" (Stufflebeam, 2001, p. 70). The evaluator presents the diverse understandings of various stakeholders, makes sense of them, and works toward a consensus.

Theory-Based Evaluation

In theory-based evaluation, the evaluator begins with a theory of how the program is supposed to work and uses the program theory to guide the evaluation (Bickman, 1987; Chen, 1990; Rogers, Petrosino, Huebner, &

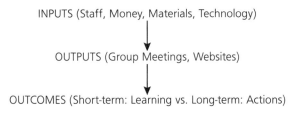

INPUTS (Staff, Money, Materials, Technology)

OUTPUTS (Group Meetings, Websites)

OUTCOMES (Short-term: Learning vs. Long-term: Actions)

FIGURE 2.2. The University of Tennessee Extension Program: Three-step logic model. From Donaldson (2007). Reprinted by permission.

Hacsi, 2000). For example, a program implementation theory might focus on the gap between program goals and program implementation, the reasons the program was or was not delivered as intended, or specific areas for program improvement. Theory-based evaluations involve logic models of the program theory and may involve stakeholders in the evaluation process (Chen, 1990). Logic models are a representation of beliefs and values about the mechanism by which the program is supposed to work.

Most federally funded programs in the United States now require a logic model to demonstrate how the program is supposed to work. Chen (2005) maintains there has been considerable interest in theory-based evaluations in health sciences and social work. The University of Tennessee's extension program, for example, uses a very simple three-step logic model consisting of inputs, outputs, and outcomes, the underlying theory being that group meetings and websites foster learning and changes in the program participants (Figure 2.2).

Other logic models are more complex versions of the same basic structure as in the previous example (Taylor-Powell & Henert, 2008). For example, the University of Wisconsin Extension Program Development logic's model shows a series of actions that describe the program, the investment, and the results. There are six core components:

1. Inputs: resources, contributions, program investments
2. Outputs: activities, services, events, and products
3. Outcomes: results or changes for individuals, groups, communities, etc.
4. Assumptions: beliefs about the program, the participants, and the context
5. External factors: the environment in which the program exists
6. Evaluation: impact

The above logic model is used for planning, program implementation, evaluation, communication, and other contexts. You can view this impressive logic model, as well as Taylor-Powell and Henert's (2008) suggestions for teaching and training with logic models at The University of Wisconsin Extension website at: *http://www.uwex.edu/ces/pdande/evaluation/evallogicmodel.html*. For suggestions on how to develop a logic model, see Krueger (n.d.).

Problems occasionally arise with the use of logic models. One problem is identifying the theory, and another is that different stakeholders may be firmly committed to different logic models. To illustrate this point, we provide examples of different values, including theories, ideologies, and goals underlying distance education and e-learning in Chapter 7. Despite these difficulties, logic models can bring stakeholders to the table to develop a shared understanding of the underlying theory, which is a worthy, if sometimes difficult, process.

Models with Consequences in the Foreground

Program evaluation models that bring consequences to the foreground include Stufflebeam's context, input, process, and produce (CIPP) model, Patton's (1997, 2000) utilization approach, and Fetterman's (1997) empowerment evaluation approach. This model emphasizes the impact of evaluations (i.e., how the findings of evaluation studies are actually used).

MODELS WITH CONSEQUENCES IN THE FOREGROUND

- The CIPP model
- Utilization evaluation
- Empowerment evaluation

The CIPP Model

With Stufflebeam et al.'s (1971) CIPP approach, evaluators work closely with program stakeholders to build a knowledge base to deliver and improve cost-effective services (Stufflebeam, 2001). CIPP's *context* refers to assessing "needs, problems, assets and opportunities to help decision-makers define goals and priorities" (Stufflebeam, 2004, p. 246). *Input* refers to assessing action plans, budgets, and staffing plans for cost-effectiveness and feasibility. *Process* refers to assessing the implementation of plans and helping users judge outcomes, and *product* refers to intended and unintended consequences and "success in meeting targeted needs" (Stuffle-beam, 2004, p. 246). The goal is to "provide a knowledge and value base for making and being accountable for decisions that result in developing, delivering, and making use of cost-effective services" (Stufflebeam, 2001, p. 56). Multiple quantitative and qualitative data sources are used to analyze the context, input, process, and outcomes, both intended and unintended (Fitzpatrick et al., 2004). This information is used then formatively to judge overall merit and worth and improve programs and services (Stufflebeam, 2001).

Utilization Evaluation

With utilization evaluation, the emphasis is on providing information to decision makers that they can use in practical ways to make an impact (Patton, 1997). The evaluator works with a select group of stakeholder representatives to clarify values, determine questions, investigate contextual dynamics, triangulate findings from different sources, and determine how the findings will be used. All aspects of the evaluation are geared toward maximizing the chances of applying the findings to their intended uses, and stakeholder consultation is important in furthering the change process (Stufflebeam, 2001). The utilization approach embraces multiple uses for the findings and does not necessarily advocate any particular social or moral agenda (Caracelli, 2000; Galston, 1999; Stufflebeam, 2001). There are several ways in which evaluation processes and findings can be used to make an impact. For example, participation in the evaluation process can foster learning in individuals and teams and change organizational culture (Patton, 1997). Another use is social betterment, defined as improved social conditions, fewer social problems, and reduced human distress and suffering (Henry, 2000). Finally, when evaluation evidence is presented to funding agents to justify funds given or to support a funding request, an investigation of unintended program and social side effects is recommended (Henry, 2000).

Empowerment Evaluation

Fetterman's (1997) approach emphasizes the evaluator as an agent of social change and evaluation as a vehicle for the self-sufficiency, self-determination, and empowerment of the disadvantaged. Stakeholders are partners in the design and analysis of evaluation studies. Miller and Campbell (2006) reviewed 46 studies based on empowerment evaluation, including school improvement for low-income children, health care

(Strober, 2005), and child abuse prevention (Lentz et al., 2004). Criticisms of the approach are conceptual ambiguity, lack of success in practice, and limited evidence of success (Miller & Campbell, 2006). Finally, it is not always clear how this approach is distinct from similar approaches such as the deliberative democratic model (Miller & Campbell, 2006).

Where Do We Diverge with Alkin and Christie?

In this overview, we agree with Alkin and Christie's (2004a) three categories of evidence, valuing, and use. We have placed almost all of the program evaluation models in the same categories. The fact that the theorists themselves agreed with Alkin and Christie's (2004b) classifications makes it difficult for us to reclassify their models, even though there were compelling arguments in some cases. For example, Alkin and Christie (2004a) classified Chen's approach under the methods category because his approach is based on the methodology of structural equation modeling. Yet we believe that Chen's (1990, 2005) theory-based evaluation should be classified under values because theories are expressions of values and beliefs. In contrast to Alkin and Christie (2004a), however, we assert that evidence, values, and consequences are present in all evaluation models, even though values or consequences may be hidden or lurking in the background.

> Evidence, values, and consequences are present in *all* evaluation models but may be difficult to identify because they are often hidden in the background. Scientific experiments, for example, are said to be "value free." But being value free is a value, so values are indeed present but not visible.

Alkin and Christie's (2004b) evaluation tree has limitations as a metaphor because the branches are separate and distinct. Messick's framework corrects for this problem because it is a progressive matrix, in which evidence, values, and consequences *overlap*. This overlap is a more accurate representation of program evaluation models over the past 50 years. In the improvement/accountability approaches, for example, the underlying values of using findings for program improvement for the common good or for the benefit of society (Stufflebeam, 2001) overlap with the social consequences of programs and even of evaluations themselves. This kind of conceptual overlap is represented by the progressive nature of Messick's framework and is one of Messick's most important insights. In sum, although program evaluation models vary in their *relative* emphasis, evidence, values, and consequences are present in all program evaluation models. Even when one or two are predominant, the others are in the background.

MESSICK'S (1989) FRAMEWORK

- Covers the same conceptual territory as Alkin and Christie (2004b).
- Is a comprehensive, omnibus program evaluation model.
- Is *grounded* in professional program evaluation theory.

Conclusions

Program evaluation is applied research and a profession in its own right (Fitzpatrick et al., 2004; Stufflebeam, 2001). Professional evaluation has a rich and diverse history of philosophies, theories, values, and practices, so that today there is a pluralistic understanding of evaluation use (Caracelli, 2000). In fact, the recurring debates over epistemology have generated the contemporary diversity of evaluation designs, approaches, and methods (Fitzpatrick et al., 2004). Alkin and Christie (2004a) classified program evaluation theories according to their "predominant focus" on (1) method, (2) values, and (3) use. These classification categories are the same as Messick's (1) scientific evidence, (2) values, and (3) consequences. For this reason, Messick's framework is a comprehensive, omnibus model of professional program evaluation.

Both professional program evaluation models and Messick's framework encompass three recurring aspects of value: scientific evidence, values, and consequences. The diversity of the models results from the relative emphasis they give to these three themes, which are, in effect, three different dimensions of program value. Classic methodologies, for example, bring scientific evidence to the foreground and ignore values and consequences. Similarly, the accreditation- and management-oriented models emphasize inputs, outputs, and consequences, but values are still *implied* because these studies usually offer directions for program improvement. Similarly, contemporary models, which affirm multiple perspectives and stakeholder participation, bring values into the foreground, and evidence is in the background. Finally, in the utilization approaches, consequences are in the foreground, whereas evidence and values are in the background. Our whole point is to show that Messick's framework provides a comprehensive, omnibus model of professional program evaluation.

CHAPTER 3

■ ■ ■ ■ ■ ■ ■ ■

Evaluation Theory and Practice in Distance Education and E-Learning

In this chapter, we review the historical context of evaluation theory and practice in distance education. We provide a brief overview of general evaluation models in distance education and e-learning and classify them by their relative emphasis on scientific evidence, values, or consequences. We then review authentic studies of evaluation practice in the literature. Finally, we show specific examples of unintended consequences emerging in distance courses, thereby providing some empirical support for Tenner's (1996) ideas and for the inclusion of unintended consequences as an explicit evaluation criterion in evaluation models in distance education and e-learning.

41

Evaluation Theory

The conceptual foundations of evaluation theory in distance education and e-learning have mostly paralleled developments in the fields of educational measurement program evaluation, with concepts from these fields coming in "through the back door" (Ross & Morrison, 1997). However, evaluation models in distance education also reflect the unique and varied characteristics of distance education contexts (e.g., Belanger & Jordan, 2000; Bates, 1995; Clark, 1994a; Van Slyke, Kittner, & Belanger, 1998). Kirkpatrick and Kirkpatrick's (2006) four-level model was designed for training contexts in general but is often used in educational evaluation. Evaluation frameworks for e-learning have grown out of distance education and are not strikingly different from distance education models. There have also been adaptations of Messick's model (Ruhe, 2002b; Bunderson, 2003). In this chapter, we group or categorize evaluation models in distance education according to their relative emphasis on scientific evidence, values, and consequences. In doing so, we show that Messick's (1989) model can be used as a model for distance education program evaluation.

Criteria for Model Selection

Because there are so many evaluation frameworks in distance education, we selected only models with a general application across diverse distance and e-learning contexts. We did not review models for specific programs or specific technologies such as video or multimedia. Using these criteria, we chose 12 evaluation models for distance and e-learning. We present these models in order based on their relative emphasis on scientific evidence, values, and consequences.

Models with Scientific Evidence in the Foreground

The first group of distance education evaluation models emphasize scientific evidence, which includes outcomes, relevance, and cost–benefit. *Outcomes* includes both quantitative data on learning outcomes, completion rates, and learner satisfaction ratings as well as interview and survey responses on learner satisfaction. *Relevance* refers to the fit between the course content and the needs of society, authentic course materials, and the transfer of learning to the real world. *Cost–benefit* refers to the cost of the course in relation to the benefits, efficiency, or effectiveness. Some models in this category are descriptive models of distance education course

- Van Slyke et al. (1998)
- Belanger and Jordan (2000)
- Bates's (1995) ACTION model
- CIAO model (Scanlon et al., 2000)
- Kirkpatrick and Kirkpatrick's (2006) model
- Hughes and Attwell's (2002) e-Learning Model
- A model of e-learning usability and learner affect (Zaharias, 2005)
- The e3Learning Model (Lam & McNaught, 2005)

FIGURE 3.1. Distance and e-learning evaluation models with scientific evidence in the foreground.

environments, which have unique characteristics. These unique features are captured in several evaluation models of the course environment and in other models that go beyond the course environment to include features of the surrounding context (e.g., learner, cost structures, and institutional features). Finally, the models we have placed in this category include *no* references to values or consequences (Figure 3.1).

Van Slyke, Kittner, and Belanger (1998)

Van Slyke et al.'s (1998) evaluation model is a model of the course environment, specifically of the relationship between contextual (input) variables and outcome (product) variables. Their two-level framework of evaluation consists of predictor variables (learner, course, distance learning, and institutional characteristics, including objectives, delivery methods, and support structure) and outcome variables (institutions and learners). Institutional outcomes include lower costs, better productivity of instructors, shared resources with other institutions, and increased geographical reach. Learner outcomes include technical awareness and skills. Although the authors believe that all these variables interact in a complex system, they do not mention underlying values or unintended consequences.

Belanger and Jordan (2000)

Belanger and Jordan (2000) proposed a framework consisting of predictor variables similar to those of Van Slyke et al. (1998). However, they include not two but four levels of outcome variables impacted by distance learning: (1) learners, (2) instructors, (3) institutions, and (4) society (Figure 3.2).

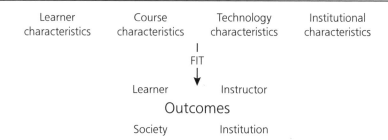

FIGURE 3.2. Belanger and Jordan's (2000) framework of evaluation.

Learner characteristics includes the learners' objectives, or personal skills such as self-sufficiency, computer proficiency, time management, interpersonal communication, problem solving, planning, previous technology experience, prior expectations, and attitudes. Course characteristics include group projects, evaluation methods, and hands-on components of the course (e.g., a series of computer-mediated technologies to support collaboration tasks). *Technology characteristics* include the "transition to an 'anytime, anywhere' environment [which] provides no inherent guarantees for quiet, comfort or ease of learning" (Belanger & Jordan, 2000, p. 189).

The lower part of the framework shows four levels of outcomes: *learner, instructor, society, and institution.* The *learner outcomes* level includes increased technology awareness and skills and higher quality of interaction with better access to the instructor. *Institutional outcomes* includes lower costs, increased geographical reach, increased productivity among instructors, and sharing of instructional resources with other institutions. Finally, *societal outcomes* includes a more professional workforce, increased quality of life, and increased access to education (regardless of culture, class, or financial status).

> Belanger and Jordan's (2000) framework is a dynamic model, where distance course variables interact in a complex, dynamic system. A lack of fit signals unintended consequences.

In this model, the arrow labeled "FIT" shows that "all of these course characteristics and contextual variables must be carefully examined, not in isolation, but together" (Belanger & Jordan, 2000, p. 189). One example is when adjustments in admissions and recruiting policies and decisions are made to meet the capabilities of younger learners, thereby enhancing the overall efficiency and success of the instructional system (Johnstone & Krauth, 1996). Similarly, learner outcomes can vary, depending on the interaction among learner, course, technology, and institutional characteristics.

Bates's (1995) ACTION model

Bates's (1995) ACTION model also emphasizes scientific evidence but not values or unintended consequences. The ACTION model consists of the following evaluation criteria:

> Access: How accessible and flexible is the technology?
>
> Costs: What is the cost structure? What is the unit cost per learner?
>
> Teaching and learning: What learning, instructional approaches, and technologies are best?
>
> Interactivity and user friendliness: What kind of interaction is provided? How easy is it? How reliable is the technology? Are there frequent crashes or breakdowns?
>
> Organizational issues: What are the organizational requirements and barriers?
>
> Novelty: How new is the technology?
>
> Speed: How quickly can the course be changed to accommodate revisions and updates?

When this model was actually used to guide an evaluation study, the Response of Adult Learners study, these questions were answered with survey and interview data. In effect, the ACTION model is a two-level model, because access, teaching and learning, interactivity, and costs are evaluated at the level of the individual, whereas organizational issues, novelty, and speed are evaluated at the level of the organization. Although frequent crashes or breakdowns are examples of unintended consequences, this model does not include an analysis of unintended consequences in general. Similarly, the model does not include any reference to the values underlying distance courses.

The CIAO Model

Scanlon, Jones, Barnard, Thompson, and Calder's (2000) CIAO model consists of context, interactions, and outcomes crossed with rationale,

	Context	Interactions	Outcomes
Rationale	Aims and context of use of CAL	Process data to understand whether, how, and why some element works	Cognitive and affective learning outcomes; attribution of outcomes to CAL is difficult
Data	Designers and course team aims; policy documents and meeting records	Records of student interaction; diaries; online logs	Measures of learning; changes in learners' attitudes and perceptions
Methods	Interview designers and course team; analyze policy documents	Observation; diaries; video/audio and computer recording	Interviews; questionnaires; tests

FIGURE 3.3. The CIAO model of evaluation. CAL, computer-assisted learning.

data, and methods (Figure 3.3). Based on 20 years of evaluation experience in course teams, the CIAO model includes an analysis of course team objectives, or intended consequences, and of policy documents and meeting records of the course teams. The authors stress learning outcomes but also acknowledge the difficulties in attributing learning outcomes to technologies. Several methods for data collection are also provided. This model emphasizes scientific evidence but not values or unintended consequences.

Kirkpatrick and Kirkpatrick's (2006) Model

Kirkpatrick and Kirkpatrick's (2006) four-level model was designed for evaluating training programs in general but is included here because it is a model that is well regarded among distance educators. This model has been around for some time (see Kirkpatrick, 1998) and can be applied to diverse training programs, including coaching, presentation skills, and sales. The model has also become popular for evaluating technology-based learning programs, especially for-credit in-service courses.

In Figure 3.4, the first level, *reaction*, refers to learner satisfaction. The second level, *learning*, refers to changed attitudes, improved knowledge, and increased skills. The third level, *behavior*, refers to new behaviors in

Level 1: Reaction

Level 2: Learning

Level 3: Behavior

Level 4: Results

FIGURE 3.4. Kirkpatrick and Kirkpatrick's (2006) four-level model of evaluation.

authentic contexts. Finally, the fourth level, *results*, refers to improved quality. According to the authors, programs should be planned in reverse order, from desired results to behaviors to learning to reaction. The evaluation tools include interviews of program participants, checklists of skills and attitudes, and performance assessment rubrics. Hard data on Level 1 are critical because learners need to respond favorably to the training before they can change attitudes or behaviors. Levels 2, 3, and 4 are implemented if funds and staff are available. In sum, the model is simple and practical but is based on evidence collected in four different levels and does not include underlying values or unintended consequences.

Hughes and Attwell's (2002) E-Learning Model

Hughes and Attwell's (2002) framework for e-learning has five major clusters of variables: (1) individual learner, (2) environmental, (3) technology, (4) contextual, and (5) pedagogic. Each of these categories is a cluster of individual variables. Individual learner variables include demographics (e.g., age, gender), learning history (including outcomes), learner attitude, learner motivation, and familiarity with the technology. The learning environment includes physical, institutional, and environment variables. The contextual variables include the political context (e.g., Who is funding e-learning and why?), cultural background (e.g., How highly is e-learning valued?), and geographic location. Technology variables include hardware, software, and connectivity, among others. Finally, pedagogic variables include the level and nature of learner support systems, accessibility, accreditation, and certification, among others. We have included Hughes and Attwell's model in this section of evidence, values, and consequences because it is fairly comprehensive, even though consequences is not a criteria.

The e3Learning Model

The e3Learning model (Lam & McNaught, 2005) is a five-step model of a complex, detailed, participatory team process to evaluate websites for e-learning (Figure 3.5). With five complex diagrams, a question pool, and a decision matrix, this model is complex and multilayered. A pool of more than 450 survey questions was compiled; these questions are grouped into five dimensions (predevelopment, environment, teaching and learning processes, learning outcomes, and others). The decision matrix consists of predevelopment, environment, process, outcome, and others. The e3Learning model is a system to allow team members to reflect and collaborate and to create a smooth workflow to enable continuous improvements that match diverse needs. The model has been used to evaluate more than 70 educational websites accessed by over 5,000 students and has supported the development of 139 more sites.

Level 1: The role of evaluation
(proposal, meetings, development, implementation, reflection)

Level 2: The evaluation process
(write plan, frame questions, collect and analyze data, make decisions)

Level 3: Communication among team members

Level 4: Work flow (logistics, monitoring, data analysis, reports)

Level 5: Chart of roles by team member by course

FIGURE 3.5. The e3Learning model (Lam & McNaught, 2005).

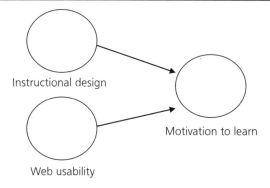

FIGURE 3.6. A model of e-learning usability and learner affect (Zaharias, 2005).

A Model of E-Learning Usability and Learner Affect (Zaharias, 2005)

Zaharias (2004, 2005) developed a conceptual framework for the usability evaluation of asynchronous e-learning applications used by adult learners in corporate training settings. The framework is an extension of human–computer interaction literature in that it is based on the notion that traditional usability measures of effectiveness, efficiency and satisfaction are not adequate for all e-learning contexts. "The usability of e-learning designs is directly related to their pedagogical value" (Zaharias, 2005, p. 1). The model predicts motivation to learn from a combination of web usability and instructional design parameters.

In Figure 3.6, the usability design dimensions include

- Content
- Learning and support
- Visual design
- Navigation
- Accessibility
- Interactivity
- Self-assessment and learnability

The model was actually used to develop a questionnaire that was psychometrically tested. To evaluate an e-learning program, then, the evaluator could use data from Zaharias's questionnaire to run a regression model.

The results of the regression model would indicate whether the e-learning instructional program predicts motivation to learn. Zaharias's approach can be used for formative or summative evaluations. We return to Zaharias's questionnaire in Chapter 6.

Models Based on Evidence, Values, and Consequences

Some evaluation models in distance education include scientific evidence, values, and consequences. *Underlying values* refers to an analysis of value labels, underlying theory, ideology, or other values such as the values of stakeholders. *Unintended consequences* refers to unintended effects, both instructional and social. We have classified seven models in this group (Figure 3.7).

Gooler (1979)

Gooler's (1979) model includes scientific evidence, values, and consequences. Data should be collected, analyzed, and used to evaluate (1) access and equality of opportunity; (2) relevancy to needs and expectations, with the recognition that shifts in needs occur; (3) quality of academic program offerings; (4) learner outcomes, including changes in learner attitudes; (5) cost-effectiveness; and (6) generation of knowledge. Gooler recommends evaluating the impact on individuals, the institution, and society and gives many varied and specific examples of unintended consequences under each of these categories. Under the access category, for example, Gooler mentions delivery problems, and under outcomes he refers to unanticipated program effects. Gooler (1979) notes that multiple stakeholders have different value systems, which underscores "the need to consider pluralistic purposes of distance education programs" (p. 47). Finally, he also includes an extensive list of "important social consequences."

• Gooler (1979)	• Lorenzo and Moore (2002)
• Rumble (1981)	
• Collis (1993)	• Baker and O'Neil (2006)
• Clark (1994a)	• Ruhe (2002b)
• Mann (1998)	• Bunderson (2003)

FIGURE 3.7. Models based on evidence, values, and consequences.

Rumble (1981)

Rumble (1981) recommends that evaluation take place on two levels. The first level is a comparison of objectives or intended outcomes with actual outcomes, in other words "the overall performance of the system under evaluation, in terms of output relative to its aims and objectives" (p. 67). The objectives are the context or the "ideal," which "has been defined and which can be used as a benchmark against which actual performance can be compared" (p. 66). The second level is an analysis of the coordination of the course subcomponents in the day-to-day course implementation.

RUMBLE'S APPROACH TO COURSE EVALUATION

Evaluation takes place at two distinct levels:

- Level 1: Overall performance (aims and objectives vs. course output).
- Level 2: Internal functioning of the system (subsystem efficiencies).

In effect, this two-level approach, which is central to Rumble's model, is a system-wide analysis of the gap between the standards of the ideal and the actual program implementation. For Rumble, outcomes includes (1) number of graduates in the shortest possible time, (2) ratio of the number of graduates to total number of learners admitted, (3) response to needs of learners and society, (4) cost-efficiency, and (5) effectiveness. Although Rumble does not use the term *unintended consequences*, this two-level approach is an analysis of both intended and unintended outcomes as they play themselves out in the day-to-day operations of the distance education system. In effect, Rumble is calling for an in-depth investigation of the course implementation system and for an analysis of unintended effects.

Collis (1993)

Based on Stake's (1967) countenance model, Collis's (1993) evaluation model has five stages:

Stage 1: Analysis of assumptions, intentions, and project planning.
Stage 2: Assessment of assumptions, intentions, plans, and success indicators.
Stage 3: Observations about underlying dynamics, such as personal ambition.

Stage 4: Assessment of the fit between what was planned and what was observed.

Stage 5: Interpretation of incongruities in the system.

The end results of these five stages are an understanding of the implementation system and a set of recommendations for changes in the course. There is a diagram for each stage, and the fifth stage diagram has no fewer than eight boxes with 11 paths between them, which would make this model difficult to use with authentic data. To analyze unintended consequences, for example, the evaluator would need to trace through various paths in all five models. In applying her framework to the evaluation data from a course using three technologies to deliver professional training to engineers and managers in electronics industries, Collis shows in considerable detail the many diverse and specific ways in which unintended consequences play themselves out in the course implementation. Collis's framework is based on Stake's (1967) model but is cumbersome, difficult to apply, and incomplete because it excludes an analysis of cost–benefit and relevance.

> Collis uses the terms *goodness of fit* and *incongruities in the system,* but these terms really mean "unintended consequences."

Clark (1994a)

Clark's (1994a) two-level framework, based on participant reactions and achievement of program objectives, includes scientific evidence, values, and unintended consequences. Surveys can be used to uncover learners' perceptions of changes in their learning and unanticipated consequences. Because media can no more influence the quality of learning than a delivery truck can influence the quality of nutrition, the effects of media should be considered separately from instruction. Therefore, program objectives should be divided into "at least two categories: those associated with delivery and those associated with instruction" (p. 69). Delivery technology includes "equipment, machines and media," whereas instructional technology includes "lessons, examples, practices and tests" (p. 64). Delivery technologies should be evaluated for their abilities to provide access and technical quality, whereas instructional technologies should be evaluated for changes in learning, transfer, motivation, and application of knowledge outside of the classroom.

Clark (1994a) recommends a cost–effectiveness analysis, with time, especially the donated time of volunteers, being included as a cost. This analysis should also include opportunity costs by comparing the costs of the program to that of an alternative delivery method for the same program. Clark also recommends an investigation and consideration of underlying values and the views of stakeholders but does not provide any direction for how this should be done. Finally, evaluation should be conducted in the early stages to identify "negative effects," which can then be corrected before the course ends. Unintended social consequences such as the unmet social needs of young learners should be reported, and unexpected effects are sometimes beneficial.

Mann (1998)

Mann's (1998) model is based on a quality assurance approach, which emphasizes the standardization of products, services, and modes of assessment. Mann's (1998) model includes quality of curriculum, quality of interaction, customer satisfaction, independent and external evaluation, and turnaround time (time between assignment submission and receipt of feedback). Mann (1998) attributed the low dropout rate of the Surrey Master of Arts (Teaching English as a Second Language; TESOL) program at the University of Surrey (United Kingdom) to the success of their admissions procedures and process. We have included this quality assurance model because customer perceptions of quality is related to brand name recognition, which is important for the success of globally delivered courses.

The Five Pillars of Quality Framework

Lorenzo and Moore (2002) proposed a quality framework consisting of five overlapping pillars, principles, and metrics that can help establish benchmarks and standards for quality based on continuous quality improvement (p. 1):

- Learning effectiveness.
- Cost–effectiveness and institutional commitment.
- Access.
- Faculty satisfaction.
- Student satisfaction.

For each pillar, several statements are provided that describe the ideal environment. The framework is also adaptive in that quality is measured by each organization "in terms of its own distinctive, dynamic mission" (p. 4). Depending on the mission and goals, evaluators can weigh each measure differently with the following equation:

Quality = $k1$ * learning effectiveness
+ $k2$ * cost effectiveness and institutional commitment
+ $k3$ * student satisfaction + $k4$ * faculty satisfaction + $k5$ * access

Measurement scales include the National Study of Student Engagement, comparative U.S. rankings of cost–effectiveness in news reports, and student satisfaction measures such as MSN's Best Party Schools. Although this model is heavy on scientific evidence, we have included it under evidence, values, and consequences because performance targets or benchmarks are expressions of values and are not based on, or derived from, scientific evidence. In addition, consequences are implied because the course either meets or fails to meet the performance targets.

Design-Centered Evaluation Architecture

Baker and O'Neil (2006) proposed three frameworks, or "design architectures," for evaluating nine overlapping conceptions of web-based instructional environments, ranging from more formal, comprehensive environments to incidental learning applications. The first architecture is from the perspective of the user and includes user variables such as access, user profile, goals, degree of control, and process. The second architecture is from the perspective of the designer and includes project time, cycle time (variations), and costs. The third is from the perspective of the funder and includes utility and "sufficient access and knowledge to build, trial and revise the system" (p. 15). These three perspectives are linked to the nine types of environments, and broad, "clinically-based guidelines" (p. 18) are provided.

Models Based on Messick's (1989) Framework

Ruhe's (2002b) Adaptation of Messick's Framework

Ruhe's (2002b) model is an early adaptation of Messick's (1989) framework and an earlier prototype of the unfolding model (Figure 3.8). Ruhe's model was used as a model of validity for assessment tasks in distance education, not for evaluating programs per se. However, Ruhe (2002b) showed that assessment tasks in distance education need to be validated as though

	Interpretation	Use
Evidential basis	• Construct/content • Learner satisfaction	• Relevance to education and training needs of society • Cost–benefit/economies of scale
Consequential basis	• Value implications	• Unintended instructional and social consequences

FIGURE 3.8. Ruhe's (2002b) adaptation of Messick's framework.

they are programs, a point made by Messick (1988). The main difference between Ruhe's (2002b) model and Ruhe and Zumbo's model (i.e., our current model offered in this book) is that the latter is an unfolding model and, therefore, more detailed, more useful, and more broadly applicable to diverse distance and e-learning environments. Ruhe's (2002b) model was an intermediate stage in the evolution of Messick's (1989) model of test validity into Ruhe and Zumbo's model of course evaluation.

Bunderson's (2003) Validity-Centered Model

Bunderson's (2003) model is an adaptation of Messick's (1989) conception of validity into a model of cyclical distance education course design and evaluation (Figure 3.9). "[Validity-centered design] VCD is a recent term and evolving method. It builds on the work of major validity theorists and applies the concept of the unified validity model in a new domain, that of blended learning and other systematically designed educational interventions" (p. 284). According to Bunderson,

> Validity embraces appeal, efficiency, values and expectations, evidence that the content, thinking processes, and structure of measures are appropriate,

- Values (e.g., reaching more students and increasing cost-effectiveness).
- Cost-effectiveness.
- Unintended negative consequences.
- Appeal.
- Efficiency.

FIGURE 3.9. Bunderson's (2003) validity-centered model.

and evidence that the treatment generalizes to different students and teachers from different backgrounds, that it relates in particular ways to other
criteria, and that the values and consequences expected are what is actually
attained. (p. 280)

Bunderson has renamed some elements from Messick's framework and
added other elements to fit the distance education context. He also recommends "continued vigilance" for unintended negative consequences.

Finally, Bunderson recommends correcting "each problem," thereby
showing that identifying unintended consequences is important because
they provide specific direction for improvement in the next design itera-
tion. The problem with Bundeson's model is that it does not reflect a thorough understanding of Messick's conception of validity, and the relabeling
of Messick's categories is cumbersome and unnecessarily verbose.

A Summary of Evaluation Models in Distance Education

The 17 models we have presented are summarized in Table 3.1. As shown
in Table 3.1, all 17 models contain outcomes as an important aspect of
merit and worth. The accreditation models are classified with the scientific
evidence group because they typically consist of checklists of measurable
items. In contrast, the quality assurance models are classified with the
scientific evidence, values, and consequences group because their consumer orientation implies values, whereas their orientation toward quality implies unintended, and undesirable, effects. Several of these models
include relevance, a broad term with multiple and related meanings such as
authenticity, transferability (Duffy & Jonassen, 1992; Willis, 2000), cognitive complexity, meaningfulness (authenticity), generalizability (Linn,
Baker, & Dunbar, 1997), and cognitive efficiency (Cobb, 1997). Several
models also contain costs, usually in relation to benefits, efficiency, or
effectiveness. A few models include unintended consequences, and fewer
still include a reference to the values, theories, and ideologies underlying
distance/e-learning courses, and of these, only two refer to stakeholders'
values (Gooler, 1979; Clark, 1994a; Collis, 1993).

Most of these models do not include value labels, or the underlying
theories or ideologies on which distance/e-learning courses are based. This
finding is surprising because new technologies are known to usher in new
values, goals, and theories of learning. Moreover, values are often *implied*
in the authors' discussions about what the course should offer: access or
geographical reach (Bates, 1995; Gooler, 1979; Van Slyke et al., 1998),

TABLE 3.1. Distance Education Evaluation Models Rated for the Facets of Messick's (1989) Framework

Author (year)	Outcomes	Relevance	C–B	Values	UC
Van Slyke et al. (1998)	Yes	Yes	No	No	No
Belanger & Jordan (2000)	Yes	Yes	Yes	No	No
Bates (1995)	Yes	No	Yes	No	No
Scanlon et al. (CIAO) (2000)	Yes	No	No	No	No
Kirkpatrick & Kirkpatrick (2006)	Yes	No	No	No	No
Rumble (1981)	Yes	Yes	Yes	No	Yes
Gooler (1979)	Yes	Yes	Yes	Yes	Yes
Clark (1994a)	Yes	Yes	Yes	Yes	Yes
Mann (1998)	Yes	Yes	Yes	Yes	Yes
Collis (1993)	Yes	No	No	Yes	Yes
Hughes & Attwell (2002)	Yes	No	Yes	No	No
Lam & McNaught (2005)	Yes	No	Yes	No	No
Zaharias (2005)	Yes	No	No	No	No
Lorenzo and Moore (2002)	Yes	Yes	Yes	Yes	No
Baker & O'Neil (2006)	Yes	Yes	Yes	Yes	Yes
Ruhe (2002b)	Yes	Yes	Yes	Yes	Yes
Bunderson (2003)	Yes	Yes	Yes	Yes	Yes

Note. C-B, cost–benefit; UC, unintended consequences.

interactivity (Bates, 1995; Clark, 1994a; Scanlon et al., 2000), hands-on course activities (Belanger & Jordan, 2000), relevance (Gooler, 1979), or cost-effectiveness (Bates, 1995; Gooler, 1979).

In sum, the purpose of this exercise is to show that the dimensions of Messick's (1989) framework are recurring themes in distance education models. Of these models, only four (Gooler, 1979; Clark, 1994a; Ruhe, 2002b; Bunderson, 2003) include *all* criteria of merit and worth of Messick's framework: (1) outcomes, (2) relevance, (3) cost–benefit, (4) underlying values, and (5) unintended consequences.

Values and Unintended Consequences

Evaluation theory in distance education has borrowed from the science of professional program evaluation theory. Table 3.1 shows that distance educators have readily adopted the traditional concepts of outcomes, relevance, and costs from the science of professional program evaluation. We found seven distance education evaluation models that included scientific evidence, unintended consequences, and underlying values, although these three categories were sometimes implied or in the background.

The values underlying distance courses are an important aspect of the merit and worth, and new technologies have always brought new values with them. Moreover, we can only take advantage of the capabilities of new technologies if we transform our fundamental conceptions about learning and institutions. Technology has moved us away from philosophies of knowledge transmission toward "a culture of collaboration capable of engaging everyone in life-long educational attainments" (Sinclair et al., 2006). Therefore, a professional program evaluation study should include an analysis of the underlying values of distance courses. As in any academic field, there is often little conscious awareness of value-laden rhetoric and underlying values and ideologies. For this reason, it is important to bring forward the values, ideologies, and theories of pedagogy underlying best practice in distance and e-learning and distinguish them from scientific evidence.

Although Rumble (1981) called for evaluators to investigate the unintended consequences of distance instructional programs, this call has been mostly avoided. Of 12 distance education evaluation models, we classified five into the category of scientific evidence. Table 3.1 shows five models that include euphemisms for unintended consequences, such as fit (Belanger & Jordan, 2000; Van Slyke et al., 1998), goodness of fit (Collis, 1993), the gap between the ideal and the real (Rumble, 1981), negative effects (Gooler, 1979), and "why and how some element works in addition to whether it works or not" (Scanlon et al., 2000, p. 4). Unintended consequences are not brought forward as an important dimension of merit and worth but are scattered, dispersed, or in the background. In fact, the term *unintended consequences* almost seems to be taboo in the distance education literature over the past 25 years. Yet because Tenner (1996) has identified various categories of the unintended consequences of technology, it is reasonable to expect to find them in distance education evaluation courses.

Evaluation Studies

From here, we review the 20-year history of authentic evaluation studies in distance education. We review only a small number of evaluation studies, which are not always easy to access. (Sloan-C has an online repository of best practices, which have been evaluated based on five quality criteria, to which the reader can refer for more information; however, not all of these reports are evaluation studies per se.) "First, only successful projects tend to be reported. If the project was not completed or . . . would embarrass the sponsors, the project will probably not make it into the academic or trade press" (Horton, 2001, p. 1). We try to answer the following three questions: To what extent are these studies guided by theoretical evaluation models? Can we find examples of values and unintended consequences lurking in the background? Are there enough of these instances to justify the inclusion of values and consequences in evaluation models?

Quantitative Studies

Evaluation studies in distance education evolved from the early experimental designs to qualitative and mixed methods as well as cost–benefit, accreditation, and quality assurance approaches. Like program evaluation, most early evaluation studies in distance education were based on experimental designs. These evaluation studies often include analyses of completion rates, grades, survey results on learner satisfaction, and attitudes toward technology and study habits. The earliest and most common quantitative studies in distance education were the equivalence studies. Popular in the 1960s and 1970s, these studies typically compare an innovative course with a traditional way of doing things (Organization for Economic Co-operation and Development, 1999). Their purpose is to demonstrate that face-to-face and distance/e-learning courses provide equivalent value even though the experiences might be very different (p. 71). These early studies helped to establish a public perception of equivalence between distance and face-to-face instruction, which was perceived as crucial for distance education to move out of the margins and become accepted into the mainstream (Simonson, Schlosser, & Hanson, 1999; Simonson, Smaldino, Albright, & Zvacek,

> Qualitative studies provide "insights about how learners are actually responding to the technology," thereby revealing the "weaknesses as well as the strengths" of distance courses (Selwyn, 1997).

2008). Today, distance education has become firmly established and continues to grow, and there is increasing recognition that distance education provides fundamentally different benefits from face-to-face courses.

Qualitative Studies

In the 1970s, evaluation came to be perceived as an essential part of **instructional design** (Ross & Morrison, 1997). In these studies, researchers use observations and open-ended interviews of learners, course designers, and instructors to obtain multiple perspectives on the characteristics of good learning in innovative environments. The focus was on "identifying particular aspects of the implementation of the design instance which helped or hindered their learning and finding ways to improve weak elements" (Reigeluth & Frick, 1999). "They should ask . . . what they did and did not like about the various elements of the instance, what helped them, what did not help them, whether they felt that the materials and activities were appropriate for their needs, what changes they would make if they could and whether they felt they had attained the objectives" (p. 641). Qualitative research also helps to define variables and generate hypotheses for future research studies (Tallent-Runnels et al., 2006, p. 95). The goal was to build theory grounded in empirical data (Lincoln & Guba, 1985; Merriam, 2002). Andrusyszyn and Davie (1997), for example, found that reflection through journal writing offered a valuable means for the transformation of knowledge to occur.

In contrast to outcomes-based evaluations, McCulloch's (1997) qualitative case study used the perspectives of the participants, course designers, and instructors to understand how the course really worked. This participatory evaluation embedded evaluation in the learners' experiences of their tutorial activities. Melton's (1995) case study of the open junior high school system in Indonesia was a process evaluation in the naturalistic tradition. McAlister (1998) did an ethnographic study of 36 mature learners that explored the effects of individual, social, and institutional factors on the outcomes of learners with low qualifications. Henderson and Putt (1999) performed a case study of different uses of audio-conferencing, including the "effectiveness of implementation strategies and the various roles of the participants in a cross-cultural context" (p. 25). These diverse approaches to qualitative research shed light on how distance/e-learning courses *really* worked as opposed to how they *should* work.

Mixed methodologies focus on both process and outcomes, thereby lending both depth and breadth to evaluation studies (Creeve & Caracelli, 1997; Tashakkori & Teddlie, 1998).

Studies Based on Mixed Methods

The Open University

There have been several mixed-methods evaluation studies in distance education. Since their 5-year project to evaluate the success of 500 first-year university students in 1973 (Woodley & McIntosh, 1980), The Open University has a long and impressive track record of evaluation studies based on a variety of mixed methodologies (Jones et al., 1996). This long history of evaluation practice culminated in Scanlon et al.'s (2000) CIAO evaluation model. In 1979, their computer-assisted learning component was evaluated for the first time (Jones et al., 1998). The study found that student interviewees had three reasons for not using optional tutorials: fear of looking "stupid," fear of breaking the software, and fear of being spied on. These findings, initially from interviews, were used to construct survey items distributed to 2,000 respondents. With this blending of methods, the interview findings were generalized to a larger population. In the 1980s, a large multidimensional evaluation involving linked projects was undertaken to determine whether the costs to learners of purchasing and maintaining personal computers were worth the benefits (Jones et al., 1996).

Jones and Petre (1994) found unanticipated consequences, such as learners reading the manual only as a last resort, a mismatch between learners' working styles and the assumptions of the instructional designers, and problems locating materials. They recommended that learner progress tracking was essential. Jones et al. (1998) found that some learners were arriving at the right answer through the wrong method. Kanuka and Anderson (1998) found that time engaged in social discourse tended to generate social discord, which served as a catalyst to the knowledge construction process. Scanlon et al. (2000) found that the narrative structure of computer simulations must be kept constant. As we show, these many Open University studies conducted over 20 years provided the empirical foundation for the CIAO evaluation model.

Master's Degree Programs

Chapman (2006) conceptualized and implemented an evaluation plan of a fully online 36-credit-hour master's degree program in training and development. A review of the literature and consultations with program administrators and faculty were used to develop an evaluation plan focused on goals, program improvement, and a framework that can be adapted to other programs. This evaluation study addressed processes, outcomes, and multiple perspectives and used a mixed-methodology approach. The authors did not compare the online program with face-to-face instruction but evaluated success on its own terms.

Martinez, Liu, Watson, and Bichelmeyer (2006) also evaluated a web-based master's degree program at a midwestern U.S. research university. Their approach reflected the participant- and expertise-oriented evaluation approaches, and they used mixed methodology. The authors collected interview and online survey data from administrators, faculty, and students and used a different interview protocol for each group. They found that the values underlying the program included:

- Enhancing the reputation of the program
- Providing research and development opportunities for professors and PhD students
- Providing remote access opportunities for those with work or family responsibilities
- Increasing the department's revenue stream

With these findings, the authors have brought into the foreground the multiple sets of values underlying the program. They concluded that "online learning environments are potentially beneficial for the key stakeholder groups including students, faculty, and administrators" (p. 6). One of the unintended consequences was that the full-time jobs and family responsibilities that provide the impetus for distance education are also the same factors that "keep these students from high levels of engagement beyond the work they do in their individual courses" (p. 272). Faculty were disillusioned with the CMS, and students appreciated the "streaming video of residential guest lectures, PowerPoint presentations, and the library e-Reserves functionality . . . but found problems in their implementation" (p. 275). Recommendations for improvement include "better informing [students] about the program before they start so that they may have more appropriate expectations about the curriculum, instructional activities, and time required to complete the program" (p. 272) and improvements to the CMS. They also recommended a cost–benefit study that included an analysis of incentives to faculty and the impact of these incentives on program quality.

Star Schools Program, U.S. Department of Education

The U.S. Department of Education provides funding to telecommunications partnerships for the Star Schools program. Star Schools grants are made to eligible telecommunications partnerships to develop distance educational and instructional programming through emerging technologies. More than 30 courses are offered, most of which are foreign language courses, followed by mathematics, science, and advanced-placement English. These courses enable students to meet high school graduation and college entrance requirements. The instructional modules are aligned with standards and benchmarks, for example:

> Indicator 1.2 of 2: Number of full credit courses or modules offering challenging content aligned with state or district standards at all academic levels (including high school credit, advanced placement, adult education, and graduate equivalency diploma courses).

Their 2006 program evaluation report available online is a summary of "pluses," "minuses," and "recommendations." Teachers reported using different and varied materials, using more cooperative learning, and greater use of multiple technologies. Because "grantees do not use a standard instrument to measure student achievement," "projects provided little data on program effectiveness, particularly regarding student outcomes," and there was considerable variation in delivery at the district and school levels (U.S. Department of Education, Office of Innovation and Improvement, 2007, p. 1). Their recommendations include "encouraging—through funding decisions, regulations, and incentives—grantees to collaborate closely with others involved in standards-based systemic reform" and "increased adoption of multiple technologies" (p. 1).

Statewide Virtual School Initiatives

State virtual schools provide web-based courses to middle and high school students. These statewide school networks have their "home" in the North American Council for Online Learning (NACOL), a virtual school association established in September 2003 dedicated to student success and lifelong learning. Many of these virtual schools are already providing the 21st-century learning environments that students need to become successful in life and in the workplace (Patrick & Levin, 2007). NACOL (2007) has also endorsed the *National Standards of Quality for Online Courses*. The SREB, Educational Technology Cooperative (2006) has also devised a list of online teaching evaluation criteria for state virtual schools. Their summary report of state virtual schools can serve as a model evaluation report, with numbers of virtual schools within the southern region, growth over the past 5 years, and lists of successes and growing pains (SREB, 2007c). A list of state-level participants in virtual school initiatives across the

United States is available at the elearners.com website at *www.elearners. com/resources/k12-online.asp.*

Human–computer interactions: technology-based subcomponents of distance courses such as webpages, computer-based learning aids, embodied agents, graphical user interface (Virvou & Kabassi, 2002).

Human–Computer Interactions

Human–computer interaction refers to the technology-based subcomponents of e-learning courses. The evaluation of components such as websites is complex and includes evaluating content, navigation, sites or pages, activities, and objectives (Nielson, 2000). "The elements of design include icons, text, color, dialog boxes and navigational systems" (p. 141). First, you need to define the learning purpose or goal. The key to interface design is the interaction of the learner with the e-learning environment to navigate through the content (p. 128). You can survey learners to determine how the site navigation worked for them, or do an analysis based on quantitative eyeball tracking. Many e-learning sites lack any theoretical foundations for content organization or interface design (Nielson, 2000).

Schaik and Ling (2005) evaluated (1) the usability of educational intranet sites by devising measures of task performance and navigation behavior and (2) the quality of human–computer interaction more generally. Conlon (2006) used classroom trials to assess a semiautomated software analyzer for evaluating students' concept maps and found that they lead to a more interactive assessment model of human–computer interaction. Finally, Mahmood and Ferneley (2006) devised a framework, based on an interpretive case study, for the evaluation of embodied agents. They found that educators prefer highly controlled embodied agents, whereas students prefer personalized, autonomous embodied agents that interface between themselves and the lecturer.

Blackboard Courses

Hazari (2002) evaluated the Blackboard course tool implemented in the Robert H. Smith School of Business at the University of Maryland. Mixed methods were used, including surveys and interviews with faculty and students. Sample items include:

- What features of Blackboard have been most useful to you?
- Have you been satisfied with the way your course instructor has used the Blackboard system?
- Do you believe that use of this system by your course instructor has contributed to your improved learning?

Hazari also conducted statistical tests of differences between faculty and student responses and found that the pattern of satisfaction with Blackboard system is the same for faculty and students. Open-ended faculty and student comments were also summarized for themes. One of the recommendations was that faculty training needs to go beyond tool use of Blackboard to include online pedagogy and that further enhanced use of course tools should be encouraged. Finally, a Student Survey Blackboard Course Tool is provided at the end of the report, available online at *www. sunilhazari.com/education/webct/bbeval.pdf.*

Cost–Benefit Analysis

Cost–benefit analysis is an evaluation tool designed to make decisions by comparing the benefits or outcome for each alternative with its costs. Costs can be categorized as fixed (e.g., technology and course development) or variable (e.g., tutor marking and Internet connections). Despite their usefulness, there are few cost–benefit studies in distance education. We have long known that start-up costs can be considerably higher than with face-to-face formats (Knapper, 1980) but need new costing models to determine the impact of learners not occupying the "desk" used in traditional cost estimation models (Belanger & Jordan, 2000). Bates (1995) proposes calculating average cost per student study hour for a given technology times the number of students over the life of a course, the grades, learner satisfaction ratings, or the number of students who complete the course. Another method is to use a detailed breakdown of costs at the student level (Bartolic-Zlomislic & Bates, 1999). Finally, educational benefits, such as the monetary value of educational benefits to society such as a university degree, can be difficult to quantify (Levin, 2001).

Evaluation Practice

In our review of the literature on evaluation studies, we found that the following models have been used to guide evaluation studies:

- Question-oriented approaches
- Cost–benefit
- Quality assurance
- CIAO model
- Collis's (1993) model
- ACTION model (Bates, 1995)
- Participatory and expertise-oriented models (Martinez et al., 2006)
- Lorenzo and Moore's (2002) five pillars

In three of these examples, the evaluation studies were led by the same person who devised the guiding theoretical models. These findings are confirmed by Tallent-Runnels et al.'s (2006) review of evaluation studies of online courses. They found 16 mixed studies and 20 qualitative studies (with a few being ethnographies or grounded theory but most being simply descriptions of the course). "Because online learning and instruction still constitute a relatively new frontier in education, informal theoretical frameworks and empirical evidence addressing some research questions are scarce" (p. 117). In our overview of evaluation studies, we found that many evaluation studies began with either a research or evaluation question or a specific methodology. What do these kinds of studies look like? Finally, Lorenzo and Moore (2002) encourage educators to apply this model to their own contexts and to share their results online, although these studies usually involve sharing findings and may not be official evaluation studies in our sense of the term.

Question-Oriented Approaches

In question-oriented approaches, the evaluation study is driven by one or more research question (Stufflebeam, 2001). In distance education, for example, the equivalence studies are question-oriented approaches because they answered the question of whether the distance and face-to-face sections of the same course were equivalent. Research questions commonly involve cause and effect, such as, did this technology-based intervention result in higher student performance, as measured by mean course grades? A question may involve multiple variables of cause and effect, such as, What are the various factors that contribute to student retention? What is the relative importance of each variable?

Method-Oriented Approaches

In the method-oriented approaches, the study is driven by an appropriate research design and methodology; the emphasis is on technical quality, not a comprehensive assessment of merit and worth (Stufflebeam, 2001). This category includes experimental studies, qualitative studies, case studies, and mixed-method studies (Stufflebeam, 2001). In experimental designs, learners are randomly assigned to an experimental or control group, and a treatment is given to the experimental group but not to the control group. When random assignment to groups is not possible, as is often the case in educational research, quasi-evaluation designs, such as an interrupted time series or a nonequivalent group design, are often used (Fitzpatrick et al., 2004). In qualitative research, learners are typically interviewed to assess their perceptions of the value of the course. The purpose of a case study is to "delineate and illuminate a program, not necessarily to guide its development or to assess and judge its merit and worth" (Stufflebeam, 2001, p. 34). A single case can provide an in-depth, stand-alone picture of a specific program, or several cases can be sampled from a range of scenarios to enhance generalizability (Reigeluth, 1999). In case research, the evaluator uses coding categories to make the conceptual connections that constitute theory building (Miles & Huberman, 1994). Mixed-methods studies combine the richness of qualitative studies with the breadth of quantitative studies. It is important to note, however, that when the orientation is on questions or methods, the emphasis of the evaluation report will be on scientific evidence, not on values or consequences.

Do Unintended Consequences Emerge in Authentic Evaluation Studies?

Although we generally do not refer to them as such, unintended consequences are not uncommon in face-to-face classes. These effects include disruptive behavior, negative response to the learning event, and inability to transfer learning (Forsyth et al., 1995). Because innovations in general tend to produce unintended consequences (Parlett & Hamilton, 1977), we would expect to see unintended consequences emerge in innovative technological applications in classrooms. Moreover, distance courses are increasingly based on new, complex, and blended technologies, so it is reasonable to anticipate unintended consequences. There is also evidence in the literature to support this notion. "The introduction of an innovation sets off a chain of repercussions in the learning milieu. In turn, these unintended consequences are likely to affect the innovation itself, changing its form and moderating its impact" (p. 12). In this section, we discuss the unintended effects that have been documented in authentic distance education evaluation studies.

Unintended Instructional Consequences

High attrition rates and bipolar distribution of grades have characterized some North American distance programs since the days of personalized systems of instruction and teaching machines (Keegan, 1993). Braun (1994) mentions unintended changes in the teacher–student relationship after technology is introduced. Jones et al.'s (1996) ethnographic evaluation of software in use found that learners used pathways through knowledge systems in different ways from those intended by course designers. Another example is the misapplication of innovative technology so that "old practices which are ineffective in a mainstream classroom can be just as ineffective using this technology (Gray & O'Grady, 1993, p. 668).

Herrmann, Fox, and Boyd (1999) classified unintended consequences of a worldwide web computer-mediated communication (CMC) system into Tenner's (1996) categories of rearranging, repeat, recomplicating, regenerating, and recongesting effects. Under rearranging effects, more time was spent learning HTML programming skills and developing and maintaining webpages than was saved by creating them. Socioeconomic factors also reduced access for many learners (p. 6) who were unable to pay ongoing maintenance costs. Repeat effects included learners spending their "saved" time surfing for more information often of doubtful or marginal use and a proliferation of e-mail messages so rapid that further "remedial" messages were needed (Herrmann et al., 1999). Recomplicating effects included the proliferation of user IDs, passwords, and PINs, while regenerating effects included transferring telecommunications costs to learners and the loss of control resulting from sophisticated hardware and software requirements. Finally, recongesting effects resulted when increasing numbers of Internet users created Internet gridlock and reduced access. Jones and Petre (1994) also found revenge effects in file management problems, problems running applications, and snags with printing. Their learners found that "the business of following instructions left them too busy to assimilate the material" (p. 32).

Hannafin, Hannafin, Land, and Oliver (1997) found that the mismatch between the rhetoric of what should happen and the design practices of what really happened in technology-based environments is most serious in emergent constructivist environments. Klinger (2002) also found unintended consequences emerging in an online discussion group for British Columbia (BC) teachers. Instead of responding to a BC Ministry of Education policy document as intended, teachers used the online forum to deconstruct the document's underlying underlying values. Because this was not the ministry's intention, Klinger's (2002) study is, in effect, a study of unintended consequences in an online discussion group.

Unintended Social Consequences

Unintended social consequences can also occur when technology is adopted in face-to-face classrooms. Brabazon (2003) mentions that online delivery undermines "intellectual interactivity" and that when the instructor is removed, so is the learning. She also deplores the erosion of student social networks, which characterize traditional campuses; the soaring workloads involved in digital communication, the marginalization of teachers; and the separation of teaching from content and facilitation. PowerPoint diminishes teachers into digital butlers and encourages mental absenteeism, even physical absenteeism because students can access the slides online (Brabazon, 2003). Another example is the domination of the worldwide web by American sites and search engines (Wilson, Qayyum, & Boshier, 1998) and the unconscious assimilation of American cultural values by learners in other countries (Fabos & Young, 1999). The larger corporate motives behind the adoption of technology in the schools are driven by the profits to be made from the sales of computers, so it is hardly surprising that little attention may be paid to pedagogy (Fabos & Young, 1999). Stoll (1999) claims that technology is used mostly for word processing and games and that the benefits associated with computers in schools are overrated. Fabos and Young (1999) documented various unintended consequences of innovative educational technology including "overly optimistic claims" (p. 218), lack of quality control in e-mail-based writing lessons, and malfunctioning classroom e-mail exchanges. Meanwhile, public funds are being misdirected into flashy multimedia of untested pedagogical quality, often at considerable expense (Lookatch, 1997).

Unintended social consequences have also been documented in the evaluation studies conducted by the distance education theorists whose models we previously reviewed. Gooler (1979) listed several "important social consequences," including forced alteration of university policies, continuous registration, faculty acceptance, internal rewards for faculty, newness to learners, and the impact on health care and poverty-oriented programs. Clark (1994a) recommends a questionnaire to participants as an "early warning system" (p. 69) to identify negative effects such as isolation and communication problems among participants. When Collis's (1993) model, based on Stake's (1967) countenance model of program evaluation, was applied to a telecommunications course, a complex chain of unintended consequences emerged. When Ruhe (2002b) used an adapted version of Messick's (1989) framework to analyze an assessment task in a multimedia-based foreign language course, a number of unintended effects emerged. In sum, when these scholars apply their models, they also discover unintended consequences in distance courses.

Positive Unintended Consequences

According to Bates (2000), instructional technologies can also result in unintended positive consequences. Ruhe (2002a), for example, found positive unintended effects in an e-mail-based writing course. At Stanford University, a distance education course resulted in the spontaneous emergence of networks or communities of practice, a positive consequence that was not anticipated by the course designers. Engineers watching a videotape of lectures would stop the tape and discuss at regular intervals before continuing with the lecture. To everyone's surprise, even though they had low credentials when entering the course, they consistently outperformed the classroom group on course material tests. According to Seely Brown and Duguid (2000), "This finding has proved remarkably robust and the courses using this 'TVI' [tutored video instruction] method have had either comparative success" (p. 222).

Another example is unintended spillover benefits of a program, such as when children who learn reading skills become more cooperative and less disruptive (Weiss, 1998). These effects include children teaching to others the skills they have learned in an innovative program (Weiss, 1998). Students with disabilities "find their voice" in online interaction and "feel more authoritative" because the low bandwidth creates an online presence equal to that of their classmates (Dede, 2005, p. 120). Ruhe (1998) found positive unintended consequences of using e-mail to teach English as a second language to foreign college students, including affective benefits and increased knowledge of cultural differences.

Finally, distance courses may bring *neither* positive nor negative unintended consequences or they may bring *both* positive and negative unintended consequences. One unintended positive consequence of Wikipedia, which recently surpassed 1 million articles and is one of the most popular online destinations, is "democratizing knowledge." Because the "read/write culture" empowers consumers to "generate their own creative product," Wikipedia has the potential to "enable free culture in schools and colleges and universities everywhere" (Read, 2006, p. 1). However, Wikipedia has also brought unintended negative consequences such as poor-quality writing and inaccurate information (Read, 2006).

Conclusions

In this chapter, we reviewed evaluation theory and practice in distance education and e-learning over the past 20 years. We classified evaluation models based on their emphasis on evidence, values and/or consequences. First we reviewed models that emphasize scientific evidence (e.g., the ACTION model [Bates, 1995] and the CIAO model [Scanlon et al., 2000]). Next we reviewed models that we believe emphasize evidence, values, and consequences (e.g., Mann [1998], Collis [1993], and the Sloan Consortium's Quality Framework and Five Pillars (Lorenzo & Moore, 2002). Third we reviewed two models based on Messick's (1989) framework (i.e., Ruhe [2002b] and Bunderson [2003]).

Although there has been a recurring call in the literature for a more professional approach to evaluation, there is little articulation of what this approach might look like. We maintain that this approach depends on an analysis of scientific evidence, values, and consequences. In this chapter, we have shown that evaluation models in distance education and e-learning have indeed been moving in this direction.

To some extent, the same can be said for evaluation practice. Most early evaluation studies were based on quantitative methodologies, that is, the questions and methods approaches (Stufflebeam, 2001). Measures include student outcomes, such as test scores or grades or comparisons of outcomes between a distance and a face-to-face version of the same course. Qualitative studies have focused on the process of teaching and learning as experienced by learners, while mixed methodologies have focused on both outcomes and process (e.g., British Open University studies). Other common approaches were cost–benefit models, models of the implementation environment (Tallent-Runnels et al., 2006), quality assurance, and accreditation studies.

More recently, evaluation studies have included some discussion of values and unintended consequences. For example, indicators or standards are used in the Star Schools program evaluation (U.S. Department of Education, The Office of Innovation and Improvement, 2007), while NACOL (2007) has endorsed national standards of quality for online courses. Martinez et al. (2006) recommend evaluation studies based on a participatory approach, a contemporary approach based on values used in program evaluation. We have also found more evaluation studies in distance and e-learning which bring unintended consequences into the foreground, for example, Klinger's (2003) study of instructional consequences and Brabazon's (2003) study of social consequences.

Compared to 20 years ago, contemporary evaluation theory and practice in distance education and e-learning reflect increasingly professional approaches to evaluation. This trend is very encouraging, especially given the steep and relentless proliferation of new technologies and course designs, which will continue to provide fertile contexts for professional evaluation studies. We have shown how Messick's (1989) framework brings trends in evaluation in distance education together into one model. In some sense, Ruhe (2002b) and Bunderson (2003) are "dress rehearsals" for the unfolding model, which responds to the call for a professional approach to evaluation by offering both a comprehensive and an adaptive approach to guide studies of the merit and worth of distance and e-learning programs.

CHAPTER 4

■ ■ ■ ■ ■ ■ ■ ■

Messick's Framework
WHAT DO EVALUATORS NEED TO KNOW?

In Chapter 2, we gave an overview of professional program evaluation models and showed that Messick's (1989) framework is an omnibus classification scheme for program evaluation. In Chapter 3, we showed that distance education evaluation models can also be categorized according to their relative emphasis on scientific evidence, values, and consequences. We also showed that evaluation practice in distance education tends to be methods oriented, even though values and unintended effects have been documented in authentic studies.

Before we get to the "nuts and bolts" of evaluation practice, we want to provide a broader, theoretical understanding of our approach to evaluation. Consisting of fewer than 20 words, Messick's (1989) framework provides important insights into evaluation in general and distance courses in particular.

The assumptions underlying Messick's (1989) conception of validity are the same assumptions underlying the unfolding model; therefore, understanding Messick's framework is essential to understanding the unfolding model. The core assumptions provide fundamental principles to guide evaluation practice in distance education.

According to Peter H. Rossi (Chen, 2005), "An evaluation should start from clarifying key assumptions underlying the program and understanding the nature of the program, exploring stakeholders' views and evaluation needs, and using these discoveries as a guide for formulating an evaluation design" (p. 209). We are doing the same thing here: clarifying the assumptions underlying the unfolding model by clarifying the assumptions underlying Messick's framework. This understanding will help distance course designers and evaluators attain a richer, more in-depth understanding of how to use the unfolding model to guide evaluation practice.

The Overlap between Test Validity and Program Evaluation

Education is one of the pillars of program evaluation, and educational evaluation has student assessment at its core (Alkin & Christie, 2004a). The term *program* has been defined as a set of resources and activities directed toward one or more common goals (Wholey, 1987). By this definition, a standardized test is a program. Therefore, test assessment and program evaluation share a common conceptual core (Mabry, 2001): determining the worth and merit of goal-oriented activities. In discussing the commonalities between Alkin and Christie's (2004a) classification scheme and Messick's (1989) framework, we showed that Messick's framework is an omnibus model for program evaluation. In fact, Messick treats tests as though they were programs, and the categories of his model overlap with categories commonly used for evaluating programs (e.g., cost–benefit, relevance, values, and unintended consequences). Messick's (1989) comprehensive approach to test validity relies on methods commonly used in program evaluation. Therefore, his framework is situated at the intersection of test validity and program evaluation (Figure 4.1). Moreover, Messick was not the first to link test assessment with program evaluation; Cronbach (1982) and Cronbach and Meehl (1955) also worked in both fields.

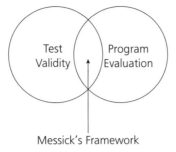

Messick's Framework

FIGURE 4.1. The overlap between test validity and program evaluation.

In adapting Messick's (1989) framework into an evaluation model for distance education, are we implying that test validity and program evaluation are the same thing? Not exactly. Fifty years ago, when the fields of program evaluation and assessment were based on experimental methodologies, there was substantial overlap between them. However, with the adoption of qualitative methodologies and the proliferation of new approaches to program evaluation, assessment and program evaluation later emerged as distinct fields. Even so, these two fields share a common conceptual core (Mabry, 2001): determining the worth and merit of educational activities. Therefore, Messick's (1989) framework can be used to evaluate both standardized tests and educational programs. Because the unfolding model is based on Messick's framework, it is a program evaluation model grounded in the science of test assessment and educational measurement.

Messick's Contributions

Our theoretical conceptions of **validity** and validation practices have changed appreciably over the last 60 years (Angoff, 1988), largely because of Messick's (1989) many contributions to our contemporary conception of validity. According to Cureton (1951), the essential feature of validity was "how well a test does the job it was employed to do" (p. 621). The American Psychological Association (APA, 1954) listed four distinct types of validity: construct validity, content validity, criterion validity, and concurrent validity. *Construct validity* refers to how well a particular test can be shown to assess the construct that it is said to measure. *Content validity* refers to how well test scores adequately represent the content domain that these scores are said to measure. *Predictive validity* is the degree to which the predictions made by a test are confirmed by the later behavior of the tested individuals. *Concurrent validity* is the extent to which individuals' scores on a new test correspond to their scores on an established test of the same construct that is administered shortly before or after the new test. Although concerns had been expressed about unintended social consequences, they were not seen as a part of validity.

Later, in the APA's (1966) *Standards for Educational and Psychological Tests and Manuals*, criterion validity and predictive validity were collapsed into criterion-related validity, thereby reducing the four validity types into three: criterion-related validity, content validity, and construct validity. These three *aspects* of validity were referred to as the "Holy Trinity" (Guion, 1980), "meaning that at least one type of validity is needed but one has three chances to get it" (Hubley & Zumbo, 1996, p. 210). As early as 1957, however, Loevinger (1957) argued that construct validity was the whole of validity, anticipating a shift away from multiple types to a single type of validity.

In the early days, validity was viewed as a property of tests, but the focus later shifted to the validity of a test in a specific context or application, such as the workplace (Angoff, 1988). The 1974 *Standards for Educational and Psychological Tests* (APA, American Educational Research Association, and National Council on Measurement in Education, 1974) shifted the focus of content validity from a representative sample of content knowledge to a representative sample of behaviors in a specific context (Messick, 1989). Professional standards were established for a number of applied testing areas such as "counseling, licensure, certification and program evaluation" (Messick, 1989, p. 18). In the 1985 *Standards* (APA, American Educational Research Association, and National Council on Measurement in Education, 1985), validity was redefined as the "appropriateness, meaningfulness, and usefulness of the specific inferences made from test scores" (p. 9). By 1985, the unintended social consequences of the use of tests—for example, bias and adverse impact—were also included in the *Standards* (Messick, 1989). In sum, successive versions of the *Standards* have slowly evolved to incorporate Messick's conception of validity.

Validation Practice

Validation practice is "disciplined inquiry" (Hubley & Zumbo, 1996) that started out historically with calculations of measures of a single aspect of validity (e.g., content validity or predictive validity). Many of these calculations are based on logical or mathematical models that date from the early

20th century (Crocker & Algina, 1986). Messick (1989) describes these procedures as fragmented, unitary approaches to validation. Hubley and Zumbo (1996) describe them as "scanty, disconnected bits of evidence . . . to make a two-point decision about the validity of a test" (p. 214). Before Messick (1989), Cronbach (1982) recommended a more comprehensive, argument-based approach to validation that considered multiple and diverse sources of evidence. This approach was the foundation for Messick's (1989) framework, which was a departure from traditional, "fragmented" approaches.

In sum, the emphasis in successive versions of the *Standards* has shifted from many types to a single, but integrated, type of validity conceptualized as Messick's (1989) framework. Validation practice has also evolved from a fragmented approach to a comprehensive, unified approach in which multiple sources of data are used to support an argument. Although Messick's framework was controversial for many years, the social consequences of high-stakes tests are now routinely investigated in professional test validation studies (Bejar, 2007; Cizek, 2001; Jones, Jones, & Hargrove, 2003). Finally, the evaluation of technology-based courses is another important area that has bridged "the gap between psychometric theory and research practice" (Hubley & Zumbo, 1996, p. 215).

Messick's Framework

Definition of Validity

Validity is "an integrated evaluative judgment of the degree to which empirical evidence and theoretical rationales support the adequacy and appropriateness of inferences and actions based on test scores or other modes of assessment" (Messick, 1989, p. 13). Validity, then, is a unified concept, and validation is a scientific activity based on the collection of multiple and diverse types of evidence (Messick, 1989; Zumbo, 1998, 2007). Messick's approach to validation is not aimed at presenting scientific proof; rather, it focuses on collecting multiple types of evidence to build an argument for

---

VALIDITY = SCIENTIFIC EVIDENCE, VALUES, AND CONSEQUENCES

Validity: an evaluative summary of scientific evidence, underlying values and potential and actual consequences (Messick, 1995a).

Validation practice: building an argument based on multiple sources of evidence (e.g., statistical calculations, qualitative data, reflections on one's own values and those of others, and an analysis of unintended consequences).

merit and worth, similar to the building of an argument in a court of law (Markus, 1998). This emphasis on building an argument, rather than providing scientific proof, is based on the modern conception that "validity is a matter of degree, not all or none" (Messick, 1989, p. 13).

The Four Facets

Messick's (1989) unified conception of validity consists of four facets, formed by crossing the evidential with the consequential bases of test interpretation and use (Figure 4.2). The two upper boxes, the evidential basis of validity, refer to traditional scientific evidence; the top left box is traditional psychometrics and the right box consists of relevance to learners and to society, and to cost–benefit. The two lower boxes, the consequential basis, include value implications and social consequences. The term *value implications* refers to underlying values, including language or rhetoric, theory, and ideology. *Social consequences* is defined as the unintended social effects of testing, including the actual and potential effects of test use, especially issues of bias, adverse impact, and distributive justice (Messick, 1989), and any other indirect effects, both actual/potential and positive/negative, of using the test on the overall educational system (Messick, 1995b).

Finally, it is important to note that the four facets of the framework are not clear-cut and distinct but "progressive" or overlapping, so that all facets contain each of the previously mentioned aspects of value. For example, values and unintended consequences are intertwined because of the significance (either positive or negative), which we assign to unintended consequences. In other words, the meaning or interpretation of scores depends on societal values. The tension between the evidential and the consequential basis is the tension between facts and values, a tension that underlies all scientific inquiry (Messick, 1989). From here, we will discuss each of the four facets of Messick's framework in greater detail.

| | **Outcomes** | |
Justification	Test interpretation	Test use
Evidential basis	Construct validity (CV)	CV + relevance/+ utility (RU)
Consequential basis	Value implications (CV + RU + VI)	Social consequences (CV + RU + VI + UC)

FIGURE 4.2. Messick's (1989) conception of validity.

Scientific Evidence

The *evidential basis for test interpretation* is an appraisal of the scientific evidence for construct validity. A *construct* is "a definition of skills and knowledge included in the domain to be measured by a tool such as a test" (Reckase, 1998b, p. 45). In validation practice, a list of the content and skill areas being tested is essential (Shepard, 1997). The four traditional types of validity are included in this first facet. Several statistical procedures are then performed on the test responses, which yield scores that are taken to be a measure of each single aspect of validity. For example, a content validity coefficient is calculated by comparing the list of content and skill areas in the course with those of the test. Correlations between the test being validated and alternate tests of the same knowledge and skill areas may be performed to generate concurrent validity coefficients. Finally, factor analysis is another kind of scientific evidence that can be used to support an argument for the validity of a test (APA, 1966).

TRADITIONAL SCIENTIFIC EVIDENCE: THE FOUR TYPES OF VALIDITY

Construct validity: how well a test is measuring the skills or knowledge it is intended to measure.

Content validity: how well test scores represent the content being tested.

Predictive validity: how well a test can predict later behaviors of individuals.

Concurrent validity: how close the scores are on two different tests that claim to measure the same thing.

The *evidential basis for test use* includes measures of predictive validity (e.g., correlations with other tests of behaviors) as well as utility (i.e., a cost–benefit analysis). Predictive validity coefficients are measures of behavior to be predicted from the test (e.g., a correlation between scores on a road test and a written driver qualification test). Cost–benefit refers to an analysis of costs compared with benefits, which in education are often difficult to quantify. To conclude, the evidential basis of Messick's framework contains two boxes, or facets: (1) traditional psychometric evidence and (2) the evidence for relevance in applied settings such as the workplace as well as utility or cost–benefit. Even so, for Messick (1989), these kinds of evidence are a part, but not the whole, of validity. The scientific evidence needs to be considered in light of the values underlying the test.

It may seem counterintuitive that Messick's framework has two upper boxes for scientific evidence but three *types* of scientific evidence. However, both relevance (to learner needs, career goals, and the contemporary workplace) as well as cost–benefit are important evaluative criteria for distance education and e-learning.

Value Implications

Values form the basis for all evaluations (Davidson, 2005). Values are shared language, theories, beliefs, and worldviews (van Dijk, 1998). Some examples of values are truth, beauty, satisfaction, and effectiveness (van Dijk, 1998). In Messick's world, an appraisal of *value implications* requires an investigation of three components: (1) rhetoric or value–laden language and terminology, (2) underlying theories, and (3) underlying ideologies "that give the theories their perspective and purpose" (Messick, 1989, p. 62; see Figure 4.3). Note that language can be easily identified because it is readily visible, whereas theories and ideologies tend to be hidden or below the surface. At the same time, those theories and ideologies can often be identified by analyzing the rhetoric, or "value–laden" language and terminology, of test manuals or course outlines.

Rhetoric: value-laden language that conveys both a concept and an opinion of a concept (van Dijk, 1998; e.g., "freedom fighter" vs. "terrorist").

RHETORIC

Rhetoric includes language that is discriminatory, exaggerated, or over-blown, such as derogatory language used to refer to the homeless. Beliefs and ideologies are conveyed not only in lexical items but also in gram-

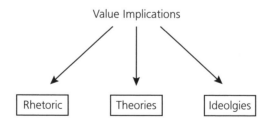

FIGURE 4.3. Value implications: The dimensions.

matical or syntactical style, as when a certain clause or word order privileges certain information or gives it more prominence (van Dijk, 1998). In validation practice, the rhetoric surrounding standardized tests should be critically evaluated to determine whether these terms are accurate descriptions of knowledge and skills said to be assessed by a test (Messick, 1989). For example, to say that a mathematics test is "world class" because it was reviewed by a few international experts may be misleading and may violate this aspect of overall merit and worth (Reckase, 1998a).

> **Theory**: the underlying assumptions or logic of how a program is supposed to work (Chen, 1990).

THEORY

The second component of the value implications category is an appraisal of the theory underlying the test. A theory connotes a body of knowledge that organizes, categorizes, describes, predicts, explains, and otherwise aids in understanding phenomenon and organizing and directing thoughts, observations, and actions (Sidani & Sechrest, 1999). For more than 30 years, evaluators have recommended making explicit the underlying theories of how programs are supposed to work and then using these theories to guide evaluation studies (Rogers et al., 2000).

> **Ideology**: a complex mix of shared values and beliefs that provide a framework for interpreting the world (Messick, 1989).

IDEOLOGY

The third component of value implications is an appraisal of the "broader ideologies that give theories their perspective and purpose" (Messick, 1989, p. 62). An ideology is "a complex configuration of shared values, affects, and beliefs that provides, among other things, an existential framework for interpreting the world" (Messick, 1989, p. 62). Ideologies are political or social systems of ideas, values, or prescriptions of groups, "belief systems," or the "social mind," which are "at work in everyday social practices" (van Dijk, 1998, p. 3). Ideologies are shared knowledge, rules, and methods that serve to regulate social practices, legitimize group actions, "stabilize particular forms of power and dominance," conceal inequities and socialize novices into established groups (van Dijk, 1998, p. 3). Science, for example, is an ideology. According to Messick (1989), the "fallout from ideological overlays is hard to avoid in educational and psychological measurement" (p. 62). One example is the view that persons with achievement scores below a certain level on a test of moral knowledge and skills are incapable of making moral judgments (Reckase, 1998a). Although "very few studies of the large numbers of studies about ideologies ever get down to the mundane job of describing what they actually look like" (van Dijk, 1998), this analysis is exactly what we do in Chapter 7, in the discussion of the ideologies underlying distance education.

MULTIPLE VALUE PERSPECTIVES

Moss (1998a) posits a dialectical view of rationality in which validity theory is not a completed project but an "ongoing critical reflection about our interpretations and theories in light of challenges from alternative perspectives" (p. 55). In the four-faceted conception of validity, "value implications are not ancillary, but rather, integral to score meaning" (Messick, 1994, p. 20). Moreover, Messick's (1989) framework is founded on Singer's (1959) view of rationality, where two different systems of inquiry confront one another in order to bring forward and make visible their underlying values and assumptions (Messick, 1989) and to bring them out into the open "for public scrutiny and critique" (p. 62).

> We live in a postmodern world characterized by multiple value perspectives. Similarly, in scientific inquiry, data can never be value-neutral (Messick, 1998).

Moss (1998a) discusses how different values or issues that are kept hidden in the background from one scientific perspective can be brought out into the foreground from another scientific perspective.

> The issue is not about what's *possible* within different perspectives . . . it's about what's emphasized, illuminated or made more likely; what's relegated to the background as trivial or impractical; and what impact this prevailing emphasis has on the actual practices of social scientists and the communities they study and serve (Moss, 1998a, p. 56). . . . This emphasis on the importance of an outside perspective to illuminate what is taken for granted (as natural, normal, the "way things are done") and thereby to provoke critical self-reflection is a theme that resonates across multiple philosophies of social science. . . . This insight is "one of the most profoundly important insights that Messick has brought to the tradition of educational and psychological measurement. (p. 62)

In sum, Messick's (1989) framework "illuminates taken-for-granted assumptions, knowledge and practices" (Moss, 1998a, p. 65), which would otherwise be "disqualified" "against the claims of a unitary body of theory" (Foucault, 1980, p. 82).

In the contemporary postmodern world of diverse values, scientific evidence can never be value-neutral (Messick, 1998). Instead, there is "a multiplicity of values including the decision-maker's values, the enhancement of individual welfare, equality and enhancement of the common good" (p. 18). Moss (1998a) recommends that evaluators assess the validity of tests "from multiple value perspectives to address a broad range of potential social consequences and to identify side effects likely to be seen as adverse by other value positions" (p. 80).

> By opening up and "problematizing" conceptual "spaces," multiple value perspectives illuminate scientific evidence and deepen and enrich evaluative findings.

According to Moss (1998a), validation practice is open to multiple perspectives that "illuminate taken-for-granted assumptions, values, and practices that alternative perspectives can provoke" (p. 65). Moss believes that a pluralistic approach to values is central to Messick's theory and brings to the foreground knowledge that would otherwise be "disqualified." "This emphasis on the importance of an outside perspective to illuminate what is taken for granted (as natural, normal, the 'way things are done') and thereby to provoke critical self-reflection is a theme that resonates across multiple philosophies of social science" (Moss, 1998a, p. 62). Moss (1998a) claims that this insight is one of the most profoundly important insights that Messick has brought to the field of educational measurement.

In sum, Messick argues that values are integral to validity; in a postmodern world, diverse perspectives must be taken into account (Moss, 1998a). Validation practice needs to reflect a multiplist view of values, which characterizes a contemporary, postmodern world. Indeed, this perspective is found in many contemporary evaluation approaches such as responsive evaluation (Abma & Stake, 2001), realist evaluation (Henry & Julnes, 1998), and constructivist evaluation (Caracelli, 2000). The value of approaching a question from these diverse value perspectives is to illuminate and probe the emergent issues and to make these issues explicit, thereby enriching our knowledge (Moss, 1998a). Moreover, evaluation in the context of multiple perspectives ensures that new alternatives, compromises, extensions, and reformulations can emerge and that a broad range of social consequences are addressed (Messick, 1989).

Unintended Consequences

The fourth facet of Messick's framework is unintended consequences (i.e., unintended effects of the test). Unanticipated consequences signal that "we may have been incomplete or off-target in test development and hence in test interpretation and use" (p. 43). Messick (1998) felt that the term *unintended consequences* needed to be defined more clearly than the terms he found in the literature. First, he categorized unintended effects into individual, institutional, systemic, and societal effects. Then he stated that his critics mistakenly believed he was using the term to refer to the consequences of the misuse or trivial misapplications of tests, but that this was not the case. In fact, Messick (1998) was concerned with "the unanticipated side-effects of *legitimate* test use" (p. 40) and not with the effects of test *misuse*.

THE UNINTENDED CONSEQUENCES OF "HIGH-STAKES" TESTING

Based on interviews with students, parents, and teachers, Jones et al. (2003) found no fewer than 67 unintended consequences of high-stakes testing mandated by the No Child Left Behind Act, including:

- Consequences for educational resources and reform.
- Consequences for students.
- Consequences for teachers.
- Consequences for instruction.
- Consequences for the community.

These authors called for an end to high-stakes testing in the nation's schools.

Unintended consequences: the side effects of *legitimate* test use, that is, of using the test in exactly the way the test was intended to be used (Messick, 1989); for example:

- Narrowing the curriculum to teach to the test.
- Placement decisions.
- Coaching.
- Gender or ethnic differences in score distributions (Shepard, 1997).

> **Test misuse**: using the test in ways in which it was not meant to be used, including procedural errors and unsound interpretations (Messick, 1989).
>
> **Note:** Unintended consequences does *not* include the side effects of test *misuse*.

The consequences of test misuse, then, are not part of his definition of unintended consequences. If unanticipated side effects arise from legitimate test use, they can be ignored if they are trivial (Messick, 1998). However, if they are not trivial, they cannot be ignored; instead, both score meaning and intended uses need to be modified.

POSITIVE UNINTENDED CONSEQUENCES

Finally, it is important to note that unintended consequences can sometimes be positive; this is referred to as "positive washback" or "beneficial by-products" (Messick, 1996).

> **SOME POSITIVE UNINTENDED CONSEQUENCES OF HIGH-STAKES TESTING**
>
> Cizek (2001) provides a list of 10 "unintended, unrecognised and unarticulated positive consequences of high-stakes testing" (p. 19). This list includes:
>
> • Better accountability systems.
> • Improved student learning.
> • Heightened scrutiny of the content of tests.

As we will see further on, it is not unusual for new technologies to usher in positive unintended consequences, and it is important to identify these aspects of value in evaluation reports.

The Overlap among the Four Facets

Construct Validity as a Unifying Force

Messick's (1989) framework is a "progressive" matrix, which means that the four facets are highly intertwined and overlap with all the other facets. "The fuzziness—or rather messiness—of these distinctions derives from the fact that we are trying to cut through a unitary concept" (p. 21). Because the meaning of scientific evidence depends on interpretation, which in turn depends on underlying values, the collection of scientific evidence is intertwined with underlying values. In other words, facts (the top two boxes of Messick's framework) and values (the lower boxes) are intertwined. The unifying force refers to combining multiple lines of evidence to support the interpretation and use of scores (Markus, 1998). The whole of validity, then, is construct validity, which is multifaceted, value laden, and consequential. It follows that validation practice is the presentation of scientific evidence and theoretical, legal, and moral considerations in a comprehensive argument based on multiple sources of evidence to support claims about merit and worth (Markus, 1998).

> **Construct validity:** the "unifying force" that makes validity a unitary concept and ties together the elements of the four cells (Messick, 1989).

The Tension between Facts and Values

"The distinction between facts and values is a conundrum: How can you have scientific evaluation if facts are objective and values are not?" (House, 2003). For example, the scientific method, from its inceptions, has been deemed to be value-free. Yet the assumption that science is value-neutral is "perverse" because the underlying principles, such as predictive accuracy, internal coherence, and parsimony, are value judgments (Messick, 1989). Moreover, science is embedded in social practice, specifically "in the meanings and values implicit in the social practices which give rise to it" (Markus, 1998, p. 12) and that "lie at the very heart of validity (p. 11). Traditional, "one-shot" scientific validity studies "are imprecise because types of validity typically remain implicit and undefined" (MacPhail, 1998, p. 137). In contrast, Messick's (1989) conception of validity is a comprehensive conception precisely because it is based on scientific evidence or facts (the evidential basis) *and* values and consequences (the consequential basis).

> Scientific evidence and values are not distinct but are blended together so that evaluative findings are "mixtures or fusions" of both (Scriven, 2003, p. 11).

The Synthesis between Facts and Values

Validity is dependent on values, and values vary widely depending on the specific contexts and applications and on the values held by evaluators and stakeholders. For example, an evaluator's values may influence the validation process, the quality of data, the interpretation of results, and even the measurement instrument (Reckase, 1998b). Markus (1998) argues that there are "multiple validities" and calls for a completion of the synthesis between the evidential basis (facts) and consequential basis (values). This synthesis between facts and values is achieved by the development of a value justification that produces a single best justified validity for a given context or application (Markus, 1998). Evaluators "should be prepared to provide justification for the values inherent in their validity arguments or else accept that their validity argument is not uniquely justified" (p. 80). In other words, evaluators need to identify diverse underlying values in the course documents, course developers, instructors, and learners; weigh, balance, and compare these values for convergence; and make a final evaluative judgment as to the extent to which these values either converge or conflict and how they play themselves out in the course implementation.

> In test validation studies, the tension among scientific evidence, underlying values, and unintended social consequences needs to be carefully negotiated (Moss, 1998a).

The Controversy over Unintended Consequences

Although Messick's (1989) conception of validity has had an enormous influence on the field of educational measurement, in the first 15 years after his framework was published, it generated considerable controversy among scholars and testing companies. Messick felt this controversy "masked conflicts in values and ideologies" (1998, p. 39), thereby proving the truth of his assumptions that facts and values were intertwined.

> **UNINTENDED CONSEQUENCES: THREE CONTENTIOUS TOPICS**
>
> 1. Are unintended social consequences a part of, or outside of, validity?
> 2. How do we collect data on unintended social consequences?
> 3. Are test developers responsible for unintended social consequences?

Messick's (1989) view that consequences are an integral part of validity has been especially contentious. His definition of validity as the appropriateness of inferences and actions based on test scores includes an appraisal of unintended social consequences. The reason is that these inferences and actions take place within a social context and have implications and consequences within a broad social context. According to Moss (1998b), testing practices transform social realities; therefore, the study of social consequences is essential.

Other scholars, however, believe that social consequences are *not* an aspect of validity. According to Popham (1997), for example, actual and potential consequences are "vitally important," but they are *not* an aspect of validity. Merging consequences with validity only "muddies the waters" and creates confusion. Mehrens (1997) argues that consequences should be moved outside of the discussion of validity because the concept confuses issues in measurement quality with issues in treatment efficacy, which is problematic. The accuracy of an inference about the amount or meaning of any trait should be separable from the treatment. Shepard (1997) agrees that including consequences overburdens the concept of validity and creates confusion.

Finding Data on Unintended Social Consequences

There are several ways that data on unintended social consequences can be obtained. The first way is by studying "the actual discourse that surrounds the products and practices of testing" (Moss, 1998b, p. 7). This qualitative evidence can provide concrete illustrations of how tests actually work in local contexts and "about the potential slippage between what we well-meaningly intend and what we in fact effect" (p. 11). Secondly, interviews with users can be held to assess concrete examples of unintended consequences in the local contexts in which tests are administered (Moss, 1998b).

An Example: The ACT Test

Reckase (1998a) suggests that the consequential basis of validity of standardized tests could be assessed by (1) an appraisal of the underlying values of the language in the test and test manual, (2) an articulation of the ideologies on which the test is based, and (3) an appraisal of actual and potential consequences in schools. In his validation of the ACT test, Reckase identified several important findings around the consequential basis of validity (Figure 4.4).

The ACT Assessment Test Battery is used for college admissions. Reckase (1998a) used Messick's framework to validate this test, with the following results:

- **Scientific evidence:** List of the knowledge and skills assessed by the test.
- **Rhetoric:** List of the language and terminology in the test manual and any "overblown" descriptors such as "world class."
- **Theory:** Grade 12 students who performed well on a test consisting of a sample of items reviewed by college faculty would do better in college. The underlying value implication, that faculty judgements are valued, is also acceptable.
- **Ideology:** A college education is valued, students should prepare themselves for it, faculty judgments are valued, and certain fields of study are prerequisites for success.
- **Unintended consequences:** Found it difficult to know when to collect the evidence for a new test and to demonstrate that an event is the effect of a test and not the effect of any number of other contextual variables.

FIGURE 4.4. Findings from a validation study of the ACT Assessment Test Battery (Reckase, 1998a).

Are Test Makers Responsible for Unintended Consequences?

Another question is whether the test maker or test user is responsible for unintended consequences (Shepard, 1997). If increased funding is offered to schools with higher test scores, then the learning consequences that follow are an important validity issue. The author recommends that test makers should do at least one study to examine the relationship between the test and the effects and check for regularly occurring side effects such as adverse impact. "When are consequences . . . the purview only of policymakers and politicians?" (p. 8). Green (1998) argues that test publishers are not in a position to obtain on their own evidence of the consequences and uses to which their tests are put. There is little hard or credible evidence, obtaining cooperation is difficult, and the uses vary widely, thereby making generalization difficult. Although publishers are disconnected from the ways in which teachers use test results, in some sense, both parties are responsible for unintended consequences, and a dialogue between them is recommended.

Implications for Evaluation

We have reviewed Messick's framework in detail because the assumptions underlying Messick's framework are the same assumptions underlying the unfolding model. Like Messick, we are interested in a comprehensive appraisal of merit and worth. A comprehensive course evaluation requires evaluators to collect and analyze multiple sources of data, both quantitative survey data and qualitative data. As we blend these data, we compare and contrast our findings and identify and reflect on our own values, the values underlying the course, and the values of interviewees and survey respondents. We bring all of these values into the foreground and weigh them carefully when interpreting what our data actually *mean*. Finally, we need to identify and investigate unintended social consequences. Whether they will be positive or negative depends in part on our own values, the values underlying the course, and those of the learners and other stakeholders. In sum, we as evaluators bring together multiple sources of evidence to build an argument about the strengths, as well as the weaknesses, of distance courses. We are not trying to prove that this course is either good or bad but rather to show how good or how bad based on multiple sources of evidence, the presentation and weighing of multiple underlying values, and full disclosure of any and all unintended consequences.

Conclusions

In this chapter, we discussed the overlap between test assessment and program evaluation and thereby justified the use of an assessment model for a different purpose: program evaluation. Messick's framework brought formerly distinct and diverse aspects of validity together into a single, comprehensive conception of validity consisting of scientific evidence, values, and consequences. Scientific evidence refers to multiple measures, including survey and interview data, relevance to learners and to society, and cost–benefit analysis. Underlying values comprises rhetoric, theory, and ideology. Next, we discussed Messick's astute insights into the meaning of the term *unintended consequences*, defined as the unanticipated effects of using the test in the ways in which it was intended. Moreover, values and consequences *must* overlap conceptually because they can be either positive or negative. Just as importantly, the four-faceted conception of validity rests on a pluralist approach to values, which requires the identification and consideration of multiple value perspectives. In sum, validity is a unified, four-faceted conception of functional worth or value, and a comprehensive test validation study must include scientific evidence, relevance, cost–benefit, reflections on underlying values, and, finally, full disclosure of unintended consequences. Messick's conception of validity is still a "hot topic," as demonstrated by Kane's (2001, 2008) work on validation. Kane's (2006) paper on validation recently won an award for research methodology from the American Educational Research Association.

The unfolding model is based on Messick's framework, and his powerful insights into test validity also apply to course evaluation. Evidence, values, and consequences also underlie the unfolding model. Like a test, a distance course is also a complex, multifaceted construct, and an appraisal of value requires an appraisal of scientific evidence, underlying values, and unintended consequences. The overlap among Messick's four boxes has important implications for distance education. In the unfolding model, evaluators should not just "drop" one of the boxes in an evaluation study. If this is done, the result would likely be a much weaker and less convincing study. The study might fail to distinguish facts from ideology, omit an analysis of costs, or sweep unintended consequences under the proverbial rug. Messick's model not only answers Rumble's (1981) call for evaluators to investigate unintended consequences but goes beyond this call by filling in another gap in the distance education literature: underlying values. Armed with these theoretical insights, evaluators in distance education will have a more informed base with which to tailor the unfolding model to diverse contexts, without losing any of the elements that comprise a comprehensive study of the value of distance courses.

CHAPTER 5

■ ■ ■ ■ ■ ■ ■ ■ ■

Getting Started

In Chapter 2, we classified professional program evaluation models based on their emphasis on scientific evidence, values, and consequences. In Chapter 3, we showed that distance education models can also be classified based on their emphasis on scientific evidence, values, and consequences. In Chapter 4, we showed that Messick's (1989) four-faceted conception of validity brings scientific evidence, values, and consequences together in a single model. As such, Messick's framework is a comprehensive model grounded in the science of professional program evaluation. By bringing Messick's (1989) insights into distance education, our unfolding model responds to the recurring calls in the distance education literature to adopt a professional model of program evaluation.

Now that we have a thorough understanding of our model, we discuss how to get started with an evaluation study. We provide an overview of important planning considerations such as formative versus summative studies. The importance of the ethics review process cannot be underestimated, so we cover tips for writing applications and obtaining consent. Next, we discuss the political context of evaluation, including political pressures, the roles of stakeholders, and the **Joint Standards on Evaluation**. We discuss using the unfolding model as a "road map" and show how the model unfolds and the kinds of evidence and analysis that are essential. We also discuss which kinds of data or evidence are optional and how to set boundaries on your study so that it is manageable, affordable, and finite. Finally, we discuss strategies to enhance the **credibility** of your study, such as representative and random **sampling**.

Planning the Evaluation Study

The first decision is whether to conduct the evaluation in the course design phase or after the course has already run. "Evaluation should be practiced continuously through the design, development and implementation cycles to ensure that things work as anticipated and intended" (Moore & Kearsley, 1996, p. 120), and evaluation is a critical component of course design (Tennyson, 1997). The best course designers go through several cycles of formative evaluation (Visscher-Voerman & Gustafson, 2004). To guide evaluation in the course design phase, Graf and Caines's (2003) WebCT Exemplary Course Rubric or Chico State University's (2003) Rubric for Online Instruction can be used as a self-evaluation tool to set and monitor guidelines for high-quality, online course design.

Formative or Summative?

Second, you need to determine whether your evaluation is formative or summative. In a formative evaluation, a course is evaluated in the course design phase to identify areas for course improvement (e.g., to make the course more effective or less costly; Baker & O'Neil, 2006). In a summative evaluation, a course is evaluated after it has already run to determine whether the course has been successful or if funding should be continued. In practice, however, this formative/summative distinction may not always be clear-cut, and there is no reason *not* to evaluate a course in the design phase (Tennyson, 1997). We emphasize that the unfolding model can be used for both formative and summative evaluation.

Use Project Tracking Software to Plan Your Study

To keep your evaluation study on track, you should use project tracking software—a time line or calendar—in which all the steps in the evaluation plan are laid out (Horton, 2001). Gantt diagrams are computerized software packages that enable you to lay out your schedule and automatically adjust it when unforeseen events arise, which may delay the entire project. You should not worry too much if the evaluation is not completed on time, because this "very rarely happens" (Jean King, personal communication, August 25, 2007).

The Ethics Review Process

All research studies in the United States and Canada need to be approved by the university's committee for the protection of human subjects. All universities are subject to federal laws on the protection of human subjects of research, which are reflected in a university's local policies. In the United States, these regulations evolved from the National Commission for the Protection of Human Subjects of Biomedical and Behavioral Research's (1979) *Belmont Report*, "which outlined not only the three fundamental principles of ethical research—respect for persons, beneficence, and justice—but also the foundation for all IRB [**institutional review board**] activity" (Oakes, 2002, p. 447). There is a dual focus: (1) to ensure that human subjects are not harmed or placed at risk and (2) to ensure that consent is freely given. Universities have strict, mandatory requirements, and there are serious consequences for noncompliance. In fact, *all* research at *any* public American university could be shut down by the federal government if even one project were in noncompliance. Although the rules and policies may seem harsh, "the situation today is a direct consequence of many documented violations of very basic ethical standards. Therefore, the importance of applying for ethics approval and strictly following approved procedures cannot be understated (Oakes, 2002, p. 467).

Evaluation versus Research

In contrast to research studies, evaluation studies are usually exempt. However, because the line between evaluation and research studies is fuzzy, you should never assume that your study is exempt, and we encourage you to apply to the IRB for an exemption. One way to distinguish research from evaluation is that research findings are generalizable, which is not the case with evaluation. Second, instructors evaluate their courses as standard practice, and most universities require evaluation findings to be reported as part of the performance management policies for faculty. Third, if you do not intend to present or publish your findings and your study is for internal purposes only, then you may not need to go through IRB. If you wish to publish your findings, present them at a conference, or use them for a master's or doctoral dissertation, then you will need to go through IRB.

> Although all research studies require IRB approval, evaluation studies may be exempt. If you have *any* doubts about whether your study is a research or an evaluation study, you should contact your university's office for the protection of human subjects for clarification *before* you begin work.

The distinction between research and evaluation also impacts your ability to collect and use data. As a general rule, gathering evaluation data does not have to be approved by university IRBs. Gathering data for research, on the other hand, does have to be approved by the IRB and, in general, researchers can do less than evaluators. For example, if you are the instructor and you intend to do research, you will need someone else to collect your data for you. If the instructor is aware of who is participating and who is not participating (even with the consent form), it is interpreted by most IRB reviewers as coercion. The students may feel they have no choice. At some universities, the IRB will deny approval to any instructor who knows which students are participating.

Tips on Writing IRB Applications

Before you write your IRB application, you need to carefully read and follow the regulations on your university's website and give a complete description of your study, including methodology and procedures. You may also have to post a notice about your study and the conditions for participation on a class e-mail list. This notice must state that participation in your study is voluntary and that the freedom to choose to participate is not limited by age, gender, employment status, or any other factors. To boost volunteer participation rates, we recommend a small monetary compensation for university students to participate in focus groups and interviews. Most students today have so many pressures on their time that it is unlikely you will find volunteers unless you offer them some compensation. Evaluation projects can usually be submitted under the "expedited review" category.

For a list of 15 tips to improve your relationships with IRBs, see Oakes (2002). There are also new, and evolving, IRB regulations around the Internet (Berg, 2007).

Recruitment

Three areas of research protocol require special attention to IRB requirements: subject recruitment, informed consent, and confidentiality (Oakes, 2002). As for recruitment, IRB requires that the selection of subjects be equitable, so that the burden of participation is equally distributed instead of being borne by the poor, the disadvantaged, or other marginal groups. The second issue is the coercion of subjects by researchers. "Coercion is subtle, and can be experienced by participants through grades or power differentials" (p. 460). "This is why IRBs generally prefer indirect (e.g., telephone and letter) to direct interpersonal recruitment strategies" (p. 460). Compensation for participation also affects coercion and "the potential for coercion is reduced when between $1 and $5 is included up front in a mail survey, as opposed to promises of payment when some task is complete" (Oakes, 2002, p. 461).

Informed Consent

"Informed consent is one of the primary ethical requirements underpinning research with human subjects" (Oakes, 2002, p. 462). Therefore, you need to provide evidence of voluntary consent from your participants. You need to attach a cover letter to your survey, which includes the name and purpose of the study, the name and contact information of the evaluator or principal investigator, the length of time required, and the topics to be discussed. You also need to assure participants that their responses are strictly confidential, that they will not be identified in the report, and that they may withdraw their consent at any time without any penalty to grades or class standing. Your consent letter must ask them to sign to indicate their consent and must state that there will be no penalties of any kind if they decline to participate. You should check with your university to see whether they have preferred models or formats.

You should write separate consent letters for survey and interview respondents and for learners, instructors, and course designers. With telephone interviews, taped consent can be given by respondents verbally over the telephone, provided that their consent is tape-recorded. Finally, because researchers have found that active consent results in low response rates, passive consent procedures are sometimes permitted (Berg, 2007). With passive consent, students sign a form if they do not wish to participate but they are not required to hand it in. All other students are deemed to be willing participants, provided the study has been explained to them clearly and in detail.

Confidentiality

In your IRB application, you need to describe in detail your procedures for protecting the well-being, confidentiality, and anonymity of your participants. You need to attach a complete list of your survey and interview questions in the appendix. Review committees will be especially concerned with any questions that may cause distress to participants such as "Do you believe your faculty supervisor would support this course?" You should state that learner anonymity will be maintained by the use of learner ID numbers instead of names on the completed surveys and interview transcripts. You also need to provide assurances that all data will be kept in a password-protected computer or locked file drawer in a secure place such as a locked office. You should state that you will not make multiple copies of any data or leave data lying around in unprotected public places such as the staff room or the photocopy machine.

Tips for Obtaining Grades and Completion Rates

Because of issues around ethics, confidentiality, and privacy, it may be difficult to obtain student grades or completion rates. Even administrators may be unable to obtain grades from their own university, unless they are in a position that normally requires them to work with student-level data. University faculty have student grades but are usually reluctant to turn them over to program evaluators. Some faculty may even believe grades are poor indicators of student learning.

> To obtain student grades and completion rates, you need to file a formal request from the appropriate department at your university, which may be the registrar's office or an office of institutional research or measurement services.

In your request, you should describe the project and submit a copy of your IRB approval form with detailed procedures to protect the confidentiality and security of the data. Any request for student grades should stipulate whether you want the grades at the student level or aggregated (i.e., grouped in some way). For example, you may receive a list of letter grades and the numbers of students who earned each grade. Depending on your purpose, these data may not be very helpful. To perform statistical analyses, you need to ask for student-level grades. You may also ask for de-identified data (i.e., data without student names or ID numbers). However, if you need student names for linking purposes, you must provide assurances of strict procedures to protect security and confidentiality. Even then, you may not get the data in the form you need. You may be asked to obtain signed consent letters from the students before their grades are turned over. The university has the right to grant or refuse your request, or to provide the data in a form that meets the university's goals, not the goals of your study. You may also need to pay a fee to the appropriate department to pull student records.

Collecting Data from Other Universities

If you are doing a multisite project and collecting data from other post-secondary institutions, you will need to obtain the approval of their IRB committees as well as that of your own university. Other universities may have additional safeguards for the protection of human subjects; for example, you may not be permitted to telephone potential participants to encourage them to complete and return the questionnaire you have mailed them. Finally, you should not be surprised if you encounter limited access to student grades, attendance records, SAT scores, or other sensitive information. One of the benefits of the unfolding model is that you collect multiple sources of data and are, therefore, less vulnerable to a failure to collect any one set of data in the desired form.

The Political Context of Evaluation

Because evaluation studies are often influenced by political considerations, they are not always, strictly speaking, scientific. Evaluation practice takes place within a political context, and the work of evaluators is situated among diverse stakeholders (i.e., individuals with "vested interests in the evaluation"; Chen, 2005, p. 8) and conflicting goals, values, or expectations (Chelimsky, 1998). Interpersonal, ethical, and political factors "pervade every aspect of the evaluation study. It is folly to ignore them . . . and moving ahead without dealing with them is both incompetent and unethical" (Fitzpatrick et al., 2004, p. 412).

Stakeholders influence evaluation in ways that do not influence research; their needs and interests must not be ignored, especially by fledgling evaluators. "Evaluation is an intensely political activity that is viewed by many as a threat" (Davidson, 2005, p. 88).

Dealing with Political Pressures from Stakeholders

Stakeholders are individuals who affect or are affected by the program, including the program head, university department director, faculty members, funding agency, and students. Evaluators need to balance scientific credibility with stakeholder credibility, which is stakeholder belief that the evaluation design gives "serious consideration of their views, concerns and needs" (Chen, 2005, p. 8). Evaluators should be neutral parties (Cronbach, 1982) responsive to, but not dependent on, stakeholders (Stufflebeam, 2001). This consideration leads to another: The values underlying a program may or may not be shared by all stakeholders, who may have conflicting goals, values, and expectations (Chelimsky, 1998). However, you need their support both to collect data from their students and to ensure that your findings will be used and will impact the wider community.

TIPS FOR DEALING WITH STAKEHOLDERS

- Plan how you will involve stakeholders at all stages.
- Identify the values, beliefs, and pet theories of faculty stakeholders.
- Meet with them to talk about the evaluation and the roles they will be playing.
- Ask them about the values and theories underlying the course.
- When stakeholders disagree, the evaluator's choices include presenting conflicting views, working toward a consensus, and balancing the views of stakeholders with established views in the literature (Chen, 1990).
- Involve them in writing survey and interview questions.
- Ask them to confirm your findings and to sign off on the report.

Stakeholders have different values and perspectives about teaching and learning, which will emerge and may even come into conflict. For example, an administrator interested in learner satisfaction and final grades may clash with a faculty member's interest in testing a theory of distributed cognition. You need to respect and value these differences, respond to any outspoken criticism, and keep the evaluation process on track. Asking stakeholders to share their insights, write survey items, give presentations on their courses, or serve as change agents will facilitate buy-in. You have an obligation to triangulate and accurately report on the multiple perspectives of stakeholders (Stake, 1995). You should also be aware of financial pressures, conflicts of interest, the dismissal of your findings, and subtle pressures from authorities to present findings in a positive light or even suppress them.

The Joint Committee on Standards for Educational Evaluation

To provide guidelines for ethical evaluation studies, the Joint Committee on Standards for Educational Evaluation (1994) has compiled standards or applied ethics of professional conduct for evaluators. The 1994 standards were developed by a broad coalition of individuals, the W. K. Kellogg Foundation, and the Western Michigan University Evaluation Center. "The goal of the standards is to develop useful, feasible, ethical and sound evaluation of educational programs" (Joint Committee on Standards for Educational Evaluation, 1994). The standards are principles of professional practice to enhance the quality and fairness of evaluations by providing a guide for evaluating educational programs. The standards are not prescriptive in nature; they are guidelines of good practice, not laws, so that compliance is voluntary, although highly recommended. These 30 principles provide a working philosophy and suggestions for observing these principles (Appendix A). *Note*: The Joint Committee's (1994) *Program Evaluation Standards* are currently under revision and the third edition is expected in 2009.

THE PROGRAM EVALUATION STANDARDS OF THE JOINT COMMITTEE ON STANDARDS FOR EDUCATIONAL EVALUATION: AN OVERVIEW

Utility: feedback to stakeholders so that the evaluation results will be used.

Feasibility: realistic, politically viable, cost-effective.

Propriety: legal and ethical conduct with due regard for the welfare of those involved.

Accuracy: independent assessment, controls for bias, valid and reliable findings.

Trade-Offs among the Standards

Evaluators need to exercise professional judgment in deciding which of the 1994 Program Evaluation Standards to implement and which ones to sacrifice; the trade-offs involved in applying the standards are a necessary part of evaluation practice (Stoesz & Zumbo, 2003). These authors used the standards as a framework to illuminate the decision making of evaluators, practical trade-offs, and the points of conflict within evaluation practice. They found that evaluators tend to make trade-offs in these areas:

- Robust data collection and reporting versus practical constraints.
- Responsibility to decision makers versus broader stakeholder groups.
- Research ideals versus sufficiently good practice.
- Humanist research principles versus traditional scientific principles.

They also found that evaluators generally agree on the points of compatibility within the standards but disagree substantially on the potential points of conflict. These results provide strong evidence of the central role that power and politics play in the perception of conflicts within evaluative practice and substantiate the claim that research ideals are often in conflict with the pragmatics around contracts, costs, schedules, multiple stakeholder agendas, and stratified "pecking orders." In other words, political considerations within the community of evaluation stakeholders tend to have the greatest impact on trade-offs. Finally, they found that mixed methods can be helpful in creating compromises, which minimize sacrifices to quality, fairness, and ethical practice (Stoesz, 2005; Stoesz & Zumbo, 2003).

> Evaluators need to balance research ideals with practical constraints, responsibilities to decision makers with responsibilities to stakeholders, and humanist principles with scientific principles (Stoesz, 2005; Stoesz & Zumbo, 2003).

Using the Unfolding Model as a "Road Map"

The unfolding model is adapted from Messick's (1989) four-faceted conception of validity. As such, it is a multifaceted, progressive matrix, based on both facts and values. Our adapted framework provides a comprehensive, integrated approach to evaluation in which multiple sources of evidence are assembled to provide a comprehensive assessment of the merit and worth of distance/e-learning courses (Figure 5.1). Although we have already presented and discussed Messick's framework in Chapter 1, we are intentionally repeating this information here to provide a smooth transition to the unfolding elements of the model.

As shown in Figure 5.1, the merit, worth, or value of any distance course can be conceptualized as a four-faceted construct: (1) scientific evidence, (2) relevance and cost–benefit, (3) underlying values, and (4) unintended consequences. The first two categories comprise the *evidential basis* of evaluation (i.e., traditional scientific evidence, including quantitative and cost–benefit analyses). Outcomes encompasses student grades, learner satisfaction, and completion rates. Process refers to the course implementation (i.e., how the course actually works). Relevance encompasses (1) the fit between the course and the educational and training needs of society, (2) the relevance of the curriculum to learners, and (3) the ability of students to transfer their learning to the real world. The consequential basis encompasses underlying values and unintended consequences. There are four kinds of underlying values: (1) course objectives, (2) value labels, (3) ideology, and (4) theory. There are two kinds of unintended consequences: instructional and social. Finally, it is important to note that the four facets of the framework are not distinct or clear-cut; instead, they overlap and cut across each other. When analyzing evaluation data, evaluators will discover how the overlap of the various aspects of value "emerges" from the analysis of the data, revealing insights into how the course functions as a complex system. From here, we discuss each of the four facets within the distance education context and then turn our attention to the overlap among the four facets.

	Interpretation	Use
Scientific basis	**Scientific evidence (SE)** (surveys/interviews)	**Relevance/cost–benefit (RC)** (SE) + (RC)
Consequential basis	**Underlying values (UV)** (SE) + (RC) + (UV)	**Unintended consequences (UC)** (SE) + (RC) + (UV) + (UC)

FIGURE 5.1. The unfolding model.

The Four Facets Unfolded

Our unfolding model is a "road map" for planning and implementing your evaluation study. The broad dimensions of the model are scientific evidence, relevance, cost–benefit, values, and unintended consequences. Each of these facets unfolds to reveal additional criteria to guide the evaluation study (Figure 5.2). For example, scientific evidence unfolds to reveal more details about the kinds of tools that can be used to collect this evidence. You will not need to use all of these tools but can choose the ones most appropriate to your course design and technologies. Similarly, you can choose relevance or cost–benefit, or you may set your boundaries so that you do not investigate either of these sources of value. In sum, an analysis of evidence (your choice of data sources), values, and consequences is essential to our approach, but within each you have considerable latitude to tailor the model to your specific needs. In this way, any concern that our unfolding model is *too* comprehensive is averted because you can tailor our model to your specific context and to constantly evolving technologies of "e-learning and beyond" (Sinclair et al., 2006). This notion of tailoring a comprehensive evaluation model is recommended by Rossi, Freeman, and Lipsey's (1999) systematic approach to evaluation.

Mixed Methods:
Blending Quantitative and Qualitative Data

Overview

Our goal is descriptive, that is, to define the significant features of the course, analyze qualitative and quantitative data, create plausible interpretations, and build a comprehensive description of how the course performs. We define *science* not as randomized trials but as a "specific and systematic way of understanding how social realities arise, operate and impact on individuals and organizations" (Berg, 2007, p. 14). This comprehensive evaluation of course performance will also yield recommendations for course improvement.

Each distance course is a case or unit of analysis, and each course evaluation is a case study. Our goal is to obtain a comprehensive, in-depth "picture" of the course as a working system. To achieve this goal, you need to:

• Collect data on some aspect of *all four facets* of the unfolding model.
• Use quantitative and qualitative methods as equal, parallel methods.

Scientific evidence
  Surveys and interviews re: learner satisfaction
  - Tutor
  - Online discussion group
  - Course package
  - Textbook
  - Course webpages
  - CMS
  Outcomes
  Grades
  Completion rates
  Checklists
  Feedback
  Webpage evaluation
  Instructor competencies
  Course management data
  Progress tracking statistics

Relevance/cost–benefit
  Relevance
  - Alignment between the course and needs of society
  - Meaningfulness of course to learners
  - Transfer of learning to authentic contexts
  Cost–Benefit
  - Costs to the university
  - Costs to learners

Underlying values
  - Course goals and objectives
  - Rhetoric (e.g., "world-class," "innovative")
  - Theory (e.g., schema theory, distributed cognition)
  - Ideology (e.g., open access)
  - Stakeholder roles and influence

Unintended consequences
  - Instructional
  - Social
  - Course implementation
  - Fit across the four facets of value
  - Negative or positive

FIGURE 5.2. The unfolding model: The four facets unfolded.

Mixed methods provide a solid foundation of evidence when the "phenomena we study are amorphous or difficult to measure directly" (Fitzpatrick et al., 2004, p. 305). Multiple measures give greater credibility to the study because you can triangulate findings across several methods with different biases (e.g., surveys and interviews; Fitzpatrick et al., 2004). "Quantitative strategies provide rigorous, reliable and verifiably large aggregates of data and the statistical testing of empirical hypotheses" (Berg, 2007, p. 14). Qualitative research provides us with "naturally emerging language, perceptions and meanings individuals assign to their experiences . . . [in] natural settings" (p. 14). "Interviews provide depth, but are not necessarily representative" (Fitzpatrick et al., 2004, p. 319). In contrast, our approach to mixed methods provides *both* the breadth and generalizability of surveys and statistics *and* the richness, and depth of interviews and focus groups, and much more besides. To quote Greene (2007):

> A mixed method way of thinking seeks better, more comprehensive understanding of educational phenomena, understanding that is woven from strands of particularity *and* generality, contextual complexity *and* patterned regularity, inside *and* outside perspectives, the whole *and* its constituent parts, change *and* stability, equity *and* excellence and so forth. That is, a mixed method way of thinking seeks not so much convergence as insight . . . and [is] fundamentally generative. (p. 80)

In sum, mixed methods provide the kind of richness, depth, and coverage required for a comprehensive understanding of distance and e-learning courses. You will be collecting and comparing quantitative and qualitative data from multiple and diverse sources. By comparing documents with interview and survey data, you can obtain a comprehensive picture of the value of the course as it is actually implemented.

Data Sources

There are several sources of data for mixed-methods evaluation studies, including documents, surveys and questionnaires, interviews, and focus groups (Figure 5.3).

Documents

First, we collect documents that give information on the history and development of the course (e.g., an application for a funding grant). We

---

Documents
- Course outline
- Course development grant
- Notes on course history
- Committee meeting notes
- Textbooks

Quantitative data sources
- Student records (e.g., grades, attendance)
- Tutor feedback
- Grades and completion rates
- Performance tracking statistics
- Webpage evaluation checklists
- Surveys

Qualitative data sources
- Interviews
- Focus groups
- Transcripts of online discussions
- Webpage evaluation checklists

FIGURE 5.3. A data-collection toolkit.

also look at the course outline and the textbook. Course history and committee meeting notes may also be helpful. The purpose is to gain a sense of the purpose of the course and the reasons behind its development and the path of development. Of these documents, the course outline is the most important; it is a critical piece of information because it tells you about the intended objectives of the course.

Quantitative Data Sources

Second, we write survey items and **interview protocols** around the four categories of the unfolding model, unfolded and tailored for additional important evaluative areas unique to that particular delivery method. Once you have your survey responses, you calculate descriptive statistics, including the mean, median, mode, and standard deviation, and then review these results for patterns of interest. Depending on your sample size and response rate, you can argue that your survey findings are representative of the opinions and perceptions of most, some, or a minority of your learners. Survey findings have the advantages of breadth and generalizability.

Qualitative Data Sources

As for qualitative data, we start out with content analysis, which refers to coding the text of transcribed interviews for themes. These textual excerpts are then grouped together in themes and displayed in boxes or matrices (Miles & Huberman, 1994). The textual excerpts under each theme are counted, and the themes are listed in order of importance in a table, with the number of comments per theme. We emphasize that "content analysis is not a reductionist, positivistic approach" (Berg, 2007, p. 308). Instead, it is a systematic way of listening to and understanding the interviewee's perspectives and determining the extent to which these perspectives are generalizable and not just the perceptions of a single individual. Moreover, our approach is not limited to content analysis; we also blend content analysis with more emergent phenomenological approaches. New themes, not specifically mentioned in our unfolding model, tend to emerge in the analysis of values and consequences and in the analysis of fit. These themes often provide unexpected and surprising insights into the course implementation, needs of learners, support services, and many other aspects of the course. We also select direct quotations from the interviews to illustrate our findings. These are salient quotations to illustrate survey findings and to provide greater depth of understanding than can be provided by descriptive statistics alone. The emergent findings can also be compared with the findings from the content analysis and used to extend or illustrate the survey findings. A convergence of results from different respondents and across different methods provides much stronger support for your conclusions than if only one method had been used.

> With mixed-methods data, compare your findings across respondents and across methods. Draw your conclusions *only* after findings from multiple sources of evidence have *converged* to build a convincing case.

We emphasize that other approaches to quantitative, qualitative, and mixed methods are available, and we encourage our readers to explore these approaches. Ongbuwezie (2006), for example, has produced a detailed taxonomy of strategies for blending mixed methods. Greene and Caracelli (1997) provide other suggestions for blending mixed methodologies and different types of data. For example, you could collect qualitative data first (e.g., interviews), pull out the emergent themes, and write your survey questions around these themes. Here your purpose would be to generalize any unexpected findings to other learners in the course.

What Is Essential to Our Approach?

Scientific Evidence

An analysis of scientific evidence, values, and consequences is essential to our approach to evaluation. Some scientific evidence, consisting of *both* quantitative and qualitative data, is essential. A survey on learner satisfaction is essential to our approach. As online enrollment increases, the study of students' perceptions of their online experiences becomes increasingly important, and these valuable data can be easily collected with web-based instruments (Bendus, 2005). In addition, we recommend outcomes, final grades, and completion rates, but these data may not be available. Some survey or interview items in the relevance category provide useful evidence of value not provided by traditional, face-to-face courses. The good news is that the analysis of these data is fairly simple. You will need to

---

Some scientific evidence is central to our approach, but you are not required to analyze *all* kinds of scientific evidence in the top two boxes of the unfolding model. You will need to collect three types of data:

- Documents (e.g., course outlines or proposals).
- Surveys.
- Interviews or focus groups on learner satisfaction.

---

calculate descriptive statistics, that is, means, medians, modes, standard deviations, sample sizes, and frequencies or, in other words, a count of the number and percentage of respondents in each survey response category. Interviews with learners can be analyzed with a blend of both content analysis and **inductive** or emergent analysis. Cost–benefit may not be of interest to your stakeholders, and one way to set boundaries on your study is by omitting cost–benefit.

In applying the unfolding model, you will find that the real action lies in two simple data analysis techniques:

- Descriptive survey statistics (mean, median, and mode).
- Themes from interview or focus group data.

Together, these results will yield a comprehensive picture of your course as a unique, complex system.

Values

You can begin collecting data on values by analyzing the course outline for goals and objectives, which is central to our approach. The course outline lays out the goals and objectives of the course, and the underlying values, theories, and ideologies are usually implicit in these documents. You can also interview the course designers about their sense of the values underlying the course. You then want to compare these findings with survey or interview findings to determine how well the course actually worked as intended.

Unintended Consequences

Third, an analysis of underlying values and unintended consequences is also *essential* to our comprehensive approach. Values and consequences *must* be included in your study. Department heads and administrators need information about whether the course is being implemented as intended as well as specific directions for program improvement. You need to compare stated goals and objectives with actual course implementation and underlying values with daily realities. You need to analyze data from these different sources to evaluate the course implementation (i.e., how the course actually works). The investigation of the underlying values and unintended consequences provides this important information and is, therefore, a crucial component of a comprehensive evaluation study. This analysis is critical because it reveals the gap between the intended and the actual course implementation. In the final stage of your analysis, you need to determine the various aspects of fit between the (1) underlying values and the course implementation, (2) multiple underlying values, and (3) course components. This analysis shows you how smoothly the course components work together as a system. Comparing the course goals and objectives with the survey and interview findings helps you to identify unintended consequences, to determine whether they are positive or negative, and, finally, to make suggestions for course improvement. In sum, our approach requires (your choice of) scientific evidence and an analysis of values and consequences. Evidence, values, and unintended consequences are the three pillars of our approach.

Tailoring the Unfolding Model to Your Needs

On first glance, our unfolding model may appear to have too many evaluation categories to be practical. However, you must remember that you

will be selecting only those aspects of merit and worth that are most informative for your delivery method (e.g., web-based course, hybrid, print
distance), subject matter, and objectives.

> The unfolding model is adaptive and responsive to the diversity of contempo-
> rary technologies and delivery methods. You can unfold and tailor the unfolding
> model to answer questions of interest to your stakeholders for your own unique
> course context.

Setting Boundaries

When you are planning the evaluation, you may need to set boundaries
by choosing which kinds of scientific evidence are critical to your study.
Because of practical constraints, you will need to make some trade-offs in
the scope of your study. Cronbach (1982) uses the term *bandwidth*, which
means that the evaluator focuses on a broad range of relevant issues rather
than aiming to achieve absolute accuracy over a smaller number of issues.
Your boundaries will be set by balancing all of these constraints.

> You can set boundaries on your study by making trade-offs among:
>
> • The technologies and delivery methods.
> • The needs of stakeholders.
> • Constraints of time and resources.
> • Limited opportunities to access data (Fitzpatrick et al., 2004).

The Technologies and Delivery Methods

The strength of the unfolding model is that it is adaptive and responsive to
the diversity of contemporary technologies and delivery methods. From
your data collection tool kit in the unfolding model, you can choose and
adapt the evaluation tools that are most suitable to the unique context
of your own distance course. For example, if you are using a CMS, you
might want to use a CMS rubric as the centerpiece of your quantitative
data-collection efforts. You could locate a rubric on the web, redesign it
to suit your own context, simplify the criteria and language and so on—of
course, citing the source of the material appropriately. You could add or
delete questions and use open-ended items to gather new ideas from users
on what additional features they would like to have. Similarly, with an
online course, you might want to use a rubric to grade student contribu-

tions to online discussions. If there are no online discussions, then you might want to write your survey to focus on other important issues, such as turn-around time. As long as you have some scientific evidence, you have considerable latitude in choosing and adapting the tools and measures found in the unfolding model.

The Needs of Stakeholders

How might the interests and values of stakeholders set boundaries on your study? For example, you may be evaluating a business course that has migrated online. The faculty in this department may be interested in redesigning a traditional course into a distance/e-learning course to maximize class size, minimize costs, and maintain benefits. In this case, you would focus on cost–benefit and may be less interested in other aspects of merit and worth. Let's look at another example. The liberal arts faculty may be interested in testing an educational theory about the personal relevance and authenticity of new technology. In this case, your focus would be on the theory of pedagogical relevance underlying the course, whether the learners are satisfied with the course materials, and whether they perceive them as relevant to their lives. In this case, you would not need to do a cost–benefit analysis. As a third example, a senior administrator may be interested in a causal analysis of learner satisfaction and final grades. In this case, you might run a regression model using learner satisfaction data and grades or completion rates. In sum, whether you choose to invest your time and energies in a cost–benefit study, a theory-driven study, or a regression model depends, at least to some extent, on the values and interests of your stakeholders.

Constraints on Time and Resources

The boundaries of your study will also be determined by constraints of time and resources. You can use GANNT project planning software, named after an engineer Henry Gannt, to set time lines for critical stages of your project in order to complete the project on time. Your evaluation grant funding may cover salaries for as short a period as 2 months or for as long as 2 years. You will need to plan how much you can reasonably accomplish in this limited time. For example, you may decide to omit a cost–benefit analysis, which can be time consuming and costly. You also need to be aware that the use of your funds for gifts, salaries, or travel may be restricted by university, state, or federal policies.

Limited Opportunities to Access Data

The boundaries of your study may also be determined by the availability of data. Data on student grades or completion rates either may not be available or may be aggregated in a form that you cannot use. If you are unable to obtain outcomes data, you can still conduct a very worthwhile study but may need to change your focus to learner satisfaction. For all these reasons, you can scale down your scientific evidence so that your study can be completed in time, with the best use of resources, and in response to stakeholder needs.

Sampling

Sampling occurs at three levels: the course, survey participation, and interview or focus group participation. In our approach to evaluation, each course is a case or unit of analysis, and each course evaluation is a mixed-methods case study. The purpose of case research is to describe a single course in depth as a working system of component parts. If you are given courses to evaluate, you will not need to sample courses. If not, then you may wish to call on faculty to participate in a grant with an evaluation component. With our approach, you will not be generalizing your results but rather presenting your findings. It is up to your reader to judge the merits of your report and to generalize to other courses. However, if you are interested in testing a theory, you will need to choose courses to represent larger entities of interest to which you will attempt to generalize your findings.

Sample Size

To maximize the credibility of your findings, your course evaluation survey should be distributed to all learners in a course. In many cases, however, you might want to survey a sample of students instead of the entire class. Sampling is less costly and time consuming, and with the results of statistical tests, you can make an inference from the sample to the population of interest. However, how do you know how many individuals to include in your sample? If your sample is too small, you may not be able to find a significant difference even if one does exist. If your sample is too large, then you may find a difference but, again, at too great a cost in time and resources. For more information on sampling, see Kish's (1995) book on survey sampling.

Power

The optimum number of participants in your sample depends on the type of statistical test, the number of variables, and the number of groups (Cohen, 1992). If you are interested in statistical tests of between-group differences, 25 learners per group is the minimum sample size. For example, if you wish to compare performance in a distance course and a face-to-face course, you would need a minimum of 25 participants in each course. The more participants are included, the more power you have to find statistically significant differences. With only 25 in each group, you will need a larger effect size to find statistically significant differences. If you are interested in a correlational study with five or six variables, your recommended minimum sample size could be as high as 300, depending on the number of variables. You can find the "right" sample size by accessing online power tables. The software program G★Power is highly recommended for sample size determination based on statistical power analysis (Buchner, Faul, & Erdfelder, 2007). G★Power is freely distributed on the web *www.psycho.uni-duesseldorf.de/aap/projects/gpower/*).

> **Response rate:** The number of individuals who completed a survey divided by the total number of course participants. A high response rate bolsters the credibility of your findings because they represent the opinions of a large number of individuals rather than just a few.

Random Selection

To generalize your findings, it is important to randomly select your participants. Qualitative findings also have more credibility if your participants have been randomly sampled so that the sample is representative of all learners in the course. If you have a heterogeneous group of learners, you can use stratified sampling, that is, samples drawn from different groups (e.g., male/female, urban/rural, young/mature). In actual evaluation practice, however, convenience sampling is often used. With convenience sampling, you use anyone who volunteers, wherever and whenever they can be found. Because students have many demands on their time, you may wish to compensate them for their participation with food, a bookstore certificate, or a cash payment if permitted by university regulations.

Response Rates

You can enhance credibility for your quantitative findings with high survey response rates. Ideally, you would like a 100% response rate (i.e., responses from the entire class). In this way, your reader will know that your participants were not "cherry-picked" to include only those who would give positively biased results. Usually, some students in your class will not consent to participate or will respond to some items but not others. The response rate is a percentage that should be reported with your descriptive statistics *for every* survey item.

Generalizability

In our approach to evaluation, each course is a case or unit of analysis, and each course evaluation is a case study. The purpose of case research is "particularization" (Stake, 1995), which means that a single case (or course) is studied in depth as a system of component parts. Our goal is to "explore significant features of the case, create plausible interpretations, test for trustworthiness of these interpretations, [and] construct a worthwhile argument" (Ross & Morrison, 1997). Therefore, you are not interested in generalizing to *other* courses, but this does not prevent your reader from generalizing to other similar courses. If you wished to provide a stronger basis for generalizing to other courses, you would need to randomly sample your courses (Reigeluth, 1999). Even then, you should use fuzzy generalizations, with tentative language such as "It is likely that" or "It may be that" (Bassey, 1999).

Conclusions

In this chapter, we discussed how to get started and provide an overview of important, preliminary considerations in evaluation studies. The importance of your university's ethics review procedures cannot be understated. Any university may be audited for noncompliance with ethics procedures. These audits are usually on short notice, and if any violations are found, all research at your university can be shut down. We also discussed the Joint Standards on Evaluation, the roles of stakeholders, and the political considerations involved in trade-offs among evaluation standards.

Next, we discussed our unfolding model, which is a conceptual road map to a comprehensive study of the merit and worth of distance/e-learning courses. An investigation of scientific evidence, values, and consequences are central to our approach; these three aspects of value are essential to a comprehensive analysis of merit and worth. The unfolding nature of our model, however, means that you have considerable choice with respect to the types of scientific evidence to collect, and among these tools, you will choose only the ones that are appropriate for the unique features of your course. You will be using a mixed methodology, including documents such as course outlines, as well as survey and interview or focus group data. The questions you write will be guided by the categories of the framework.

The boundaries of your study will be set for you by the technologies and delivery methods, the needs of stakeholder, and the constraints of time, resources, and limited data access (Fitzpatrick et al., 2004). The two most important ways to enhance the credibility of your findings is to randomly sample participants and to obtain large response rates. Finally, our approach requires little statistical expertise, is easy to use, and has, in our experience of evaluating distance courses, proven to be very effective. In Chapter 8, we show the rich findings that resulted from applying our framework to survey and interview data from two authentic postsecondary courses. We now proceed to a discussion of how to collect data on the evidential basis, the top two boxes of the unfolding model.

CHAPTER 6

■ ■ ■ ■ ■ ■ ■ ■

The Unfolding Model
SCIENTIFIC EVIDENCE

In the first two chapters, we laid out the background and context of evaluation of contemporary distance/e-learning courses and reviewed the history of professional program evaluation. We contrasted traditional questions-and-methods models with contemporary social advocacy models. In Chapter 3, we showed how evaluation frameworks in distance education are based largely on scientific evidence, including grades, retention, and cost–benefit analysis. Although a few of these evaluation models are grounded in the science of professional program evaluation, they are still unlikely to provide a comprehensive evaluation of distance/e-learning courses because they omit underlying values and unintended consequences. We showed that, in authentic evaluation studies of distance/e-learning courses, unintended consequences emerge in myriad and diverse ways, but that the reporting of these effects tends to be dispersed or in the background, rather than in the foreground, of evaluation studies.

In Chapter 4, we discussed Messick's (1989) framework on validity and showed that Messick has already done a comprehensive, theoretical analysis of the value of tests, which consists of scientific evidence, values, and unintended consequences. In Chapter 5, we elaborated on the unfolding model as an evaluation framework for distance/e-learning courses. We showed that the facets of our model include recurring themes in evaluation models in both distance education and program evaluation, specifically outcomes, process, relevance, cost–benefit analysis, underlying values, and unintended consequences. Because these categories also occur in our model, it is clear that Messick's (1989) framework provides a conceptual bridge between professional program evaluation and evaluation models in distance education.

Definition of "Scientific Evidence"

After your ethics review protocol has been approved by your university and you have set the boundaries of your study, you are ready to begin collecting your scientific evidence. As you will recall, evidential basis, the upper two boxes of the unfolding model, refers to the kinds of scientific evidence to be collected. In our approach, the term "scientific evidence" includes both quantitative and qualitative data, provided they are collected and analyzed according to rigorous standards in educational evaluation. Mixed methods are used as equal and parallel methods (Tashakkori & Teddlie, 1998); in other words, both quantitative and qualitative methods are used to investigate how the program actually works (course implementation) and the outcomes of the program (e.g., grades, learner satisfaction, scores on checklists). Mixed methods is powerful because it combines the breadth of quantitative methods with the depth of qualitative methods.

What kind of data do you collect for the evidential basis (i.e., the two upper left boxes of the unfolding model; Figure 6.1)? (To give our

> **Scientific evidence**
> Surveys/interviews/focus groups/online ethnographies
> to measure learner satisfaction with course components
> - Tutor
> - Online discussion group
> - Course package
> - Textbook
> - Course webpages
>
> Outcomes
> - Grades
> - Completion and retention rates
> - Student assessment and feedback
>
> Checklists and rubrics to measure environmental quality
> - Course management systems
> - Webpage quality
> - Learning objects quality
> - Accessibility for learners with disabilities
> - Instructor competencies
>
> Data/statistics to track learner progress
> - Course management data

FIGURE 6.1. The unfolding model: Scientific evidence unfolded.

readers an overview of this section, Figure 6.1 and the accompanying text intentionally duplicates Figure 1.5 and related information in Chapter 1.) The scientific basis consists of both the upper left box, scientific evidence, a list of scientific measures and the context of their application, and the upper right box, relevance and cost–benefit, which are additional aspects of value or constructs that are also commonly scientifically measured. The scientific basis includes traditional scientific measures such as surveys and interviews on learner satisfaction, outcomes such as grades and completion rates, checklists, and rubrics to measure environmental quality such as web evaluation, instructor competencies, and data/statistics to track learner progress.

Learner satisfaction refers to satisfaction with the course components, as measured by quantitative survey ratings or revealed in depth through qualitative interview findings. Feedback refers to instructor feedback on learners' assignments and the quality of the assessment tasks. Instructor competencies refers to a checklist of instructor performance on tasks. Checklists can be used to evaluate both webpage quality and instructor competencies. Course management data refers to summary progress tracking statistics found in CMSs, for example, the number of minutes that each learner spends on each webpage or the number of lessons completed in any given time period. In this way, instructors can instantly see what their students are doing, even though they are not physically present.

To summarize, the top left box of the unfolding model encompasses scientific evidence from multiple sources (e.g., outcomes, surveys, interviews, and checklists). Relevance can be measured with all of the tools in the upper left box, while cost–benefit is measured with its own unique set of tools, strategies, and techniques.

Scientific Evidence

Measuring Learner Satisfaction

From the beginning, learner satisfaction has been an important construct in distance education, just as it continues to be in e-learning. As online enrollments increase, students' perceptions of their online experiences become increasingly significant. Learner satisfaction is also related to learner persistence, which in turn is related to completion rates. Satisfied learners are more likely to recommend the course to others, and more course registrations will enable the course to be "scaled up," thereby increasing revenues and lowering operating costs. Student satisfaction measures also put the learner in the role of customer and have important implications for services as students "shop around" for the optimum course experience (Sener & Humbert, 2002). "As with any expanding universe, the need to broaden and deepen our knowledge of satisfying students is growing in all directions" (Sener & Humbert, 2002, p. 12).

Student satisfaction, in addition, is a "complex, multi-faceted, and challenging area of evaluation" (Sener & Humbert, 2002, p. 2). The construct can be broken down into distinct areas, such as satisfaction with individual courses, satisfaction with the program, or satisfaction with the type of learning environment (e.g., fully online or blended) (Sener & Humbert, 2002). It can also be broken down into satisfaction with the course components (e.g., access, materials, technology, and interaction). You can measure learner satisfaction with surveys consisting of closed- and open-ended items. The items on the survey should be written around and grouped by the kinds of categories we have just listed. Alternatively, to obtain more detailed, unexpected information that might not be captured in a survey, you could also conduct interviews with an interview protocol written around any of these dimensions of learner satisfaction.

Surveys

To collect data on leaner satisfaction, you can write surveys, conduct interviews or focus groups, and use web-based instruments (Bendus, 2005). Surveys are questionnaires to measure educational and psychological attributes such as opinions, attitudes, and behaviors. Before you begin writing, we recommend that you peruse surveys in the literature of educational measurement or distance education to develop a sense of the characteristics of good surveys. Scholarly journals in distance education are a good place to locate surveys developed for the unique context of distance education. Roberts, Drani, Telg, and Lundy (2005), for example, used data from 194 students to refine an instrument that measures student attitudes on course-related components such as the instructor, overall course effectiveness, technical dimensions, technical support, and convenience of registration. Other surveys in distance education measure attitudes toward distance teaching (Cheung, 1998) and assessment (Harrison et al., 1991). To learn more about surveys, consult Groves et al. (2004), Nardi (2006), or Saris and Gallhofer's (2007) work on survey methodology.

Finding Surveys on the Web

On the web, you can find several popular test banks, with surveys on diverse educational and psychological constructs. The Buros Institute of Mental Measurements (2008) database provides free information on almost 4,000 tests and test reviews for a small fee. This survey bank is available at *www.unl.edu/buros/*. Plake and Impare's (2001) *Fourteenth Mental Measurements Yearbook* contains more than 400 tests and attitude surveys. The Educational Testing Service has an online data bank of more than 20,000 tests. Black, Ferdig, and DiPietro (2008) provide a comprehensive list of evaluative instruments for virtual high schools. Again, these listings may not provide information or guarantees on the quality of the surveys; nevertheless, these websites are excellent places to start. The Flashlight Project, under the auspices of the American Association for Higher Education, provides a range of very useful surveys and other assessment tools to help institutions evaluate technology-based educational practices (TLT Group, 2008a).

Surveys in the E-Learning Literature

A good questionnaire developed to measure student satisfaction with online courses can be found in the appendix of Picciano's (2002) study of interaction, presence, and performance in an online course at Hunter College in New York City. This questionnaire has a blend of closed- and open-ended items. The items are simply and clearly worded and are likely to be interpreted the same way by respondents (not always the case with surveys!). The survey contains demographic variables and sections on web-based tools and affective response. The survey provides an excellent model of good survey design and can be found at *www.aln.org/publications/jaln/v6n1/v6n1_picciano.asp*.

There are also surveys that have been developed for particular online environments. For example, Zaharias (2004, 2005) developed a questionnaire for e-learning applications according to an established methodology in human–computer interaction research. The questionnaire items are based on a conceptual framework that combines web and instructional design dimensions with an affective learning dimension. The web dimensions include content, visual design, and navigation, and the affective dimension includes intrinsic motivation to learn. The questionnaire was used in two large empirical studies that reported significant evidence for reliability. Finally, if your institution subscribes to the Teaching, Learning, and Technology (TLT) Group, you can use and adapt their flashlight templates—a bank of surveys and instructions for teaching and learning (TLT Group, 2008b).

Problems with Using Existing Surveys

Often, however, you cannot just locate existing surveys and use them in your evaluation study. Even if you could, there are several problems with using existing surveys in your evaluation. First, all written material, from student lecture notes to standardized tests, is copyrighted, even without any written notice. Copyrighted material cannot be reproduced without permission. To obtain permission to use commercial surveys, you will likely have to pay fees to the author or publisher. The National Survey of Student Engagement (NSSE), for example, is a high-quality fee-based commercial survey widely used in American universities. With surveys in journal articles, you may not have to pay fees, but you still need to obtain permission from the author and/or the journal. Moreover, because different journals have different copyright rules, you will need to do a search in the Sherpa/Romeo site, a database of the copyright rules of most academic journals available at *www.sherpa.ac.uk/romeo.php*.

Second, most surveys in the literature have no guarantee of quality, so you should look for psychometric information on test quality. Some scholarly journals in educational measurement often publish validation studies of surveys, which include tables of "factor loadings." These tables group the survey items into dimensions or subscales, which can be very helpful in defining the construct. Survey items in this chapter can be used as examples to guide item writing.

The most important problem with using existing surveys, however, is relevance for your purpose. Surveys from the literature or test banks may measure some dimensions in the unfolding model but not all of them. You will probably find it difficult to locate a survey that measures all of the dimensions relevant to your particular course, or if it does, the survey may be written for a different context, such as K–12. For all of these reasons, you will probably want to write your own survey.

How to Write Good Survey Questions

As the plan for your evaluation study, the unfolding model provides the outline for writing your survey questions (Figure 6.2). We recommend writing your survey questions around the dimensions of value identified in the unfolding model (e.g., learner satisfaction). If you substitute similar constructs, you may discover that they are difficult to measure and that you get "bogged down." One example of a difficult construct is "student engagement." Although this construct appears similar to "learner satisfaction," it is much more difficult to define and measure with a list of survey

---

Step 1: Identify your construct and its dimensions.

Step 2: Write each item to measure only one dimension.

Step 3: Follow guidelines for good item writing:
- Write short, simple, and clearly worded items (about five items for each dimension).
- Add a mix of closed- and open-ended items.
- Use five to seven response choices on Likert-scales.
- Write Likert scale descriptors to measure equally increasing amounts of the dimension being measured.
- To increase the reliability of your survey, write more items.

Step 4: To test the quality of your survey, do a factor analysis and calculate Cronbach's alpha.

FIGURE 6.2. Steps to writing good survey questions.

items. The National Survey of Student Engagement (NSSE), developed at Indiana University, Bloomington, measures "student engagement" indirectly through an extensive list of proxy behavioral variables. The NSSE is the "gold standard" for this particular construct and more information on ordering this survey can be found at *nsse.iub.edu/index.cfm*.

Identify the Construct and Its Dimensions

The first rule for writing good survey questions is to identify the construct you are measuring, for example, student satisfaction or web usability. The second step is to break this construct down into its various dimensions. For example, if your construct is student satisfaction, you can break it down into the following dimensions: satisfaction with the instructor, satisfaction with the feedback, and satisfaction with opportunities for interaction. Another example is the construct of student performance, which can be broken down into the dimensions of study habits, prior knowledge, communications skills, time available for study, teacher effectiveness, and so on (Picciano, 2002, p. 22). Once you have mapped out your dimensions, you should then write four or five survey questions for each of these dimensions. Zaharias (2005) developed a conceptual framework for the usability evaluation of asynchronous e-learning applications. In the classification tree diagram shown in Figure 6.3, the construct is web usability and the branches are the dimensions that make up the construct.

Write Each Item to Measure Only One Dimension

It is very important to write each survey item so that it measures one, and only one, dimension. This can be more difficult than it sounds because educational constructs often overlap. To produce meaningful results that

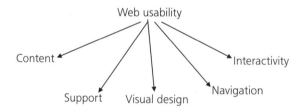

FIGURE 6.3. Web usability: The construct and its dimensions (Zaharias, 2005).

are easy to interpret, you should write a cluster of survey items for each dimension. In this process, you may discover other dimensions that you had not previously considered. For example, Picciano (2002) found that student presence was a separate dimension of the construct of student interaction. In this case, a cluster of items would be written around student interaction and another cluster around presence. It would be hard to imagine how a thermostat could measure both temperature and mass, but this situation is analogous to long, complex, and ambiguously worded survey items that are really measuring more than one dimension.

Follow Guidelines for Good Item Writing

The next rule of good item writing is to write questions that are short, simply worded, clear, unambiguous, and easy to understand. Survey items that are long and complex and that contain difficult vocabulary, qualifiers, or phrases joined by conjunctions, such as "and/or" and "if/then," are more difficult for participants to answer and adversely affect the quality of the data. You should write about five questions for each dimension. Next, you should add some closed- or open-ended items so that you have a mix of different item types. Closed-ended items have forced choices such as yes/no. Likert scales should have from five to seven response choices with both numbers and descriptors. The numbers enable you to easily enter the data in a data file, and the descriptors below the numbers should be carefully worded to reflect increasing quantities of the attribute. To increase the reliability of your survey, you can always write more items around the same dimensions. More items will provide a more complete content coverage of your area of interest and help to even out measurement error from poor wording on any individual item. Finally, you will need to write different survey items for course designers, faculty, and learners. For more information on how to write surveys, see Fowler (2001).

Test the Quality of Your Survey

Finally, to test the quality of your survey, you could do a factor analysis and calculate Cronbach's alpha. These analyses are available in a software package like Statistical Package for the Social Sciences (SPSS). A factor analysis tells you whether each survey item is measuring one or more than one dimension, as well as whether the items you have written for each dimension are, in fact, measuring that dimension or whether they overlap with other dimensions. If your items overlap, then technically they are not good items because each item should measure one, and only one, dimension. When an item measures more than one dimension, you should throw it out or rewrite it and run your factor analysis again. You should repeat this process until you get clean results. Cronbach's alpha is a measure of reliability, which again, will flag poor items (i.e., items that are not highly correlated with the construct of interest). Again, you should throw out or rewrite these items and run your analysis again.

Let us examine an example of this process. As you may recall, Zaharias (2005) was interested in evaluating web usability of asynchronous e-learning applications. We saw how he broke this construct into dimensions. To develop a questionnaire, he then wrote 10 items for each dimension. To evaluate the questionnaire, Zaharias analyzed the data from the first administration with Cronbach's alpha and factor analysis. This analysis enabled him to identify poor questionnaire items, which he then threw out or rewrote. He administered the questionnaire a second time and went through the same psychometric analysis. He tested two revisions of the questionnaire until he obtained acceptable psychometric results, which were imperative if he was to obtain acceptable results on his regression model predicting motivation to learn from web usability. Another excellent example of the complete process of instrument development and testing, including a list of dimensions (table of specifications) and confirmatory factor analysis, can be found in Chaney et al. (2007).

Run a factor analysis and Cronbach's alpha when:

- You plan to publish your survey and recommend its adoption by others.
  or
- You plan to run more sophisticated analysis (e.g., multivariate statistics).
  or
- You plan to publish your results in a prestigious journal with high standards.

Using the Unfolding Model to Write Survey and Interview Questions

To begin, you can write your survey and interview questions around the evidential basis (i.e., the upper two boxes of our framework). The first box, scientific evidence, consists of learner satisfaction, outcomes (e.g., grades, completion rates), checklists, and progress tracking statistics (see Figure 6.1).

After you have set your boundaries on the scope of the evaluation, the next step is to narrow down these broad topics by writing more specific questions under each broad group. As mentioned, you should include both Likert response scales, which will help you to aggregate results for the group, and some open-ended responses, which will enable you to probe for richer, and sometimes unexpected, insights from individuals. We now cycle through each of the categories of our framework and provide examples of survey and interview questions.

Outcomes: Enrollment, Grades, and Completion Rates

If you are unable to obtain student records or grades, you can survey learners about their grades and completion rates (Figure 6.4).

Learner Satisfaction with the Course Components

The next group of questions deals with learner satisfaction with the course components. You can list your course components and write your survey questions around each component (Figure 6.5). Again, you want to have a mix of closed- and open-ended items (Figure 6.6). As shown in Figure 6.6, your closed-ended items should have a Likert scale with between five to seven response choices along with descriptors.

Grades
- What was your grade point average last term? _____ %
- What grade do you expect to obtain in this course? _____
- The grades on my assignments are fair. Y _____ N _____
- The midterm exam was fair. Y _____ N _____
- I was satisfied with my grade on the final project. Y _____ N _____
- I was satisfied with the assignments. Y _____ N _____
- I knew how to get a good grade in the course. Y _____ N _____

Course completion rates
- Why did you not complete the course? _____
- If you did not complete any other postsecondary courses last term, please check here. _____

FIGURE 6.4. Survey questions for learners about grades and completion rates. Based on Ruhe and Bates (1999a, 1999b) and Ruhe, Qayyum, and Bates (1999).

Instructor
Course materials
- Textbook
- Print package

Technology:
- Web
- E-mail
- Interactive video
- CD-ROM

Course activities:
- Online discussions
- Group projects
- Video-conferencing sessions

Feedback:
- Instructor comments
- Assignments
- Midterm and final exam
- Grades

CMS
Course web pages
Support

FIGURE 6.5. Course components unfolded.

Administering Surveys

Surveys can be disseminated in person (in courses with face-to-face meetings), by mail, e-mail, telephone, or the web. Regardless of how you make the initial contact, you need to explain the project, ask for volunteers, and distribute the subject consent form and surveys. In face-to-face meetings, it is better to wait for learners to complete the surveys right then and there instead of returning later to collect them.

For online courses, you can set up a survey on the web or e-mail questionnaires to learners. A program like SurveyMonkey provides a quick and easy approach to putting surveys on the web. You can select from more than a dozen types of questions, including multiple-choice format, rating scales, and drop-down menus. You can put a link on your blog, send a survey invitation to your own e-mail list, track respondents, and send follow-up reminders. SurveyMonkey is available at *www.surveymonkey.com/*. Finally, you should try to set your web surveys as "sticky forms"; that is, the data entered by respondents remain in the fields even

Instructor

The instructor knows a lot about the course content.

1	2	3	4	5
Strongly disagree	Disagree	Neutral	Agree	Agree strongly

I learned a lot from my conversations with the instructor.

1	2	3	4	5
Strongly disagree	Disagree	Neutral	Agree	Agree strongly

Course Materials

I was satisfied with the course package.

1	2	3	4	5
Strongly disagree	Disagree	Neutral	Agree	Agree strongly

I learned a lot from the course textbook.

1	2	3	4	5
Strongly disagree	Disagree	Neutral	Agree	Agree strongly

How did the technology in this course help your learning? _____

_____

Course activities

I was happy with the online discussions.

1	2	3	4	5
Strongly disagree	Disagree	Neutral	Agree	Agree strongly

How did the technology help your learning?

_____

_____

(continued)

FIGURE 6.6. Sample learner satisfaction survey questions.

My project team worked well together.

1	2	3	4	5
Strongly disagree	Disagree	Neutral	Agree	Agree strongly

Effort

This workload in this course was too heavy.

1	2	3	4	5
Strongly disagree	Disagree	Neutral	Agree	Agree strongly

How many hours per week did you spend working on the course?

Almost none _____

1 or 2 hours _____

2 or 3 hours _____

4 or 5 hours _____

More than 5 hours _____

Overall learner satisfaction

I didn't get as much out of this course as I expected.

1	2	3	4	5
Strongly disagree	Disagree	Neutral	Agree	Agree strongly

What aspects of the course worked well/didn't work well for you? _____

_____

_____

_____

Is there anything else about the course you would like to tell us? _____

_____

_____

FIGURE 6.6. *(page 2 of 2)*

after respondents exit the survey so that they can return to complete the survey without having to reenter data.

In your participant consent form, you can stipulate that anyone who sends in a completed questionnaire is deemed to have consented to be contacted for a telephone interview. The anonymity of both survey respondents and interviewees is protected by assigning a numerical code to each participant instead of writing their names on the surveys or interview transcripts.

Mail, E-Mail, and Web Surveys

Several articles have been written about the relative merits of mail, e-mail, and web-based surveys. Mail yields higher response rates, but response times are longer and costs are higher (Shannon & Bradshaw, 2002). To increase response rates to mailed surveys, King, Pealer, and Bernard (2001) recommend a cover letter offering an incentive, return envelopes, and postage. The benefits of e-mail and web-based surveys are "reduced cost, ease of data entry, format flexibility and ability to access different populations" (Granello & Wheaton, 2004). The disadvantages are measurement error, low response rates, and possible nonrepresentativeness of the data (Granello & Wheaton, 2004). Another disadvantage of e-mail surveys is that the data may need to be rekeyed into a database. Finally, it is important to remember that we sometimes need paper surveys to assess consumer satisfaction; for example, if the computer does not function well or if students have problems, they will simply not respond to your online survey unless you also give them the option of a paper survey. These kinds of issues affect your data collection, your results and analysis, and your ability to generalize from a sample to all of the learners in a course.

We recommend web-based surveys over e-mail or paper surveys for several reasons. First, web-based data protect respondents' confidentiality and anonymity better than e-mail because IP addresses show which computers were used, but e-mail addresses can identify individual users. Second, data collected over the web with a program such as Cold Fusion is automatically compiled and stored in a database, where it can be saved as a .csv file and easily converted into a program similar to Excel or SPSS.

When setting up a web-based data-collection system, your web designer needs to obtain a list of data specs from an experienced data analyst before designing the system. Failure to set up all of these specifications before you implement your data-collection system can cause major problems later with data storage, cleaning, and analysis. First, your data-collection system must be in compliance with IRB and Health Insurance Portability and Accountability Act (HIPAA) regulations. Your survey should be preceded by a screen ensuring respondents' confidentiality and anonymity and a check box with "I agree with these terms and conditions" to obtain participants' consent. Your data should then be collected on a single screen, not on multiple screens. This way, all your data will be delivered into a single "flat" data file, thereby freeing you from having to link data across multiple data files. If you do need to link data across multiple forms, you will need to use student names, IDs, or other identifiers as your linking variables.

Second, to reduce measurement error, we recommend pull-down menus, radio buttons and check boxes, clear formatting, and minimal use of graphics for faster downloading (Granello & Wheaton, 2004). Third, to be in compliance with state mandates, care must be taken to ensure that the survey is accessible to the disabled and visually impaired and that instructions are provided on how to access an alternative format such as a telephone survey. To increase response rates, Sheehan and Jafari (2003) recommends sending several follow-up e-mail messages referring the participants to the web address with the survey. Finally, after you have finished designing your web-based data-collection system, we recommend entering dummy or fake data to test how well your system works.

VIGNETTE

Your colleague says that scientific evidence is not essential to evaluating instructional programs but is merely one of many convincing ways to tell a story. How would you respond?

Analyzing Survey Data

Downloading Your Data

If you are using a web-based survey, you should download your data at least once a week into a password-protected computer to preserve its integrity and confidentiality. You can XML or save text in a delimited form and export it across programs, for example, from EXCEL to SPSS, SAS, or Statistica. Next, you will need to convert your data into a statistical software package. To do descriptive statistics and produce charts and graphs, you could use a program similar to Excel. However, if you want to do more complex statistical analysis, you will want to use a program similar to SPSS. With powerful statistical packages, you will need to prepare the data for analysis, for example, by defining your variable type (i.e., nominal, ordinal, interval or ratio) and variable codes (e.g., 1 = *disagree strongly*, 2 = *disagree*). With other software packages, there may be little preliminary work that is needed before you can analyze your data, but you may have less flexibility, speed, and power in analyzing results.

Cleaning and Exploring Your Data

After you have downloaded and converted all your data, you need to clean your data (i.e., search for and correct data entry errors such as missing, inaccurate, or impossible values). You should review each line of data to ensure that the numbers appear in the correct columns, that respondents have not hit the submit button twice, and that you have not mistakenly deleted any test data. If you have a small data file, you could also visually scan the data for suspiciously large or small values. These values may be data errors, which you need to correct, delete, or replace with a "missing value" code.

You also want to explore your data to get a clear understanding of the spread and shape, or distribution, for each variable. You can do this by running a frequency analysis, stem and leaf diagram, or histogram for each variable. A frequency analysis is a vertical list of the number of responses in each response category. A stem and leaf diagram provides the same information in a horizontal list. Histograms provide a visual display of your data in the form of a graph. A normal distribution has a bell-shape curve, whereas a bimodal distribution has a cluster of scores at the extreme ends of the scale and few scores in the middle. These techniques will show you how spread out your data points are from the mean and how flat or peaked your distribution is. They will also reveal outliers (i.e., suspiciously large or small values). If these data points are data entry errors, you need to correct, delete, or replace them. These visuals help you answer these questions: How frequently does each score occur? How spread out are the scores? Are there any outliers, that is, unusually high or low scores? Are these outliers authentic data points or could they be data entry errors? Finally, if you are interested in subgroup differences (e.g., young first-year students vs. mature adult learners), you can also select cases by group and run an analysis for each subgroup separately.

TABLE 6.1. Response to "Support Services for This Course Are Unsatisfactory"

1		2		3		4		5	
N	%	N	%	N	%	N	%	N	%
0	0	1	6	8	47	6	35	2	12

Note. N = 17. Judgments were made on a 5-point scale (1 = *strongly disagree*, 2 = *disagree*, 3 = *neither agree nor disagree*, 4 = *agree*, 5 = *strongly agree*). Data from Ruhe and Bates (1999b).

Descriptive Statistics

"Many important questions of concern to stakeholders can be answered with descriptive statistics or graphs" (Fitzpatrick et al., 2004, p. 359). Our approach relies heavily on simple descriptive statistics and *not* on complex statistical analyses. Descriptives include the mean, median, mode, standard deviation, total sample size, and frequencies (i.e., a count of the number and percentage of responses in each response category). Descriptive statistics are easy to calculate and convey important information to your stakeholders about the program. Table 6.1 is an example of how to report the following results from a single survey item about satisfaction with the support services: "Forty-seven percent of respondents were dissatisfied with the support services, 47% were neutral, and 6% were satisfied." In your evaluation report, you can provide a list of similar tables, one table for each survey question, along with a one-sentence summary. This simple reporting technique for learner satisfaction survey items is the foundation of our approach to evaluation.

However, you should be aware that means and standard deviations can be misleading. For example, a bimodal distribution of scores on learner satisfaction show that some learners were very satisfied, some were very dissatisfied, and few were in the middle, a finding that is not uncommon in distance and technology-based education. For this reason, we recommend you use frequency tables to report the number and percentage of responses in each response category.

Qualitative Data:
Interviews, Focus Groups, and Online Ethnographies

Qualitative data are used to obtain rich, in-depth information about the day-to-day workings of the course implementation system, as experienced by those individuals who are closest to the system. With interview and focus group data, you can use the perceptions and beliefs of a small number of individuals to "understand experiences and reconstruct events in which you did not participate" (Rubin & Rubin, 2005, p. 3). West, Waddoups, and Graham (2007), for example, used qualitative data to understand the experiences of instructors as they adopted a CMS. Their findings lead to specific recommendations for improving faculty adoption rates.

Qualitative data can be collected from open-ended survey questions, one-on-one face-to-face or telephone interviews, or focus groups. In focus groups, a group of respondents sit down together to have a guided conversation. Data can also be collected over the Internet (e.g., in chat room or online discussions). Interviews and focus groups should always be recorded, for example, with tape- or video recorders. Next, the interviews can be transcribed, or written down word for word, so that the text of the interviews can be analyzed. One way to save time is to use transcription machines or the Voice to Text feature in Microsoft Office.

Interviews

To obtain a comprehensive picture of the course from multiple perspectives, you can interview a sample of learners, course designers, and instructors. Interviews provide additional rich information that may not be available from surveys. For example, West et al. (2007) interviewed instructors and obtained valuable insights into the experiences of instructors as they adopted a CMS. Similarly, Shea's (2007) analysis of data from 386 faculty teaching online in 36 colleges in a large state university system identified the most significant factors that support and undermine motivation to teach online. The top motivator is a more flexible work schedule. The top demotivator is inadequate compensation for perceived greater work than for traditionally delivered courses, especially for online course development, revision, and teaching.

In your evaluation studies, you will find that interviews of students, instructors, and course designers provide multiple and diverse perspectives on the course and enable evaluators to perform triangulate data across the three groups. In an interview, an investigator guides a conversation partner through an extended conversation to "understand experiences and reconstruct events in which you did not participate" (Rubin & Rubin, 2005, p. 3). Respondents should be made to feel comfortable enough to talk at length on subjects that are important to them. Qualitative data are tape-recorded and transcribed. The evaluator then reads and reflects on the transcripts for recurring themes and salient quotations that are insightful and supportive of key findings of the report.

Writing Interview Questions

A list of interview questions is called a *protocol*, of which there are three types: (1) structured, (2) unstructured, and (3) semistructured (Berg, 2007). With structured protocols, all interview questions are listed in advance and are asked in order, with little or no deviation or follow-up. In unstructured interviews, the researcher may not be sure of the questions or even the vocabulary that participants might use. Therefore, the questions will evolve in real time from the conversation. With semistructured questions, you begin with a list, but can ask additional follow-up questions, probe for richer information, or even deviate from most questions on your list if topics need to be investigated in depth.

We recommend a semistructured protocol. To write your interview questions, an outline is recommended (Patton, 2000). And we recommend using our framework as your outline. Unlike survey items, interview questions are usually open ended and tend to be broader in focus. They should be written to capture extended information about learners' perceptions of the course components and the workings of the course as a whole. A sample interview protocol is given in Figure 6.7. When formulating questions, avoid affectively worded, double-barreled, and complex questions, from which it is "almost impossible" to analyze data (Berg, 2007). Because this protocol is semistructured, you do not need to ask every question, but can spend more time on informative responses and ask additional follow-up questions to obtain richer data. Finally, you should write one set of interview questions for learners and different sets of questions for instructors and course designers. For more information on how to write interview questions, see Denzin & Lincoln (2005) and Rubin and Rubin (2005).

Should You Write Survey or Interview Questions First?

You could write the survey and interview questions at the same time and analyze the results of both together. Another option is to conduct your interviews first and then use your interview findings to give you ideas for writing survey questions. With this approach, your survey findings will enable you to obtain a larger, more representative sample, thereby allowing you to generalize your interview findings to a larger population. Alternatively, you could collect survey responses first, review them for response patterns of interest, and use these findings to write your interview questions, which would explore some of the survey issues in greater depth.

- Why did you enroll in this course?
- What is your overall opinion of the course?
- How much do you feel you are learning in the course? What have you been learning?
- Did you learn what you wanted to, what you expected, what you think the course intended?
- How do you feel about the ways in which technology is used in this course?
- Do you find the technology easy to use? If not, why?
- How much do you feel you are learning in the course?
- What strengths/weaknesses does the delivery mode have?
- Would you use it again? Would you recommend it to others?
- What problems, if any, have you had with the technology?
- How comfortable were you with the technology to begin with? How comfortable now?
- What (technical, personal, financial) support was provided?
- Is it important to be a self-directed person with good time management/ good study habits to complete this course? Did you have those skills or did you learn them?
- How do you feel about the way your learning was assessed?
- What changes in assessment would you recommend?
- What do you think is important to successfully complete this course?
- Where have you focused your efforts? Why? What activities/preparation seem most important?

FIGURE 6.7. Sample interview questions for learners.

Conducting Interviews

Interviewees can be selected randomly from the course list or from the names of learners who sent in completed surveys. There are several excellent books available on interview training procedures (e.g., Patton, 1990). Face-to-face interviews can be taperecorded. As for telephone interviews, you can purchase an inexpensive voice recorder at most major electronics outlets and attach it to your phone. When interviewing course participants overseas, it is important to determine the time difference and schedule the day and time of the interview by e-mail. It is especially important to avoid using cordless phones, which can make speakers in countries with poor service and few land lines almost inaudible. Your interviews should last from 45 minutes to 1 hour.

INTERVIEW DOS AND DON'TS

Do:
- Depart from your interview protocol by asking follow-up questions.
- Check your tape-recorder and batteries before you begin the interview.
- Be friendly, sound interested, and make your interviewee feel at ease.

Don't:
- Use a cordless phones for interviews with overseas speakers.
- Ask leading or suggestive questions to obtain specific answers.

To conduct the interview, you should use your interview protocol to provide a common overall direction. However, you should also feel free to depart from this list based on the respondents' replies, to introduce new ideas or topics, to pursue emergent areas of interest, and to follow up on or clarify important points. If you need someone to expand on their answers, you can express interest and say "Tell me more." By probing beyond your protocol, you will increase the richness and depth of your findings (Agar, 1996). After all the interviews are conducted, you should hire a professional transcriber to type your interviews.

Focus Groups

Focus groups are commonly used as a research method in adult education (Chioncel, van der Veen, Wildemeersch, & Jarvis, 2003). The primary benefit of focus groups is that they create a synergistic effect, which makes findings richer than interviews with a single individual (Krueger & Casey, 2004). Because the participants' contributions are dynamic and shaped by the group in real time, focus groups are less susceptible to researcher bias than telephone interviews with a single participant (Fitzpatrick et al., 2004). In face-to-face focus groups, you want eight to 10 participants, and the session should last from 1½ to 2 hours; in addition, the focus group leader should be unknown to the participants so as to avoid unduly influencing the results (Fitzpatrick et al., 2004).

To conduct successful focus groups, you need to prepare ahead, have good facilitation skills, and use more than one tape-recorder or video camera. You could give the group some work to do in advance, such as making a list or thinking about some questions (Krueger & Casey, 2004). During the session, you could use a flip chart to go over these issues in a group. The leader asks questions, moderates the discussion, keeps participants on track, and links their contributions. Participants could talk about their reactions to innovations, their needs and concerns, what they gained from the course, barriers to success, and changes they would recommend (Fitzpatrick et al., 2004). Face-to-face focus groups should be videotaped and the audio portion transcribed. For more information on focus groups, see Greenbaum (2002).

Moderating Chat Rooms

Focus groups can also be held electronically in chat rooms. With chat rooms, you should have no more than five or six participants; otherwise it can become difficult to link contributions and follow threads in the conversation. The main advantage of chat room groups is that transcripts are instantly available, so that you will not have to transcribe your data. Other advantages are preserving participant anonymity, saving time on transcription, and allowing learners in diverse locations to participate without having to schedule or travel to a meeting (Berg, 2007). The main disadvantages are a loss of spontaneity, as respondents edit and reflect on their contributions, and a loss of any visual data, such as body language, which can sometimes help to clarify meaning (Berg, 2007).

Online Ethnographies

The practice of observing and taking notes of cultural or educational phenomena is called *ethnography*. There are three ways to do ethnographic observations. For distance/e-learning courses with occasional face-to-face meetings, you could sit in on and observe these classes. Second, Goldman-Segall (1995) offers a proposal for analyzing ethnographic multimedia narratives. Third, for fully online courses, you could "lurk" in online discussions, chat rooms, asynchronous discussions, or blogs. Whether observing or lurking, you could take detailed notes of your observations and record the length of each learning activity. Because you are collecting data from a class in progress, you need to inform learners that you will be observing and collecting data and give them the option to opt out of participating.

Scoring Participation in Online Discussions

Provided you have obtained written consent from learners and you do not identify them by their real names, you may print out transcripts of online discussions and analyze them for themes. There are several protocols available for coding online discussions. For example, they can be scored quantitatively for number of messages or message threading (Henri, 1992), for discussion skills such as linking contributions and summarizing, or for social constructivist principles and higher order thinking skills (Kanuka & Anderson, 1998). In addition, these scoring methods play an instructional role by shaping online interaction to reflect the values embedded in the scoring method. For example, giving learners points for making connections with previous postings shapes learners' postings so that they do not take on the appearance of disconnected texts with no thread. Finally, it is important to note that because computers generate written records, scoring techniques for online discussions are more reliable than those for face-to-face discussions that are not tape-recorded or videotaped (Bates, personal communication, November, 2000).

Qualitative Data Analysis

There are many diverse approaches to analyzing qualitative methods. Our preferred approach is to group excerpts of salient text according to theme and then count the number of text excerpts coded for that theme. As recommended by Miles and Huberman (1994), these themes can then be reported in as shown in Table 6.2. In this way, you can extract the most frequently recurring themes and list them in order of importance. However, some evaluators feel that this is a quantitative approach to qualitative data analysis. We, therefore, encourage you to explore other approaches to qualitative data analysis, including ethnographic, phenomenological, hermeneutical, netnographic approaches, among others (Miles & Huberman, 1994). The term "netnographic" refers to an ethnographic study of computer-related environments such as blogs, online communities, chat rooms, and online forums (Kozinets, 2002). These diverse approaches reflect different epistemological perspectives and are legitimate and equally worthy. Your choice of which approach to use depends on your own values and preferences.

TABLE 6.2. Benefits and Drawbacks of the Course

Benefits

No conflicts with work/child care/other responsibilities	8
Can complete at my own pace/time/location	6
Variety of teaching methods (text, video)	4

Drawbacks

Inconvenient/insufficient tutor office hours	8
Delays in receiving mailed course material/grades/transcripts	7
Miss the interaction with instructor	2
Miss the interaction with other learners	2
Limited times for exam writing	1
Lack of motivation	1

Note. N = 18. Data from Ruhe and Bates (1999b).

Using Qualitative Data Analysis Software

Qualitative data analysis consists of (1) data reduction, (2) data display, and (3) verification and conclusions (Berg, 2007). According to Richards (2005), using qualitative data analysis software has become almost mandatory. "Once software is learned, [researchers] can achieve much more in considerably less time and at far less risk" (p. 3). To find the most appropriate computer-assisted qualitative data analysis package for your needs and use it to best advantage, see Lewins and Silver (2007). For more information on handling qualitative data, see Richards's (2005) practical advice and running examples on using qualitative data analysis software, modeling, and documenting the data analysis process and working in teams on large projects.

Coding

Qualitative data are transcribed and coded for themes that emerge from the data. The term *coding* refers to reading over and reflecting on the data, writing down themes in the margin, and connecting the themes to understand how the course works as a whole. The purpose of the qualitative analysis is to provide a rich, "thick" description (Merriam, 2002), which helps you to understand how the course works as a system. You also want to identify salient quotations to include in your report; these quotations can be very insightful and can be used to illustrate or flesh out your survey findings. There are two ways to code qualitative data:

(1) Use a highlighting pen and paper transcripts or (2) import electronic copies transcripts into a qualitative data analysis software package such as NUDIST.

Deductive

Our approach to coding qualitative data is the deductive–inductive approach recommended by Miles and Huberman (1994). The first stage is the **deductive** stage, where you use the categories of our unfolding framework as a priori coding categories. First, you need to read over the interview printouts, reflect on them, and use a colored pen to highlight salient quotations. When you find text that illustrates any of the categories of our unfolding framework, highlight the text and write the category beside the text in the margin. The first stage of coding will be deductive; that is, you hold the data up against the framework, highlight segments of text that illustrate or provide an example of each category in the framework, and write the name of the code (e.g., unintended consequences) next to the text segments. Because words can take on different and ambiguous meanings depending on their contexts, your comments and coding categories should also be written directly beside salient interview quotations.

As you code deductively, patterns and connections will emerge. A pattern refers to a recurrence of the same theme (e.g., different student respondents identifying different barriers to success). You may also use the adapted framework to build a matrix of coding categories and organize your highlighted quotations as evidence under each of the categories of the four boxes. By assembling data beneath the construct they measure, these matrices perform a similar function to factor analysis; that is, they produce sharply defined, measurable constructs, thereby bolstering construct validity (Eisenhardt, 1989). You can learn more about constructing these matrices and other practical procedures for data reduction, organization, and analysis of qualitative data from Miles and Huberman (1994).

In the next stage, you compare your categories across respondents. When the same category keeps emerging, it is a confirmed theme or pattern. You need to constantly compare your margin notes across respondents (e.g., tutors, students, designers, and course administrators) to identify recurring patterns or themes and areas of convergence or agreement among participants. You can also compare data across respondents; the convergence of multiple perspectives increases the confidence of accurate interpretations. You also need to be alert for differences among respondents' perceptions, either within or across different respondent groups. These differences in perceptions can help you to identify unintended consequences.

Inductive

As data are compared across cases for recurring patterns and critical differences, the focus of your analysis will shift toward induction, and your findings may need to be reexamined, qualified, or extended in response to emergent themes. You can also bring in new coding categories and make the conceptual connections that constitute theory building (Miles & Huberman, 1994). You need to continue with your analysis until no new themes emerge from the data, in other words, until the data are saturated. At this point, you then need to count the number of instances of each recurring theme. You then list these themes in a table, as shown in Table 6.2. You then need to select which of your most memorable quotations to insert as direct quotes into your report. You can select quotations that are intriguing findings in their own right or that are especially illustrative of recurring themes or patterns.

The Limitations of Qualitative Analysis

Although there are many approaches to qualitative analysis, no approach is perfect, and the choice of approach depends ultimately on the evaluator's values, beliefs, and preferences. One limitation of qualitative case methodology is that findings are context dependent and cannot be generalized. Another issue is researcher **bias** and a tendency to read one's own expectations into the data, thereby verifying one's own preconceptions. Flyvberg (2006) argues that these perceived limitations are really misunderstandings. For example, a case study has its own methodological rigor, but this rigor is different than that of quantitative studies. According to Kuhn (1987), case research has much to contribute to scientific disciplines, which need a large number of thoroughly executed case study exemplars to be effective. By using distance education courses as case studies, instructional designers can gain "a nuanced view of reality" and "develop their own skills to a high level" through "concrete, context-dependent experience" and "feedback from those under study" (p. 223). Finally, we believe that case studies can best be approached through mixed methods, which can counter the limitations inherent in using *only* a qualitative *or* a quantitative method.

Outcomes

Student performance is open to many definitions including course completion and added knowledge and skills (Picciano, 2002). The term *outcomes* refers to measures of student performance such as student grades, retention rates, and year-end test scores. Student performance in university courses is often based on multiple measures such as tests, written assignments, and group projects (Picciano, 2002). Final grades are commonly based on a composite of these grades and are reported as percentages, letter grades, or pass/fail. Retention rates refers to the number and percentage of students who did completed the course. You should also remember that dropout may have nothing to do with the course (e.g., inability to access local university libraries; personal reasons such as illness, pregnancy, or change of employment status or residence) and try to determine whether course improvements can be made to increase completion rates. "Ultimately, student performance is a key measure of the overall success of the course" (Picciano, 2002).

Grades, Retention Rates, and Completion Rates

After you have reviewed the documents, you need to decide which learner outcomes data to collect. "The importance of student success in higher education is incontestable" (Yorke & Longden, 2004). There are several broad questions that can guide your collection and analysis of grades, retention, and completion rate data (Figure 6.8).

Grades

The final course grade is probably the most valid measure of student performance. You could report or compare mean ABC (pass) or DFW (failure) rates, attendance rates, and retention or completion rates between the distance and face-to-face course. Distance education evaluation reports have a long history of statistical differences in final course grades. For example, you could use a t test to compare mean final grades between a distance course and face-to-face course equivalent. You could use chi-square, a simple statistical test, to compare scores on any of these measures (expressed as percentages) between subgroups of interest (e.g., mature learners vs. young high school learners). When analyzing by subgroups, you need to be careful that your groups are not so small that the identities of your participants could be known.

Grades
- Are the data in raw scores, percentages, or letter grades?
- How is the final grade calculated?
- Are student assignments, tests, and final grades norm referenced or criterion referenced?
- How well did learners do on the course overall?
- How will you determine how well they did on the course?
- Can you get IRB permission to obtain student grades?
- What form are the data in (e.g., student level or aggregated)?
- Are student grades available electronically?

Retention and completion rates
- How many students completed the course?
- What was the course retention rate?
- What percentage of students completed the course?
- How were final student grades distributed (e.g., normal or bimodal)?
- What percentages of all learners earned a grade of A, B, or C compared with D, F, and W?
- What was the attendance/participation rate?

FIGURE 6.8. Questions about grades, retention, and completion rates.

However, you should be aware that student grades may not be as useful for a cross-course comparison as you might expect. Postsecondary grading systems reflect the diverse values and priorities of individual faculty members. A final grade in a course may be based on performance or discrete content knowledge. Another problem is when grades are norm referenced or criterion referenced. **Norm-referenced test** scores are rescaled on the normal curve. **Criterion-referenced test** scores are calculated by comparing student performance with a rubric or checklist of criteria.

NORM-REFERENCED VERSUS CRITERIA-REFERENCED TESTS

Norm-referenced tests: Raw test scores are rescaled to fit a normal curve.

Criterion-referenced tests: Student performance is scored against a list of criteria.

Some departments, like business or law, have policies to rescale or norm their grades at the end of term and then assign failing grades to learners in the lower end of the distribution. Learners may fail the course even if they have a mean final grade of, for example, 60% or even 70%. When grades are normed, the mean and shape of the grades distribution are identical across different sections of the same course. For this reason, you will not be able to perform statistical comparison of mean final normed grades between traditional and distance sections of the same course. Even with raw scores, these comparisons will be difficult to interpret because of the influence of confounding variables. You should be aware that not finding a statistically significant difference does not justify the inference that the two courses are equivalent; in fact, you may not have had enough statistical power to find a statistically significant difference.

Retention and Completion Rates

Retention and completion rates signal "a focus on effectiveness and efficiency of an institution or system" (Yorke & Longden, 2004, p. 5). However, life-long learning and more flexibility for students may "give rise to patterns that are quite different from residential education," patterns that might "create headaches for universities with regard to the prediction of income streams and provision of resources" (Yorke & Longden, p. 9). Therefore, a "measure of 'success per study unit' might be more appropriate for distance and e-learning" (Yorke & Longden, p. 6) because this measure reflects a more student-centered view than traditional retention rates. You might want to report or compare how course completion rates vary with demographics (e.g., student maturity or access to high-speed computers).

Data Format and Availability

You also need to find out in what form the data are available (e.g., whether you need individual deidentified student-level records or aggregated data such as mean final course grades). The term *student records* refers to student scores on tests, essays, or assignments and attendance data. These records can be an official collection of data prepared by the university or a private or government agency (Lincoln & Guba, 1985) or a list compiled by the professors and stored in their web-based CMSs. If you request student records from the faculty or from your university's office of institutional or measurement services, you must provide the name of your study, your title and department, evidence of IRB approval, and very clear data specifications such as the course name, number, section number, professor, and semester.

In sum, outcomes data should be analyzed because an evaluation study "should authenticate claims that the provided interactions result in the planned outcomes, that is, allegations that students learn, are supported" (Baker & O'Neil, 2006, p. 78). However, if these data are unavailable or readily open to interpretation, then you should rely on surveys of student satisfaction or perceptions of their learning. "Ultimately, student perceptions of their learning may be as good as other measures because these perceptions may be the catalysts for continuing to pursue course work and other learning opportunities (Picciano, 2002, p. 24).

Student Assessment and Feedback

Given how technology and distance learning can transform assessment (Messick, 1988; Ruhe, 2002b; Ruhe & Zumbo, 2006), it is important to understand how learners respond to assessment tasks and to instructor comments on their assignments. "Managing student assignments, providing feedback to students, and assessing students' learning are all key factors in any course, whether face-to-face or online (Tallant-Runnels et al., 2006). "Feedback" covers innovative assessment tools such as research paper rubrics, learner self-assessment checklists, and peer writing checklists. In e-learning environments, the web provides new and efficient means of collecting these data. For example, learners use instructor guidelines to evaluate their peers' team contributions by completing web-based peer evaluation forms and generating reports (Derntl & Motschnig-Pitrik, 2004), or they share, validate, and refine their evaluation decisions with online evaluation blogs and online focus groups (Horton, 2001).

In addition to rubrics, you can also use survey items to measure learners' perceptions of instructor feedback (Figure 6.9). Instructor feedback can also be evaluated with a quality assurance approach. The Common-

---

- The feedback on my assignments was helpful.
- The instructor returned my marked assignments promptly.
- When I asked the instructor about my grades, he/she was helpful.
- The instructor's feedback encouraged my learning.
- I felt the assignments were a good use of my time.
- I was generally satisfied with the instructor's comments on my papers.
- Is there anything more you would like to tell us about your instructor feedback?

FIGURE 6.9. Examples of survey questions on instructor feedback.

wealth of Learning, for example, scored instructors' comments on students' papers by their proximity to an ideal feedback model, ranked the total scores of all instructors, and used this ranking to award future contracts to instructors (Ruhe, 2002a). For more information on the current state of student assessment practices in online courses, see Roberts' (2006) and Comeaux's (2005) work in this area.

The Evaluation of Environmental Quality

Course Management Systems

CMSs are comprehensive gateways with course and program information, message boards, chat rooms, and links to university databases. Indiana University, for example, has a single CMS for all campuses, which can be accessed at *https//oncourse.iu.edu/portal*. Support needs include both technical (i.e., issues of accessing the course, problems with computers or software) and academic (issues with the course content, tutoring and counseling; Watson, 2007). Depending on your course design and the interests of your stakeholders, you may choose to evaluate any of these course components.

Webpages

There are several protocols for evaluating webpages. Because technologies are continuously evolving, there is a proliferation of innovative, online learning environments that facilitate navigation, reinforce context, expand learner control and interaction with the environment, and redefine simulation and games (Tennyson & Elmore, 1997, p. 56). There is even a web-based online psychology lab where learners can conduct and monitor their lab experiments at a distance (O'Graw & Williams, 2006).

Several checklists have been developed to evaluate human–computer interaction, including webpage response and navigation. These checklists typically include criteria such as download time, browser variability, webpage design, content design, and the design of the overall site architecture (Nielson, 2000, p. 5). Tools such as Jacobson's (2006) knowledge mediator framework, with the design features for adaptive hypermedia, are useful. Gouli, Gogoulou, Papanikolaou, and Grigoriadou (2005) devised a web-based concept map assessment tool that provides personalized feedback to help learners reconsider their beliefs and accomplish mapping tasks successfully.

Readers interested in human–computer interactions might consult Robson's (2000) framework for evaluating an online open learning course. It is a multistaged model of the contextual variables involved in the interaction between students and technology. Her evaluation foci include human–computer interfaces, fit with course design and learning theories, and students' use of computer technology for learning. Her model includes a series of evaluation forms and time lines for multistaged, course evaluation studies. According to Schaik and Ling (2005), there is a need for more psychometrically validated instruments for the evaluation of websites.

Learning Objects/Digital Modules
The Advanced Distributed Learning Initiative

The Office of the Under Secretary of Defense for Personnel and Readiness created the Advanced Distributed Learning (ADL) Initiative to implement learning technologies across the Department of Defense (Fletcher, Tobias, & Wisher, 2007). This initiative focuses on using content or instructional materials as digital modules or learning objects to make them readily accessible, "digital, sharable, and reusable" (p. 96). "ADL objects may range in size from entire courses to more granular assets, such as video clips, audio messages, single graphics, and animations" (p. 97). "ADL is building toward a future in which human knowledge, held in instructional objects, is identified and collected from the global information grid (currently the web) and is then assembled on demand for real-time interactions tailored to each learner's knowledge, goals, interests, and needs" (p. 27). The Office of the Under Secretary of Defense for Personnel and Readiness (2007) anticipates that learning in the future may take place through goal-driven, tutorial, and problem-solving conversations involving handheld (or perhaps worn) devices wirelessly linked to one another and to the global information grid" (p. 27).

> ADL objects can store indexes of learners' prior knowledge and their progress toward instructional objectives. As a student progresses, a representation of his or her mastery and progress is created by the learning system to tailor successive instructional interactions more precisely to the student's needs. The objects can also store other characteristics that can be used to individualize instruction, such as motivation, attitude, personality indexes, and metacognitive skills (Strijker, 2004; Tobias, 2006). (Fletcher et al., 2007, p. 98)

The Sharable Content Objects Reference Model

The ADL vision has inspired a set of standards for e-learning environments. The Sharable Content Objects Reference Model (SCORM) enables objects to be reused across browsers, authoring tools, and programming languages (Duncan, 2005; Fletcher et al., 2007). The SCORM criteria for instructional objects are: accessibility across learning systems; interoperability across platforms, browsers, and CMSs; durability across software and operating systems; and reusability (Dodds, 2004; Dodds & Fletcher, 2004). There are successive versions of SCORM, and the current version is available at *www.adlnet.org.*

The Southern Regional Educational Board's Checklist

To help colleges and state agencies review determine the quality of digital learning content, the Southern Regional Educational Board (SREB) (2007a, 2007b) has devised the following checklist of evaluation criteria for learning objects:

- Content quality
- Learning goal alignment
- Feedback
- Motivation
- Presentation design
- Interface usability
- Accessibility
- Re-usability
- Standards compliance
- Intellectual property and copyright

For more information about learning objects, including a list of repositories, see Moisey, Ally, and Spencer (2006).

Accessibility for Learners with Disabilities

American universities commonly provide guidelines on designing websites in ways that are accessible to learners with disabilities. The University of Maryland University College's website on Accessibility in Distance Education (ADE), for example, provides guidelines and strategies for developing accessible online learning materials for people with disabilities (The

Center for the Virtual University [CVU], The Office of Distance Education and Lifelong Learning, University of Maryland University College, 2007). This website includes topics such as the definition of accessibility, legal issues, types of disabilities, characteristics of accessible websites and best design practices. For more information, you can consult their website at *www.umuc.edu/ade/*.

The World Wide Web Consortium is made up of organizations around the world to develop specifications, guidelines, software, and tools to maximize the potential of the worldwide web. Their Web Accessibility Initiative guidelines are widely regarded as the international standard for web accessibility. You can find international standards for web accessibility, strategies, guidelines, and resources and support materials at *www.w3.org/WAI*. They also have resources on evaluating websites for accessibility and a list of interactive tools to test webpages for conformance to various accessibility guidelines and to flag areas for improvement.

Instructor Competencies

We have seen that instructor performance can be evaluated with student satisfaction survey items. The second way is to use a checklist of instructor competencies. Pesl Murphrey and Dooley (2006) list the key competencies (knowledge, skills, and abilities) required by e-learning specialists based on a needs assessment and focus group findings at Texas A&M University. Another tool is Klein, Spector, Grabowski, and de la Teja's (2004) International Board of Standards for Training, Performance and Instruction standards, which list instructor competencies in online and blended settings. These competencies cover the many roles of instructors, including facilitator, coach, mentor, critic, and stage crew.

Progress Tracking Data

CMSs usually collect data to track the progress of hundreds of learners who are not physically present. These systems include records of completed tasks and assignments, grades, and even summary statistics of the number of minutes that each learner spends on each webpage. In this way, instructors can instantly see what their students are doing and how well they are doing it. An automated tally of learners' online posting, for example, can give instructors a sense of participation patterns, levels of involvement, and the relative success of various conference topics (Harasim, Hiltz, Teles, &

Turoff, 1996). Evaluators can report descriptive statistics on these data, which can be very helpful in understanding course implementation.

Relevance

In our framework, the evidential basis for test interpretation encompasses relevance and cost–benefit analysis (Messick, 1989). Relevance encompasses (1) alignment between the course and the contemporary educational and training needs of society, (2) the meaningfulness of the course to learners, and (3) the ability of learners to transfer their learning to authentic contexts, that is, the real world. Let us begin with the first aspect of relevance.

THE DIMENSIONS OF RELEVANCE

- Alignment between the course and needs of society.
- Meaningfulness of the course to learners.
- Transfer of learning to authentic contexts.

Alignment between the Course and the Needs of Society

The first aspect of relevance is the degree to which the course is aligned to contemporary educational and training needs. Distance education has long been coupled with the theoretical context of the Information Age and beliefs about the transformative power of technology. In the Information Age, the wealth of nations is determined by intellectual and creative production (Duderstat, 1999). The 21st-century economy calls for a new paradigm of teaching and learning. Educational technology can be innovative, useful, authentic, and relevant provided it develops the knowledge, abilities, and skills needed by the information society. The new economy requires training that is customized, flexible, learner centered, and team based (Reigeluth, 1999).

However, there seems to be a mismatch between current skill sets and the needs of the new economy. According to NACOL and Partnership for 21st Century Skills (2006), U.S. students are falling behind their peers on international assessments that measure 21st-century skills, U.S. innovation is in decline, and workplace jobs and skill demands are not being filled. Similarly, in *Charting a New Course*, the Ministry of Advanced Education, Training and Technology, Government of British Columbia (2000)

expressed concern that the traditional postsecondary sector is not changing fast enough and the workforce is not undergoing the constant skills
retraining and upgrading needed for BC to transition to a knowledge-
based economy.

To help students compete successfully in the global economy, NACOL
and Partnership for 21st Century Skills (2006) have articulated a vision to
support their acquisition of 21st-century skills. These skills are defined as
follows:

- Global awareness
- Self-directed learning
- Information and communications technology (ICT) literacy
- Problem-solving skills
- Time management and personal responsibility
- Technical (computer) skills

NACOL and Partnership for 21st Century Skills (2006) feel that a demonstrated mastery of 21st-century skills should be a set of educational
outcomes. Finally, virtual universities are being created as consumer-
oriented models that respond to corporate needs for a highly skilled workforce (Cremer, 2001). When students learn these skills in their distance/
e-learning courses, then these lessons are an important aspect of the value
provided by these courses to society.

Meaningfulness of the Course to Learners

The second aspect of relevance is the perceived meaningfulness and usefulness of the curriculum to learners. "Course design which matches the
needs of learners with the content is essential for student success" (Tallant-
Runnels et al., 2006, p. 110). After all, the young people of this millen-
nial generation grew up with the Internet and thrive in a multimedia,
highly communicative environment. Learning online is natural to them,
as much as retrieving and creating information on the Internet, blogging,
communicating on cell phones, downloading files to iPods, and instant
messaging. Online learning and virtual schools are providing 21st-century
education and more opportunities for today's students (Watson, 2007).

Young adult learners enjoy considerable control in their personal use
of technology; it makes sense that they should enjoy the same kinds of control in their educational programs. Moreover, research shows that when
learners can control the pace of the lessons, satisfaction and engagement
improve (Tallant-Runnels et al., 2006). Instructional design then becomes

---

**How Can Writing Skills Instruction Be Designed
to Be Meaningful to Learners?**

University of Minnesota undergraduates are often required to take writing-intensive courses to fulfill their program requirements. One such course is HMED 3001, The History of Medicine, a Western survey course that covers Ancient Greece to the present. The problem was how to teach writing skills to students who either felt they did not need instruction and/or had little background in grammar. Working with Professor Jole Shackelford, Christine Manganaro, the graduate teacher assistant, found the solution. She developed a series of online modules organized around "I" statements that had emerged in her tutorials (e.g., "Help! I can't get started" and "I'm not really sure what historians do"). By organizing the modules around her students' problems instead of around grammar points, Christine designed an online writing instruction curriculum that was relevant to their needs.

FIGURE 6.10. A case study in designing writing instruction for relevance.

the development of favorable learning environments, where students take precedence over teachers, and the criteria of evaluation are functionality, meaningfulness, and enhanced quality of life, not the achievement of predetermined, discrete objectives (Peters, 1993). Figure 6.10 provides a case study in designing writing instruction, which is relevant to students.

Transfer of Learning to Authentic Contexts

The third aspect of relevance is the ability of learners to transfer their knowledge and skills to authentic contexts. Learning experiences should be "representations of life itself" and an "improvement in the quality of living" (Peters, 1993, p. 57). The Information Age economy requires "initiative, teamwork, higher order thinking skills and diversity" (Reigeluth, 1999, p. 27) and new skills such as "accessing information (searching, downloading from multiple formats), selecting, storing and reordering information, communicating online, incorporating accessed material into work documents, sharing and manipulating information and accessing, combining, creating and transmitting audio, video and text and data as necessary" (Bates, 2000, p. 21). In this age of rapid and persistent technological change, keeping these skills updated requires lifelong learning and a continuous cycle of retraining (Bates, 2000; Rowley, Lujan, & Dolence, 1998). "It is reassuring that the skills identified as crucial . . . for the twenty-first century . . . higher order cognitive skills, affective and social skills . . . have not changed dramatically in the last fifteen years or so . . . [they] are not just fads or shifts in the workplace" (p. 122) but will continue to have ongoing relevance for the future (Dede, 2005). Are learners using their skills after the course had ended? Is the course material meaningful, authentic, and generalizable? Are the course topics of interest and relevant, to learners, so that they are motivated to remember information and transfer it to other contexts outside of the classroom?

Writing Survey or Interview Questions about Relevance

As we have shown, relevance is a construct with multiple and varied dimensions in distance education. Under relevance, you could write questions to measure learners' perceptions about how well this course fits their needs, academic and professional goals, and their lives more broadly. You could also write items about their ability to transfer the information to authentic contexts outside of the classroom (e.g., to use course content to understand contemporary issues). You could write items about their perceptions of the richness, depth, meaningfulness and authenticity of the course activities. Finally, you could write items about the currency and ease of use and updating of the technology, the acquisition of computer-based literacy skills, and the appropriateness of the technology for the subject matter (Figure 6.11).

When writing questions around relevance, you might want to refer back to the literature for our discussion of this concept and its many applications in distance education. Your choice of which aspects of relevance to measure depends on your evaluation focus.

Cost–Benefit Analysis

The final facet of the evidential basis is cost–benefit analysis, an evaluation tool designed to systematically compare benefits with costs (Kee, 1994). A cost–benefit ratio is a mathematical calculation in which the costs of a course are divided by quantifiable benefits, both tangible and intangible. The first step in calculating cost–benefit ratios is calculating costs. Levin's (1983) "ingredients" approach is still helpful in determining costs, which can be fixed (e.g., technology and course development) or variable (e.g., instructor marking and Internet connections). Because it is easier to calculate costs than benefits, you should first define and list your cost items. Your first decision is whether you mean costs to the university or costs to learners.

Alignment between the Course and Needs of Society

1. How well did the course activities help you to understand contemporary issues?

   1 = Very well
   2 = Somewhat well
   3 = Neutral
   4 = Less well than expected
   5 = Not at all well

2. How much did the course help improve your computer skills?

   1 = Very much
   2 = Somewhat
   3 = Neutral
   4 = Less than expected
   5 = Not at all

3. The technology used in this course is contemporary and up-to-date.

   1 = Strongly agree
   2 = Agree
   3 = Neutral
   4 = Disagree
   5 = Strongly disagree

4. What suggestions do you have to make this course more contemporary? ___
   _____

   _____

Meaningfulness of Course to Learners

1. I am taking this course because it is a requirement.

   1 = Strongly agree
   2 = Agree
   3 = Neutral
   4 = Disagree
   5 = Strongly disagree

2. The course materials will help me achieve my career goals.

   1 = Strongly agree
   2 = Agree
   3 = Neutral
   4 = Disagree
   5 = Strongly disagree

(continued)

FIGURE 6.11. Sample survey questionnaire on relevance.

3. The technology motivated me to study hard in this course.

    1 = Strongly agree
    2 = Agree
    3 = Neutral
    4 = Disagree
    5 = Strongly disagree

4. How does this course help prepare you for your career? _____

_____

_____

5. What suggestions do you have to make the course more relevant to your career goals? _____

_____

_____

_____

Transfer of Learning to Authentic Contexts

1. Do you plan to use what you've learned in this course after the course is over?

    Yes _____   No _____

2. If so, how do you plan to use what you've learned? Be specific. _____

_____

_____

3. Use checkmarks to indicate which of the following skills you plan to use after the course is over.

    _____ Computer skills

    _____ Writing skills

    _____ Thinking skills

    _____ Project management skills

    _____ None of the above

FIGURE 6.11. *(page 2 of 2)*

Costs to the University

If your focus is costs to the university, you need to ask administrators to list and estimate their costs. You may find that online programs have cost savings as a result of fewer physical classrooms and facilities. "These savings are offset by the need for hardware, software, and connectivity for classes, on-going technical support, comprehensive student support, course development or licensing, and other costs, especially while a program is starting" (Watson, 2007, p. 7). If you are not sure of the exact numbers, you need to continue searching until you determine where this cost information is located, whether it is accessible, and if so, how to obtain it. You should not be surprised if even university administrators either do not have access to these data or do not have them in the form you need. Figure 6.12 shows how to break down the costs and benefits for the university.

Your next step is calculating quantifiable benefits, such as learner satisfaction ratings, the number of students who complete the course (either each term or over the life of the course), the number who complete in the shortest possible time, and the ratio of completers to the total number of learners enrolled (Bates, 1995). Alternatively, benefits could be operationalized as mean grade point average, distribution of grades, mean learner satisfaction scores, or ABC/DFW rate, which is a ratio of successful to unsuccessful learners. Another strategy is to report mean scores on survey questions about benefits provided by the technology such as access and flexibility. You need to determine whether you will use one or more than one measure and how you will combine and weight multiple measures. The next step, the quantification of intangible educational benefits, is more difficult. These intangible benefits are autonomy and convenience

Costs	Benefits
• Purchase of new technology and upgrades • Course development costs • Maintenance costs • Tutors salaries and benefits	• Cost savings (e.g., instructors' salaries, classroom space, parking space) • Intangible savings (e.g., less traffic congestion) • Increased enrollments • Higher levels of student satisfaction

FIGURE 6.12. Costs and benefits for the university.

(Tallant-Runnels et al., 2006). Convenience covers both learners' ability to access or participate in an educational course or program, regardless of geographical location, and flexibility, which is the freedom to participate regardless of schedule (Bourdeau & Bates, 1997). You then plug your cost and benefit values into the cost–benefit ratio and divide costs by benefits to calculate the ratio. In the example in Figure 6.13, costs and benefits are defined as the costs and benefits to the university, not to learners.

Step 1: Calculate cost–benefit ratio of the distance course.

$$\text{Cost–benefit ratio}_{\text{distance course}} = \frac{\text{Costs}}{\text{Benefit}}$$

Step 2: Calculate costs.
Costs = course development + technology investment and maintenance + tutors' salaries

Step 3: Calculate benefits.
Benefits = mean student satisfaction scores or mean final grade score or completion rate or ABC/DFW rate

Step 4: Calculate cost–benefit ratio of the face-to-face course.

$$\text{Cost–benefit ratio}_{\text{face-to-face course}} = \frac{\text{Costs}}{\text{Benefit}}$$

Step 5: Calculate costs.
Costs = classroom space + salaries + parking space

Step 6: Calculate benefits.
Benefits = mean student satisfaction scores or mean final grade score or completion rate or ABC/DFW rate

Step 7: Divide costs by benefits for both courses.

Step 8: Is cost–benefit ratio of the distance course *smaller* than the ratio of the face-to-face course?

FIGURE 6.13. Steps in calculating cost–benefit ratios. In this example, costs and benefits are defined as the costs and benefits to the university, not to learners.

Costs to Learners

If your focus is costs and benefits to learners, you need to decide which cost items to include and list them in a survey for learners, an approach used by Bartolic-Zlomislic and Bates (1999). Figure 6.14 shows examples of survey questions about costs and benefits for learners. You should be aware that there can be wide variation in how students determine their costs. More information on costs are in Van Dusen (2000) and information on how to calculate cost–benefit ratios are given by Bartolic-Zlomislic and Bates (1999).

Calculating Cost–Benefit Ratios

Horton (2001) provides some very detailed information about how to calculate costs relative to benefits and equations and worked examples for e-learning. First, you need to classify your benefits into three types (Figure 6.15). Next your work will be easier if you can work with hard benefits. Hard benefits are easily quantified, whereas it is more difficult to convert soft benefits to a dollar value. Fuzzy benefits are intangible and even more difficult to quantify.

Costs

Tuition
Technology fees
Computer
Travel to study centers
Accommodation
Postage
Textbooks
Connectivity costs
Student fees
Other (please specify) _____

Benefits

What are the most important benefits of this course for you? _____
_____

FIGURE 6.14. Survey questions about costs and benefits for learners. Based on Ruhe and Bates (1999a) and Bartolic-Zlomislic and Bates (1999).

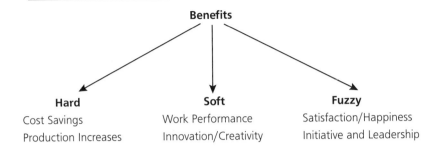

FIGURE 6.15. Three types of benefits (Horton, 2001).

Total costs = (development costs per course × number of courses)
+ costs of offering course × number of years

Benefit = number enrolled per course per year × number of courses
× number of years

In the final step, you compare costs to benefits by using the spreadsheet from Horton's website at *www.horton.com/evaluating*.

Cost-Effectiveness

Another approach is cost-effectiveness (Claeys, 1999; Levin, 1993), which includes opportunity cost. At a time of shrinking budgets, productivity improvements are important. Productivity can be defined as some ratio of quality, access, and cost as opposed to simply the costs of mass production and delivery. For research-intensive universities, a cost–benefit analysis can determine whether productivity gains should be made by enhancing quality of small-scale delivery methods or by increasing access at reduced cost (Garrison & Anderson, 1999). A related notion is the "replaceability challenge"; that is, are there other media or set of media attributes that yield similar learning outcomes with comparable cost structures and opportunities for access (Keegan, 1993)? For this purpose, baseline measures of the set of conditions that are being replaced by technology should be used (Clark, 1994a). To compare cost–benefit ratios between a distance course and a face-to-face course, for example, you calculate the cost of both courses and then the benefits of both. You then divide their respective costs by their respective benefits. The course with the lower ratio is the more cost-effective course.

Return on Investment

Another way of measuring productivity is return on investment (ROI), which involves the calculation of a ratio of net program benefits divided by program costs. Projections for future scalability are also important components of productivity. Scalability refers to using technology to increase the number of learners, thereby decreasing costs per learner. According to Hannafin, Land, and Oliver (1999),

> We need greater utility from the resources we have and from those in the future. We need to use resources more flexibly, extensively and efficiently . . . accommodate diverse goals and needs using identical (or similar) resources rather than redeveloping the same resources. The growth of both information and technology requires that scalable models be advanced, along with designs that permit ready access, updating and inclusion of growing bodies of resources. (p. 139)

To forecast future trends, a Delphi survey is both a useful research methodology and a synergistic approach to the complexity of educational environments (Keegan, 1986; Ritchie & Earnest, 1999). With Delphi surveys, successive rounds of a survey are sent to experts, with the goal of arriving at a consensus on the final round. These estimates can be used to project future benefits in cost–benefit ratios. For more information and case studies on cost–benefit, cost-effectiveness, and ROI studies in e-learning, including calculations, see Horton (2001), Bartolic-Zlomislic and Bates (1999), and Finkelstein, Frances, Jewett, and Scholz (2000).

Conclusions

Finally, the issues around the costs and benefits of designing and delivering distance and e-learning courses can be expected to evolve along with new technologies. Print, for example, is still used in many countries, especially developing ones, because it is cost-effective (Bates, 2005, cited in Awalt, 2007). According to Bates (2005), although there may be agreement about the methods of measuring costs, there are few case reports "where costs have been carefully measured and analysed under operational conditions" (p. 153). Bates (2005) continues:

> Most importantly, there has been a lack of business models built on the experience of running Web-based programmes in a cost-effective manner. Business models should investigate likely revenues from student tuition fees

and/or government funding, the number of students required to break even at a given level of income, and the costs of sustainable operations that avoid teacher and student work overload. Business models should also include market research and risk assessment. (p. 153)

To summarize, new technologies require new models of cost that need to go beyond fixed and variable costs to include projections and risks of future earnings. Also, questions need to be resolved (e.g., does the number of clients served justify the program's continued existence?; Chen, 2005). Although an analysis of costs relative to benefits is one approach to answering this question, future projections must also rest on solid assumptions about who these future clients will be. For example, Awalt (2007) points out that traditional student enrollment has declined in recent years because of low birth rates and maintains that the future of distance and e-learning is in lifelong learning and, in particular, in the growing numbers of senior citizens. To be accurate, then, future earnings streams must be based on correct, which in our rapidly changing world often means innovative, assumptions.

Bringing It All Together: Mixed Methods

After you have collected all of your data, you will have a mix of data from diverse sources, for example, surveys, interviews, cost–benefit formulas, and checklists. This diversity overcomes the limitations inherent in any one data source used alone. Mixed methods combine both the breadth and generalizability of quantitative data with the richness and depth of qualitative data. As we will see in the case studies in Chapter 8, mixed methods findings illuminate both the course implementation and the course outcomes, have more credibility from triangulation across methods, and provide a more comprehensive picture of merit and worth.

Conclusions

To summarize, the top two boxes of the unfolding model refer to scientific evidence, both quantitative and qualitative data, collected around themes listed in these two boxes. The upper two boxes have been the traditional focus of several distance education evaluation models and of almost all authentic evaluation studies of distance education courses. The upper left box, scientific evidence, encompasses outcomes, grades and completion rates, surveys and interviews of learner satisfaction, checklists, instructor competencies, and course management data. The upper right box encompasses relevance and cost–benefit analysis. The use of some kind of mixed-methods scientific evidence is essential to our approach, as is an analysis of values and consequences. You can choose among the various types of scientific evidence in this chapter, depending on the kind of course you are evaluating.

CHAPTER 7

■ ■ ■ ■ ■ ■ ■ ■ ■

The Unfolding Model

VALUES AND CONSEQUENCES

In the previous chapter, we discussed how to use the upper two boxes of the unfolding model, that is, the diverse types of scientific evidence, including surveys, interviews, and cost–benefit data. In this chapter, we discuss the two lower boxes of the unfolding model. Although we already presented this information in Chapter 1, we are intentionally reproducing it here to provide an overview of the key concepts in this chapter. As a reminder, these lower boxes are called the *consequential basis*, and comprise underlying values and unintended consequences (Figure 7.1).

Underlying values
- Course goals and objectives
- Rhetoric/value labels (e.g., "world class," "innovative")
- Theory (e.g., schema theory, e-learning cognition)
- Ideology (e.g., open access, learner centeredness)
- Stakeholder roles and influence

Unintended consequences (negative and positive)
- Instructional
- Social
- Course implementation
- "Fit" across the four facets

FIGURE 7.1. The unfolding model: The consequential basis unfolded.

As shown in Figure 7.1, underlying values encompasses course goals and objectives, ideologies, and theories underlying distance courses. They include broad beliefs (e.g., open learning, geographical access, flexibility, and learner centeredness). In contrast, the term *theory* refers to more specific beliefs about cause and effect (e.g., that active learning techniques enhance motivation and student performance). These are the kinds of values you will want to identify and see working in authentic distance/e-learning courses.

First, you use course documents to identify the value labels, theory, and ideology underlying the course. Then you use survey and interview questions as sources of data on values and consequences. At first, you will code your qualitative data deductively (i.e., by using the categories in the unfolding model), but as unanticipated effects emerge into patterns, your emphasis will gradually shift toward a more inductive approach. As you compare the intended goals and objectives for the course with the fit across the four facets of the unfolding model, unintended instructional and social consequences will fall out of your analysis.

Underlying Values

What Are Values?

When evaluating any distance course, you need to identify, articulate, and bring forward the values underlying the course. When people hear the word *values*, they often think of personal values; however, there are several kinds of values that are not personal values but rather are attributes or outcomes that are valuable in a particular context (Davidson, 2005). Some examples of values are truth, satisfaction, and cost-effectiveness.

According to Scriven (2003), some value claims can be rational and objective (e.g., children in an orphanage should have enough nutritious food, be kept warm, and have medical care; Davidson, 2005). In other cases, we need to identify relevant values, often by consulting the literature or stakeholders (Davidson, 2005). "The values on which an evaluation is based are defensible insofar as there is sufficiently widespread agreement within the relevant context about those values that they can reasonably be treated as givens" (Davidson, 2005, p. 95).

The Dimensions of Value in Distance and E-Learning Courses

Distance/e-learning courses are designed for a wide range of purposes, including geographical reach, flexibility, pedagogical richness and depth or to increase revenues and cost cuts. Therefore, your evaluation study should include an analysis of the underlying values of distance courses. As in any academic field, there may be little conscious awareness of value-laden rhetoric and underlying values and ideologies. For this reason, it is important for evaluators to bring these underlying values into the foreground (Figure 7.2). (To provide an overview of the dimensions of value, we are intentionally reproducing this same figure on the dimensions of value from Chapter 1.) *Rhetoric/value labels* refers to rhetoric, such as "world-class," "innovative," and "cutting-edge technology" in course outlines and grant proposals. *Theory* refers to theories of teaching and learning, such as constructivism, whereas *ideology* refers to broader underlying values, such as team-based learning, on which more narrow theories are based. *Standards* refers to specific goals for distance and e-learning courses that can be found in the literature (e.g., Lorenzo & Moore, 2002,

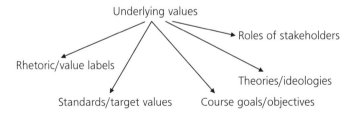

FIGURE 7.2. Aspects of values underlying distance and e-learning courses.

five pillars of quality). *Target values* refers to setting measurable goals based on standards for specific courses. *Course goals/objectives* refers to specific goals for the course. *Roles of stakeholders* refers to persons with a vested interest in the evaluation findings and raises the question of what the roles of stakeholders will be in your study. You do not need to investigate all of these dimensions in your study, but you can pick and choose those dimensions that are most relevant to your course.

How to Identify the Values Underlying Your Course

Underlying values infuse distance course goals and objectives and are found in the value-laden language, the theory underlying the course, and the ideology in which the course is embedded. To identify underlying values, you need to review course documents, such as the course outline and webpages. A content analysis of these documents will provide you with a picture of the intentions of the course designers (i.e., the intended course implementation). Later, when you analyze unintended consequences, you will compare this "rhetoric of intent" with the actual course implementation. The distance between the two is what Rumble (1981) referred to as the gap between the ideal and the real. You can begin to get a sense of this gap by asking learners survey and interview questions about underlying values.

Value Labels

Value labels refers to the value-laden language found in course proposals and course outlines. We believe that evaluators need to deconstruct the rhetoric around distance courses so that the rhetoric of intent does not interfere with an impartial analysis of actual performance. Because this language reflects the ideology and theory underlying the course activities, the analysis requires not only identification of the rhetoric but a comparison with the underlying ideologies and theories and a comparison of these findings with the course activities. These aspects of values, then, overlap because value labels are an expression of both ideology and theory.

There has been an influx of value-laden language into distance education from fields such as educational psychology, media studies, and educational technology. The history of terminology in distance learning reflects historical advances in media and communications technology, developments in distance education (Bourdeau & Bates, 1997), the system of attitudes and beliefs underlying the educational technology movement

(Knapper, 1980), and the perspectives of various authors (Sauve, 1993). There has also been a proliferation of new technology-related vocabulary. Terms such as *virtual reality, cyberspace,* and *real time* may have been trendy in the mid-1990s (de Kerckhove, 1995) but have now moved into the mainstream. The term *digital artifact* used to refer to applets or animated graphics but has evolved to mean visible defects, whereas a *jaggie* is a kind of defect in which jagged lines appear around a web image because there is not enough resolution to portray a smooth line (*http://en.wikipedia.org/wiki/Jaggies*).

According to Evans and Nation (1993), one of the mandates of distance education is to support learners by creating new language and reflecting new values that challenge traditional educational structures. New language has emerged around customer orientation, philosophies of learner centeredness, and the proliferation of new private distance universities. Ljosa (1993) describes distance education as "a value-oriented service system," in which organizational back-up services such as production, procurement, logistics, marketing, information, and administration "have to be adapted to the values and qualities we want to offer our customers." Some other novel terms are *faculty centered* (Duderstat, 1999) and *supply-side focus,* terms used by Blustein, Goldstein, and Lozier (1999) to refer to a lack of attention to the needs of potential "clients," or students.

Because new language has radically changed the values we hold around postsecondary education, distance education has been said to be "inherently subversive" (Evans & Nation, 1993). For example, what are the values underlying the shift from "student" to "customer" or "client"? The first term is situated within classic apprenticeship models of medieval universities, with entrenched social relations handed down, mostly unchanged, from the preindustrial age. In this expertise-based evaluation model, students are assessed by professors and have few rights and little legal recourse. Customers, on the other hand, are equal partners who exchange money for goods or services and are bound by a legal contract. Under contract law, both parties have rights and obligations as well as legal protection if they are violated. In universities, this shift is reflected in course outlines, which are often seen as quasi-legal contracts and may even be the focus of lawsuits when the course activities do not follow the course outline. Another example is the term *legacy media,* which was coined to reflect the new social reality that evening television news programs are becoming obsolete, because anyone with a cell phone can capture a video image that can be uploaded on to a site like You Tube, which provides interactive, customized, and immediate "news" services to viewers.

Standards and Target Values

Standards refers to specific goals for distance and e-learning courses that are found in the literature. A standard is the "specification and articulation of the characteristics and level of performance required" (Smith, Armstrong, & Brown, 1999). Target values refers to setting specific, quantifiable goals based on standards (e.g., to obtain a specific retention rate such as 85%). It is important to note that standards are based on values, although target values may be based on both values and on data obtained from previous years. There is increasing discussion about standards and benchmarks for distance and e-learning courses. Seok (2007) provides an excellent review of standards, accreditation, benchmarks, and guidelines in distance and online education, while Klein et al. (2004) discuss standards for instructor competencies in online and blended settings.

Sloan-C's Five Pillars

As we saw in Chapter 3, Sloan-C proposed five overlapping pillars, defined as principles and metrics that can help establish benchmarks and standards for quality based on continuous quality improvement (CQI). These five pillars are (1) learning effectiveness, (2) cost-effectiveness and institutional commitment, (3) access, (4) faculty satisfaction, and (5) student satisfaction. For each pillar, the ideal environment is described, and quality is measured by each organization in light of its unique mission and goals.

The NACOL Standards

In September 2007, NACOL articulated national standards of quality for online courses. These standards are, in effect, a list of values by which to judge the quality of online courses. These quality standards were evaluated and assembled into a document entitled *The National Standards of Quality for Online Courses* (NACOL, 2007) and can be used as benchmarks. The standards consist of the following major categories:

- Content—for example, measurable goals, objectives focused on what learners will be able to do after the course.
- Instructional design—for example, multiple learning paths to master the content, based on student needs.

- Student assessment—for example, grading rubrics, appropriate readability levels, timely and frequent feedback about student progress.
- Technology—permits the online teacher to add content, activities, and assessments to extend learning opportunities; is easy to navigate; makes maximum use of the medium and makes resources available by alternative means (e.g., video, CDs, and podcasting).
- Course evaluation and management—the results of peer review and student evaluations of courses; multiple strategies are used to evaluate the course.
- 21st-century skills—for example, ICT literacy, self-directed learning, and global awareness.

Each of these categories is broken down into a list of criteria, of which only a few examples are given. You may use the NACOL standards as coding categories to see how closely your course approaches these benchmarks. NACOL's standards for online courses are available at *www.nacol. org/nationalstandards/NACOL%20Standards%20Quality%20Online%20 Courses%202007.pdf.*

Benchmarks for Internet-Based Courses

Phipps and Merisotas (2000) also developed a list of 24 benchmarks to ensure quality in Internet-based courses. Commissioned by the National Education Association, a major professional association of higher education faculty in the United States, and Blackboard Inc., their report consists of six case studies of universities with Internet-based degree programs. The case studies were designed to ascertain whether various measures of quality are reflected in the policies, procedures, and practices of these universities. These benchmarks provide indicators of the quality of Internet-based distance education courses.

Setting Your Own Performance Standards

In her book *Evaluation Methodology Basics: The Nuts and Bolts of Sound Evaluation*, Davidson (2005) devotes three chapters to values, with several practical strategies and procedures to help determine values and standards. She also identified the following evaluative criteria, which could be applied to distance courses.

- Has a positive impact on students, community, etc.
- Is more cost-effective than other options.
- Has features or attributes that enhance the experience of consumers.
- Corresponds to objectives.
- Meets needs of participants.
- Makes sense as a "package."

Strategies for determining values also include using stakeholder input, specialist judgment, and results from a needs assessment (Davidson, 2005). Davidson shows how to use a matrix to determine the importance of various criteria, weigh and synthesize data from mixed methods, and draw evaluative conclusions. This book is highly recommended for any work on setting performance standards.

Course Goals and Objectives

Data Sources

The first step in identifying the values unique to your course is to review documents about the course (Figure 7.3). The course outline is a critical document that describes the course goals and objectives, in other words, how the course is expected to work. The course outline describes the course components, the underlying values and pedagogical theory, and the purpose and role of the technology. For example, when technologies are blended, the course outline describes what each of these technologies is expected to contribute and how they should work together to achieve the course objectives. You should collect as many relevant documents as possible to identify the rhetoric, goals and objectives, underlying theory, and ideology of the course. Documents on paper, such as course outlines, can

Documents	Surveys and/or Interviews with Stakeholders
• Course outline • Preface of the course textbook • Course development grant • University and course webpages • Notes of committee meetings	• Course developer, faculty, students

FIGURE 7.3. Data sources for identifying underlying values in a course.

be scanned into a computer and analyzed using content analysis software (Fitzpatrick et al., 2004).

Rationale

The first step in your analysis is to identify the course goals and objectives. This information can be found in the course outline, preface of the course textbook or materials, course webpages, and the course development proposal. In some cases, you should also review the university or department webpages to identify the underlying ideology, values, and philosophies of the institution. These statements of goals and objectives describe the course's "intended effects," that is, what the course was designed and intended to accomplish. This information provides you with clear statements of the *desired* course implementation. You then compare these statements with the *actual* course implementation (i.e., how the course really works). This gap between the ideal and the real can provide you with valuable recommendations for course redesign and improvement. Now that you know how to look for information on underlying values, we explain the kinds of ideologies and theories that underlie distance courses, so that you can identify how these aspects of value are reflected in your course as well.

Ideology

An ideology is an organized collection of ideas, a comprehensive vision or worldview that offers change in society through beliefs and values of how the world *ought* to be (Wikipedia, 2006). van Dijk (1998) defines the term *ideology* as a "social system of ideas" with a very broad cultural base. Ideologies are "shared knowledge, rules or methods held by groups or collectives, and which are expressed or lived in everyday life and at work and which serve to regulate social practices" (p. 8). Messick (1989) defines ideology as the broader context of philosophies, beliefs, and values in which theories and value labels are embedded.

It is the work of evaluators to distinguish scientific evidence from values, ideologies, and theories, even though, as Messick (1989) points out, this distinction is not always clear-cut because evidence and values overlap and cut across each other. Although scholars who theorize about ideologies define general principles or characteristics, they seldom describe what particular ideologies actually look like (van Dijk, 1998). One interesting example of turning a traditional ideology on its head is Capella University's perspective on online learning.

- The Information Age paradigm
- The aura of technological change
- Consumerism
- Open learning
- Learner centeredness
- Constructivism
- New social roles for instructors and learners

FIGURE 7.4. Ideologies underlying distance education.

It is often asserted in the literature that face-to-face learning is preferable to stand-alone online learning. But Capella University questions this . . . argument. Rather than asking when or how online might supplement face-to-face learning, we ask "When is face-to-face interaction necessary to blended learning?" In effect, Capella's pedagogical philosophy and practices turn face-to-face instruction into a supplement of the primary activity of delivering learning online. (Offerman & Tassava, 2006)

From here, we name and describe some of the predominant ideologies underlying distance courses and e-learning (Figure 7.4), although, as the previous example shows, these philosophies are continuously evolving in response to new technologies.

Technological Change

Because we have already discussed the Information Age paradigm, we begin with the ideology around technological change. In her book, *Digital Hemlock*, Brabazon (2003) claims that technology is not neutral but is invoked and applied as if it were a god or supernatural force. Technological change is driven by the rhetoric and the unquestioned acceptance of the notion that use of technology per se is an improvement. The field is characterized by "motherhood" statements about flexibility and the illusion of access, that education occurs when content is downloaded. After the huge amounts of money invested in online education in the late decade, there is still a top-down push, with religious overtones and evidence of worship of the new god. "It is part of a discourse that frets over the digital divide, not out of a true concern with racial or class discrimination, but in order to place fear in the minds of consumers (and university administrators) that they will be left behind by the technological revolution" (Cremer, 2001, p. 2).

Consumerism

According to Cremer (2001), there is a consumerist ideology underlying distance education, which makes education just another commodity delivered by corporate, for-profit institutions driven by efficiency, performance, marketing, and productivity. Although there are several guides to distance education programs in the United States (e.g., Deane, 2005), most of these practical, how-to guides explain the principles and guidelines for choosing online courses but fall short of being true consumer reports. A related concern, that could be perceived as an ideology, is profitability, a perspective that underlies e-learning development to a greater extent than distance education (Awalt, 2007).

Open Learning

According to Collis (1996), after "more than a decade, there is still no consistently used definition of open, flexible or distance learning" (p. 339), although there has been an overlap between the terms *distance learning* and *open learning* from the beginning (Keegan, 1986). Bates (1995) defines open learning is "a goal or an educational policy; the provision of learning in a flexible manner, built around the geographical, social and time constraints of individual learners, rather than those of an educational institution" (p. 27). This definition puts the emphasis on flexibility and the importance of learner centeredness. Bates (1995) includes the concept of "open admissions."

> Open learning may include distance education, or it may depend on other flexible forms of learning such as independent study and face-to-face teaching. It may also include other concepts such as open access without prior requisite qualifications. Both open-ness and distance education are never found in their purest forms. . . . Thus, there are degrees of open-ness and distance. (p. 27)

This emphasis is echoed in the Athabasca University calendar, where open learning is defined as removing traditional barriers to a university education by providing flexibility, affordability, and a year-round entrance policy (Athabasca University, 2007).

Constructivism: Learners construct their own personal understandings of structures of meaning through reflection and action in the world (Piaget, 1967).

Constructivism

Distance education and e-learning have been heavily influenced by constructivism (Hiltz & Goldman, 2005), which has radically transformed deeply held assumptions about teaching and learning. We believe that constructivism is an ideology rather than a theory, because it provides a broad foundation of values on which a wide variety of more specific theories of teaching and learning are based. Constructists believe that knowledge is "constructed, not transmitted" and that knowledge is a personal interpretation of experience that embraces multiple perspectives (Jonassen, Myers, & McKillop, 1996). Learners are not "empty vessels" but active participants who use prior knowledge to select information from available resources to construct mental models (Dorr & Seel, 1997). Learners "assemble" knowledge, which should be embedded in contexts that are relevant, useful, and meaningful (Cobb & Bowers, 1999; Greeno, 1997; Jonassen et al., 1996).

Although constructivism has a long history, it first came to the attention of North American instructional designers when Jonassen (1991) challenged instructional designers to abandon the "objectivist epistemologies" that underlie behaviorist and cognitivist learning theories and move toward design models with a greater emphasis on learners' construction of meaning (Molenda, 1997). *Constructivist learning environments* are "places where learners may work together and support each other as they use a variety of tools and information resources in their guided pursuit of learning goals and problem-solving activities" (p. 5). Constructivism provides the foundation for learners to explore new integrated multimedia environments (Dorr & Seel, 1997), to learn in physical isolation from others (Greeno, 1997), and to participate in online learning communities. Instructors provide experience with the knowledge construction process, facilitate multiple perspectives, foster ownership, voice and self-awareness, embed learning in social experience, and encourage multiple forms of representation through media (Honebein, 1996). To this end, instructors model desired behaviors, coach individual learners, lead them to resources, and facilitate collaboration on tasks that may range from preparing for an exam to solving ill-structured problems (Reigeluth, 1999). Instead of occupying a central role, instructors take a guiding role and "fade out" when appropriate (Brown, Collins, & Duguid, 1996; Grabe & Grabe, 1998). However, constructivism does not imply that a free-for-all for learners is appropriate (Wellburn, 1999).

APPLIED CONSTRUCTIVISM: A COURSE IN NEW MEDIA WRITING

One example of an innovative practice based on constructivist principles is COMP 5250, New Media Writing, a course at the University of Minnesota. Craig Stroupe (2007) uses Blackboard to teach students how to write hypertext fiction. Learners are given a paragraph about a main character in a social situation.

> Tim is a freshman at his first off-campus party in the fall at UMD. It's Friday night, and he's walked over from the dorm with some guys that he doesn't know very well. He's holding can of Old Milwaukee Lite in one hand. He's decided that hardly anybody knows him here, and he can be anything he wants. He can hear a group of jocks behind him teasing a girl about going home to the Twin Cities every weekend to see her boyfriend. She just laughs. Tim notices that a trickle of people keep going out the backdoor of the run-down house, and come back in a few minutes all red cheeked. Tim notices how nearly everybody is looking over the shoulders of the people their talking to, like someone more important is about to show up.

Learners are asked to create tension by describing the action from the point of view of a newcomer, a stranger, or a character who knows the culture intimately but now feels alienated. Example paragraphs are also given in hypertext. In this way, learners can make use of not only text but also images and even voice recordings to make writing more engaging and to broaden out from writing on paper to learning a host of 21st-century skills associated with Blackboard.

ANOTHER EXAMPLE: PARTICIPATORY EXAMS

Another example of an innovative practice based on constructivism is student-constructed participatory exams used in a graduate course in information systems at the New Jersey Institute of Technology over three semesters (Shen, Hiltz, & Bieber, 2006). Virtual Classroom and Web-Board were used as synchronous conferencing tools, and students wrote exam questions, posted them online, and designed their own evaluative rubrics. Participatory exams were designed as a means of advancing the active construction of knowledge. Students wrote the items and designed the scoring rubrics, all of which were posted online, where it could be accessed by learners. "Students could read everything their peers posted— questions, answers, grades and disputes—and many did. We believe this is a vital aspect of constructivist learning as students think over their peer's understandings" (p. 96). The model for the participatory exams was based on Benbunan-Fich, Hiltz, and Harasim's (2004) online interaction learning model, an integrated theoretical framework for learning networks. Although Shen et al.'s (2006) longitudinal evaluation study of this innovative exam format is based on quantitative data, we would add that one major strength of the participatory exam model that it is grounded in theory and is an application of a further refinement of constructivism by Benbunan-Fich et al. (2004).

Theories

The third dimension of underlying values in the unfolding model is the theory underlying distance education and e-learning courses. The underlying theory is the rationale for how these innovative courses are *intended* to work. "Online instructors [should] design their courses in accordance with sound educational theories. Students in well-designed and well-implemented online courses learned significantly more than those in online courses where teaching and learning activities were not carefully planned" (Tallent-Runnels et al., 2006, p. 116).

There is no comprehensive one-size-fits-all theory of distance education (Institute for Higher Education Policy, 1999). Instead, the full range of pedagogical theories, from those based on behaviorism to those that rest on contructivism, apply to the diverse contexts of distance education and e-learning (Figure 7.5). Breuch (2004), for example, discusses the social theories underlying virtual peer review. In your final evaluation report, you should identify these theories, even if they are not explicitly stated in the course outline but are implicit in the course design. After that, you can compare the intentions expressed in the theory with the actual course implementation or how the course *really* works. From here, we will go on to discuss a sample of pedagogical theories that are most relevant to evaluation studies in distance and e-learning.

Behaviorism

Behaviorism is based on Skinner's (1965) theory of stimulus and response, developed in laboratory studies with pigeons. These principles came into education through Thorndike's (1913) measurement principles, which are based on the mastery of discrete, measurable "bits" of content knowledge. Behaviorism led to linear models of instructional design, including the first teaching machines, programmed instruction, and assessment activities based on the mastery of discrete, measurable bits of content

Behaviorism
    Programmed instruction

Cognitivism
    Schema theory
    Assimilation theory
    Anchored instruction

Constructivism
    Problem-based learning
    Distributed cognition
    Situated apprenticeship
    Human-computer interaction

FIGURE 7.5. Theories underlying distance education.

knowledge. These instructional designs reflected the education needs of the industrial era (Reigeluth, 1999; Tennyson & Elmore, 1997). Maki, Maki, Patterson, and Whittaker (2000) found that rewarding learners with points, based on behaviorist reinforcement schedules, were effective in reducing last-minute cramming. Behaviorist principles continue to be the foundation of many contemporary web-based learning activities such as NASA's Virtual Skies web-based simulation and in computer-based environments where gold stars, points, and other extrinsic motivators are used as a reward system, as first introduced by Thorndike and now a milestone in CD-ROM's, websites, and other e-learning environments (Gilliani, 2003).

Cognitivism

The cognitivist paradigm maintains that learners are actively processing or transforming material (Cobb & Bowers, 1999) within the "black box" of the mind. This view of learners as active and reflective participants is a sharp reaction to behaviorism. Under the cognitivist umbrella are various theories such as schema theory, assimilation theory (Tennyson & Elmore, 1997), and anchored instruction. Interactive media have led to new learning theories for instructional design that present a more holistic picture of learning (Bourdeau & Bates, 1997; Gilliani, 2003). Cognitive approaches have been used to make computers adaptive and responsive to individual needs and abilities (Seel, 1997), give learners active rather than passive roles (Tennyson & Elmore, 1997), and teach for transfer of learning material to contexts outside of the classroom. Transfer is stimulated by the learner's perception of similarities between the classroom context and the real world (Dijkstra, 1997) by anchoring instruction in meaningful technology-based contexts for solving "ill-structured" problems (Cognition and Technology Group [CTGV], 1993; Bransford, Sherwood, Hasselbring, Kinzer, & Williams, 1990) and by basing instruction on employment-related needs (Tennyson & Elmore, 1997).

ANCHORED INSTRUCTION

With anchored instruction, students investigate a problem, identify gaps in their knowledge, research information, and find solutions (Bransford et al., 1990). Learning activities are designed around an "anchor," which is based on a contextualized case study or problem situation. Curriculum materials should allow exploration by the learner (e.g., interactive sites) to allow active manipulation, questioning, and involvement in the situation (NASA Dryden Learning Technologies Project, 2007). Students take ownership of problems related to everyday life and become actively involved in generating solution, so that the knowledge and skills are highly transferable to other situations (NASA Dryden Learning Technologies Project, 2007). The worldwide web can support anchored instruction by providing a context for the problem, including news clips, pictures or graphics, virtual tours, simulations, and images to set context and information to help them develop a solution to the problem (NASA Dryden Learning Technologies Project, 2007).

Constructivism

As we previously discussed, constructivism emphasizes learners' active construction of meaning as opposed to the mastery of an "objective" body of knowledge. Constructivism is a conceptual umbrella that encompasses several theories of learning. We cannot elaborate on all of these theories but will briefly discuss the theories in Figure 7.6. We have included human–computer interaction because of its close conceptual proximity to distributed cognition.

PROBLEM-BASED LEARNING

Problem-based learning was developed at McMaster University in Hamilton, Ontario. In problem-based learning, authentic situations are used to give students experience in solving real-world problems. Problems

> - Problem-based learning
> - Distributed cognition
> - Situated apprenticeship
> - Human–computer interaction

FIGURE 7.6. Theories based on constructivism.

are presented to small groups of learners. Early guidance is provided by instructors, but this guidance is faded out as learners become more proficient (Merrill, 2002). Merrill (2007) also suggests using worked examples early on, then introducing smaller less complex problems and finally more realistic, complex problems. Gail Wortman at Iowa Learning Online used Blackboard to create GenBio, a course designed for at-risk and special needs high school students. These learners need instruction in reading and study skills and may require pacing adjustments. Aligned with the National Science Education Standards, this innovative course won Blackboard's Greenhouse Exemplary Course Award.

DISTRIBUTED COGNITION

Distributed cognition refers to the effects of interaction between an individual and media on the individual's mental representations and cognitive functions; it is the fundamental basis of the relationship between media and learning (Seel & Winn, 1997). Distributed cognition focuses on the individual's construction of meaning in a social context (i.e., the activity, context, and culture; Brown et al., 1996). Cognition is "heavily dependent on the learner's ability to strategically manage and organize all information resources, especially the external environment where media plays a central role" (p. 293). Consequently, tools are integral to the learning process rather than external aids to internal cognitive processes (Cobb & Bowers, 1999).

Different media also affect the individual's mental representation, schema encoding, and cognitive and semiotic processes differently (Seel & Winn, 1997); these interactions have psychological and educational consequences (Salomon, 1993). The traditional lecture, or knowledge transmission approach, originated with the technology of the medieval manuscript, which monks in a university would read to their students for the purpose of analyzing the language of a text in depth (Bates, 1995). With its unique capabilities, however, contemporary media can complement or support the learner's cognitive operations by fulfilling totally new instructional functions in discovery-based learning environments (Seel & Winn, 1997). For example, information via television, which is fast paced and crowded with information, is processed differently than information in print, which allows for reflection and cognitive rehearsal.

SITUATED APPRENTICESHIP

In situated apprenticeship models, learning is "interaction in a situation which uses an anchor or focal point to trigger problem-solving activities, thereby creating knowledge which is not inert" (Bransford et al., 1990, p. 107). Media can provide unique environments in which learners can construct their own understandings (Tennyson, 1997), reduce the gap between prior knowledge and current experiences (Seel & Winn, 1997), explore virtual realities, and control their own learning (Tennyson & Elmore, 1997) based on self-determined needs and interests (Seel & Winn, 1997).

Cognition and Technology Group at Vanderbilt, CTGV, a moderate proponent of constructivism, has been developing "powerful instructional strategies" around multimedia to facilitate learners' construction of knowledge (Molenda, 1997, p. 51). In contrast to passive listening to lectures, an active, team-based approach to learning is exemplified by hypermedia and computer simulations such as SimLife and The Oregon Trail (Grabe & Grabe, 1998). These kinds of simulations "play a critical enabling role for the information-age paradigm of instruction" (Reigeluth, 1999, p. 88) and are appropriate for today's digital generation.

> They have spent their early years surrounded by robust visual electronic media . . . Unlike those of us who were raised in an era of passive, broadcast media such as radio and television, today's students expect—indeed demand—interaction. They approach learning as a "plug and play" experience; they are unaccustomed and unwilling to learn sequentially and instead are induced to plunge in and learn through participation and experimentation. (Reigeluth, 1999, p. 7)

More recently, Schwartz, Bransford, and Sears (2005) have extended the notion of adaptive, innovative learning by arguing that it is blended with, and inseparable from, content knowledge. Any learning trajectory is a blend of content expertise and innovative expertise. The issue is how an instructor should blend these two kinds of expertise in a curriculum or a program. When using tools such as graphs and spreadsheets, students can perform much better at answering "clients' questions" than groups who use only calculators. With the Internet, "working smart" assignments can foster students' abilities to innovate and learn to solve significant challenges delivered online. "For example, individuals, classes, or even random samples from a region could receive a challenge online, have several days to prepare, confront the challenge, revise as needed, complete the challenge again, and so on, with the number of cycles to proficiency being one measure of interest. Additionally, each cycle could use increasingly difficult challenges to gauge student gains throughout the year" (Schwartz et al., 2005, p. 59). In effect, Schwartz et al. have been rethinking the notion of transfer.

HUMAN–COMPUTER INTERACTION

Finally, the literature on human–computer interaction could be considered as a kind of "off-shoot" of distributed cognition. Both areas emphasize the interaction between learners and their environments. Research into how course management systems (CMS) systems are used for learning is in an early stage. Malikowski et al. (2007) recommend a model for research in CMS that considers both technical features and research-based theories about how people learn, with implications for developing learning activities in these environments. This model was developed by using findings from current CMS to increase its relevance and adaptability. They also synthesized research in CMS from different vendors, which had similar features but different labels. Finally, they presented research-based implications for developing learning activities.

Writing Survey/Interview Questions about Underlying Values

The best way to identify underlying values is from the language, or rhetoric, of the course outline, course materials, course development proposal, and any documents on the course history. Most of the work in identifying values is done when you read these materials, but you might also want to write a few questions about the course objectives in your surveys to faculty, course designers, and learners (Figure 7.7). Once you have a clear sense of the underlying values, you can then write your survey and interview items to measure learner satisfaction with these values and the extent to which they were realized. Information about underlying values can also be obtained by interviewing the course designers and the instructors (Figure 7.8).

1. How well do you think the course objectives met your needs? Explain. ___

_____

_____

2. The course objectives were confusing.

1	2	3	4	5
Strongly disagree	Disagree slightly	Neutral	Agree	Agree strongly

3. I feel that the course activities fulfilled the course objectives.

1	2	3	4	5
Strongly disagree	Disagree slightly	Neutral	Agree	Agree strongly

4. I feel that the goals and objectives of this course were achieved.

1	2	3	4	5
Strongly disagree	Disagree slightly	Neutral	Agree	Agree strongly

5. Did you read the course objectives? _____ Yes _____ No

6. How could the course be changed to better meet the course objectives?

_____

_____

FIGURE 7.7. Survey questions about underlying values for learners.

Analyzing Data on Underlying Values

Coding Qualitative Data

In the analysis stage, you want to identify patterns in the values underlying the course. There are three aspects of value—rhetoric, ideology, and theory—and you will want to code the course documents and interview data using these three themes as coding categories. You can begin by reviewing the course goals, objectives, theories, and ideologies in the course documents such as the syllabus or the course proposal. You might want to take a critical look at these values by comparing them with the NACOL standards. You may find that the values underlying the course are incomplete in some way and need to be extended. The course goals and

1. Why was this course created?
2. What are the goals and objectives of the course?
3. In designing this course, what did you intend to accomplish?
4. What benefits does this course offer that would not be provided by a face-to-face course?
5. Do you have any favorite theories of teaching and learning?
6. When you designed the course, did you base the design on a theory?
7. Do you think the course "works" according to the theory?
8. Do you think the learners understand the goals and objectives of the course?
9. Do you feel that this course is a high-quality course? Why?
10. If you could change anything about this course, what would it be?

FIGURE 7.8. Interview questions about underlying values for course designers.

objectives, then, show you how the course was conceptualized and how it was intended to be implemented. The course objectives are, in some sense, standards of quality for the course.

Course Implementation

Once you have analyzed the course documents, you then compare these statements of *intent* with the *actual* course implementation to (1) develop an understanding of *how* and *why* the course is supposed to work and to (2) determine the extent to which the course was implemented as intended. You might want to draw a diagram of the course components to develop a clear sense of what each component (e.g., technology) is contributing to the whole, whether the activities are redundant, and whether all the components are necessary. Hybrid courses, which blend different technologies, are especially complex.

Multiple Underlying Values

You should also ask whether the course was designed around a single set of values or around *multiple* sets of values. In the latter case, you need to determine how complementary these multiple values are or whether they are incompatible. You should not be surprised to find multiple values working at cross-purposes in the course implementation, sometimes resulting in confusion for learners. In this way, identifying multiple underlying values leads to your next stage of analysis: identifying unintended consequences.

Because distance courses are designed for diverse purposes, there can sometimes be different, and even conflicting, sets of underlying values. For example, courses can be designed to provide access or flexibility (the ability to participate without attending regularly scheduled classroom meetings); to inject richness, depth, and relevance into the course content; or to increase revenues and cost cuts. Although distance courses are usually designed around one consistent set of values, some courses may also be designed around more than a single set of values. Some examples are provided in our authentic case studies in Chapter 8. "The problem is that many important values are likely to remain relative to their community of believers or stakeholders" (Messick, 1998, p. 38), and tensions can arise when stakeholders, or even course design teams, approach distance courses with conflicting sets of values. When a course is designed on a foundation of conflicting values, these differences can be reflected in the course implementation, creating confusion and frustration for learners. For example, when an instructor is designed out of a course in order to cut costs, mature learners who have grown up with instructors in traditional roles may be frustrated if they are not provided with an instructor to help them with the course materials or explain the answers to their assessments (Ruhe, 2002a).

Roles of Stakeholders

The final aspect of underlying values is the roles of stakeholders. You will need to identify who the stakeholders are (e.g., students, faculty, administrators) and develop some intuitive sense of their beliefs and values. This stage may or may not require interviewing or surveying them, depending on the boundaries of your study. Aggarwal (2003), for example, includes an informative analysis of stakeholders' perspectives on e-course management. The roles of stakeholders in evaluation studies range from peripheral involvement to being interviewees and participants to data analysis and report writing. We would not recommend the latter because of the intrusion of bias. You should also be aware that if you are paid by a university to write a report, you may or may not have rights to publish or disseminate the findings and would be advised to establish your authorship rights in writing.

Unintended Consequences

The fourth facet of the unfolding model is unintended consequences. Distance education courses, especially third-generation designs, are complex, innovative, multidimensional systems (Collis, 1996). Unintended consequences are the inevitable products of complex systems (Tenner, 1996). According to Tallent-Runnels et al. (2006), researchers have just begun to understand the variables of online courses, the similarities and differences with face-to-face instruction, and the use of scaffolds and other strategies to improve online interaction. Because new hybrid courses are always evolving, "we will always be in beta" (Qayyum & Bates, 1999), and there will be an ongoing need to evaluate how new courses *actually* work, in contrast to how they are expected to work (Figure 7.9).

Instructional Consequences

In our framework, there are two kinds of unintended consequences: instructional and social. Unintended instructional consequences manifest themselves in ways that adversely affect the quality of instruction, possibly reducing or even eliminating anticipated gains (Tenner, 1996). Unanticipated implementation problems range from routine technical

Unintended instructional consequences
- Bugs, glitches
- Redundant course materials
- High attrition rates
- Bipolar grade distributions
- Course drift away from theory
- Unrealized cost savings
- Failure to achieve expected scale-up

Unintended social consequences
- Learner isolation and impoverished interaction
- New social roles for instructors
- Corporate, consumerist influence
- Less privacy and more surveillance

FIGURE 7.9. Unintended consequences unfolded.

bugs and glitches to a lack of fit between the technology and the subject matter. "The complexity of mechanical systems makes it impossible to test for all possible malfunctions and makes it inevitable that in actual use, some flaws will appear that were hidden from designers" (Tenner, 1996, p. 13). Another type of unintended consequence is course materials that are redundant or unhelpful. Mayer, Heiser, and Lonn (2001), for example, found that no beneficial learning resulted when redundant text was added to narrated animation. In addition, according to Gray and O'Grady (1993), "The presence of the visual link per se does not necessarily improve the lesson's educational effectiveness. Often, it simply served to demonstrate that old practices which are ineffective in a mainstream classroom can be just as ineffective using this technology" (p. 668). One example of course drift away from constructivist theory is Clark's (1994b) description of how turning off a microphone in a video-conferencing room generated peer discussion, which was then treated by the instructor as a discipline problem and silenced.

A recent advertisement in a local, Midwest newspaper (Learn while you drive!, 2006) read:

Learn While You Drive! Study with the World's Most Distinguished Professors Without Attending a Single Class!

Questions:
• What are the values underlying this course?
• What might be some unintended instructional or social consequences?

In early North American distance programs, high attrition rates and bipolar distributions of grades first emerged as unintended effects with personalized system of instruction in the days of teaching machines (Keegan, 1993; Knapper, 1980).

> The distribution of marks is usually bi-polar, with a large number of students scoring very high (because by repeated effort they attain the necessary performance criteria) and a few failing (because they give up somewhere along the way.) Instructors . . . invariably encounter reactions from department heads and deans who find it difficult to understand why . . . marks are not distributed in the customary way. This ultimately leads to a debate as to whether the purpose of education is to sort out the students or . . . to train [them] to perform certain minimum levels of competency. (Knapper, 1980, p. 59)

In this case, the grade distribution ran headlong into traditional expectations for a normal distribution of student grades. The bivariate distribution led to the perception that distance education was of inferior quality. Other examples of unintended consequences are unrealized cost savings and the failure of technology to bring about predicted benefits. The U.S. Open University, for example, was closed after they were unable to reach their predicted enrollment, probably because they were competing with so many high-quality distance providers.

Social Consequences

Examples of the unintended social consequences of educational technology abound, and we will give only a few examples. First, distance learners have long been perceived as isolated, and this concern persists even today. Brabazon (2003) claims that embodied experience, which cannot be measured, is crucial to the university experience. Teachers encounter former students years later and express gratitude for a teachable moment that changed their lives; there is simply no replacement for the exhilaration and inspiration of embodied interaction. In contrast, online education impoverishes interaction, capable only of providing competencies. Brabazon joins others who call Internet teaching into question and argues that online education in itself, as disembodied interaction, is an impoverished interaction, capable only of providing competence. Technology upstages and diminishes the presenter, encourages "mental absenteeism" in the audience, and discourages students from attending classes at all (Brabazon, 2003). Similarly, Noble (1998) deplores the "automation" of higher education, assault on academic freedom, and monitoring and surveillance of teacher–student interactions. Finally, in many states, online programs continue to be "guided and overseen by rules and regulations created for traditional schools . . . Many states are only beginning to address these policy issues, and in some states there has been controversy surrounding the effectiveness and legality of cyberschools" (Watson, 2007, p. 7). Funding for online students and programs is not always a given, nor is equal access to hardware or the Internet for students in low-income inner-city and rural areas. Students with learning or physical disabilities may not always have access to text or images (Watson, 2007).

New Social Roles for Instructors

We have seen that new language such as "open learning," "access," and "flexibility" reflects a shift in values, roles, and expectations underlying distance education courses. This shift in values may have raised the status of learners but has also accelerated the displacement of instructors from their traditional, central roles. The instructor is now a coach or "guide on the side," responsible for empowering students as "thinkers and problem-solvers" (Sandholtz, Ringstaff, & Dwyer, 1997, p. 176). Instructors have become "information brokers" (Van Horn, 1998), "digital butlers" (Brabazon, 2003), or "human back-up support" (Leslie Buffam, Open Learning Agency, personal communication, March 23, 1999). In the future, instructors may be replaced by media (Bourdeau & Bates, 1997) or may become designers of learning experiences, processes, and environments (Duderstat, 1999). This discussion shows how the categories of the unfolding model overlap; that is, new terminology and rhetoric overlap with underlying values and with unintended social consequences.

Corporate Influences

"One agenda for global higher education . . . is who is to set standards . . . and arbitrate and decide on matters such as degrees and exchange of course credit" (Rossman, 1992). According to Cremer (2001), an ideology of corporate, for-profit consumerism underlies the merger of computing and higher education. The workplace, for example, has been transformed, so that women can work from home for lower wages, workers' communications are electronically monitored, and access to information is restricted (Menzies, 1996; Noble, 2003). "The academic enterprise [is reduced] to another commodity . . . the student . . . to a consumer of intellectual property [and] the professor, to a facilitator of this consumption, all in the name of efficiency and increased market-share" (p. 1). There is corporate influence on curriculum, and the unconscious assimilation of American cultural values by learners in foreign countries (Fabos & Young, 1999). Public funds are diverted into flashy multimedia of untested pedagogical quality often at considerable expense (Lookatch, 1997). Stoll (1999) also presents several examples of the misguided adoption of technology in the absence of pedagogical considerations.

The emergence of for-profit providers has put pressure on colleges and universities, thereby reducing their enrollment numbers. "The results for faculty are a decreasing share of the university's budget, higher faculty–student ratios, and a transformation from content expert to 'leader of a learning-process'" (Cremer, 2001, p. 3). Learning is reduced to a management problem, and there is a steady overhaul of tertiary education by managerialism (Brabazon, 2003). Administrators would rather invest in machines that go "ping" instead of in students, or teachers, whose work is reduced to facilitation.

Finally, there is concern not only about the automation of higher education but also the deleterious effects on academic freedom, the privacy of the teacher–student relationship, and a trend toward using technology for surveillance (Noble, 2003). The transparency of online communication to third parties not only impacts academic freedom but also represents a "far larger political concern" (p. 95). Noble claims that web-based courses at University of California, Los Angeles are routinely audited by the administration, that the U.S. Air Force was given a list of names of foreign students without their knowledge or consent, and that online postings can result in charges of "hate crimes." In the post-9/11 world, the implications for privacy and civil rights go far beyond the classroom.

How Can You Identify Unintended Consequences?

One way to identify unintended consequences is to ask whether the course was originally offered in a face-to-face format, because the conversion to a distance course has raised a number of issues, including the migration of paper materials onto the web, lack of fit between the course activities and technologies, and increased workload for students. You may also want to find out whether the course was designed by a team of professional course designers or by a professor and graduate student. If the latter, then you should be especially alert to the emergence of unintended consequences. Another way to identify unintended consequences is to write open-ended survey or interview questions, which will elicit information from learners about their experiences. The third way is to analyze the fit of the data across the four facets of the unfolding model. Before we discuss each of these points, we emphasize that unintended consequences can be positive as well as negative. The University of Maryland University College, State University of New York, University of Central Florida, Pennsylvania State University, and University of Massachusetts have witnessed positive, unintended spillover effects from online learning into face-to-face learning (Bourne & Moore, 2004).

Writing Survey/Interview Questions about Unintended Consequences

Your next set of questions is about unintended instructional and social consequences. You may find it difficult to write these questions because it can be difficult to identify unintended consequences in advance. After all, if they could be anticipated, they would probably be designed out of the course. The best way to anticipate unintended consequences is to review the literature, which can alert you to the kinds of effects that may emerge. However, with the ongoing integration of more and newer technologies in distance/e-learning courses, unintended consequences will very likely continue to emerge in new and unexpected ways.

It follows that most of your survey questions about unintended consequences will be open ended. You could ask learners how well the course met the course objectives and whether they encountered any problems. You could also ask them to identify any problems in accessing the course from home or at convenient times. You could ask them a series of questions to identify any problems with the course components (e.g., the technology, the materials, and the activities; Figure 7.10).

Instructional

1. Was there anything about this course that didn't work the way you expected? Explain. _____

2. Did you encounter any problems with the technology? ____ Yes ____ No

3. Did you have any problems accessing the course?   ____ Yes ____ No

4. Did you encounter any problems with the support services?
   ____ Yes ____ No

5. Were there any other problems you encountered? Explain. _____

Unintended Social Consequences

1. Was your role as a learner different from what you expected? Explain. ___
   _____

2. Was the instructor's role different from what you expected? If so, how? _
   _____

3. Did you encounter any problems participating in the group projects? Explain.
   _____

4. Did the small group activities work the way you expected? If not, why not?
   _____

5. Did you encounter any unexpected social or cultural issues in this course?
   Explain. _____
   _____

FIGURE 7.10. Questions about unintended consequences.

Analyzing Data on Unintended Consequences

Unintended consequences emerge in the analysis stage of your evaluation study. By blending quantitative and qualitative data and identifying both outcomes and processes, you can identify unintended consequences by analyzing how well the course functions as a complete system of interacting components. However, how do we actually do this analysis? There are several ways to analyze your data for unintended consequences (Figure 7.11).

The first step is to compare the theory, ideology, and value labels with how the course is actually functioning. Is there a gap between how the course was expected to work and how it actually worked? Identifying the rhetoric, goals, and objectives is the first step to determining whether there is a gap between these intended goals and the course implementation. You also want to analyze learners' perceptions of how well the course fits with the course objectives and whether they have identified areas where there is a lack of fit.

The second way to identify unintended consequences is to research the history of the course. Evaluators should find out whether the course was originally designed as a face-to-face course and subsequently converted to a distance course. In such cases, especially when there is little course development funding, the evaluator should look for technology-based add-ons, which may increase student workload without adding much to their learning. Reviewing committee notes is another way to determine how the course developers valued different theories or tech-

---

- Is there a lack of fit between the course outline and course implementation?
- Find out about the course history.
    - Was it converted from a traditional course?
- Is there a lack of fit among the underlying values?
- Analyze the course as a "system."
    - How complex is the course design?
    - Is the course a blended or hybrid model?
    - How new are the technologies?
    - What problems emerged from the data?
- Is there a lack of fit between your respondents' perceptions?
- Is there a lack of fit between your survey and interview responses?

FIGURE 7.11. How to identify unintended consequences.

nologies and how these differences were negotiated as the course was designed.

The third way to identify unintended consequences is to determine whether there are multiple conflicting values or ideologies underlying the course, and there may be a considerable gap between the rhetoric and the actual course implementation. These myriad values are not always compatible, nor are they always reflected in the coherent workings of distance course systems. With qualitative and ethnographic methods, our attention is drawn to "what *does* happen as opposed to what *could* happen" (Selwyn, 1997, p. 306), thereby yielding empirical findings about how the course functions as a system. As we mentioned, distance/e-learning courses are complex implementation environments or systems of interacting components (Banathy, 1999; Moore & Kearsley, 1996). Systems theory, then, is useful in modeling distance/e-learning courses as systems made up of interacting components. In this stage of analysis, you compare findings within and across participants in the interviews and surveys (i.e., among tutors, students, designers, and course administrators) and across the components of the system. You need to understand the entire system in context, as a rich and complex case, and be alert for a lack of fit between various course components. A good course will function smoothly, much like a good car, whereas a poor course will have lots of "bumps" and "rattles," which interfere with the intended outcomes. You should be especially alert for unintended consequences that interfere with the smooth running of the course. How well do the components work together? How did the course implementation influence outcomes? Were there mediating variables that intervened in unexpected ways between the process and the outcomes?

VIGNETTE

Unintended consequences cannot be identified in advance and designed out of the course because if they could be anticipated, they would not be unintended consequences. How would you respond?

To determine how the course works as a system, you need to closely scrutinize all qualitative and quantitative evidence, which will allow you to map out the system and judge for yourself how well it functions. You need to compare the qualitative and quantitative findings for convergence. You need to compare coded interview transcripts, open-ended questionnaire responses, course outlines, and webpages. You need to compare the survey and interview responses of course designers, faculty, and learners when they were asked to identify problems with the course components. For example, you may find a pattern in the qualitative data that students are encountering unexpected and recurring barriers to access, despite the fact that the university is dedicated to distance learning and the removal of conventional barriers to access. For example, you may wonder why two interviewees complain about long lines in the university computer labs to access an online course that was designed to be accessed from home.

Assessing Fit across the Four Facets of the Unfolding Model

Once you have analyzed your survey and interview data, your next step is to assess the fit across the four facets of value. Based on Messick's (1989) framework, our unfolding model is also a progressive matrix, which means that evidence, values, and consequences are not distinct but instead overlap and cut across each other. This overlapping quality reflects the current research in distance education, which has shifted toward investigating the complex and synergistic relationships among learner characteristics, course design, and constraints of the delivery system (Tallent-Runnels et al., 2006). For example, the theories underlying learner control overlap with cost–benefit because learner control and self-pacing are benefits for learners; moreover, when learners can control the pace of the lessons, satisfaction and engagement improve (Tallent-Runnels et al., 2006). As this example shows, an investigation of theories, cost–benefit, course implementation, and both affective and learning outcomes overlaps. This overlap shows that the value of distance/e-learning courses is a complex, multidimensional construct and that it is difficult, if not impossible, to "cut through" this unitary construct by artificially dividing it into the four distinct boxes of our framework, which is purely for heuristic purposes. Instead, the tensions between scientific evidence and social consequences "must be carefully negotiated" (Messick, 1998, p. 38).

The progressive nature of our framework means that as evaluators assess scientific evidence, their attention will be directed to the presence of values and consequences that are always present but lurking in the background. To provide a comprehensive assessment of merit and worth, evaluators need to bring *all* of these aspects of value into the foreground.

For example, evaluators of distance courses should ask whether access should be broadened to include conditions that facilitate course completion (Institute for Higher Education Policy, 1999). If learners are driving to campus to access an online course, is the course successful in providing access (Ruhe, Qayyum, & Bates, 1999)? Similarly, bimodal grade distributions and high dropout rates, which are not uncommon with distance delivery methods (Zigrell, 1991), should also be included in any analysis of access (Rumble, 1981). The objective of providing access is not being achieved if 50% of learners drop out. How high do dropout rates have to be before they are unacceptable, and who decides and on what basis? These questions reflect the overlap among outcomes, values, and unintended consequences.

At this point, you may wish to proceed deductively by using the fit elements in Figure 7.12 as coding categories. For those inclined toward inductive approaches, however, the alternative at this stage is to shift your analysis to a more inductive approach to qualitative research, where you code the data by just allowing unanticipated themes and connections to emerge in a "chain," which may either deepen or extend our deductive categories. You will also be making connections between survey and interview findings. All of these emergent connections will lead to an understanding of the dynamics of the course implementation, the gap between the intended and the actual course, unintended effects, and suggestions for course improvement. In fact, this final stage of the analysis, where everything finally comes together, is the most fluid and exciting stage of the study, and you should not feel compelled to force any analytical categories on the data but instead should just follow where your chain of associations takes you, until you feel that you have no further questions about how the course actually works. In the following discussion of the elements of fit below, we show where our chain of associations leads us in analyzing the data from the case studies in Chapter 8.

> - Fit between media and the subject matter.
> - Fit between learners and the course.
> - Fit between relevance and the course implementation.
> - Fit between theories and the course implementation.
> - Fit among evidence, values, and consequences.

FIGURE 7.12. Determining "fit" across the four facets of value.

Fit between Media and the Subject Matter

Although specific course designs tend to be associated with different media, there is still no proven method for fitting media to the subject matter (Moore & Kearsley, 1996). According to Moore and Kearsley (1996), instructional media need to fit with the course objectives and activities, the students, the learning environment, economic or organizational factors, and feasibility. Some best practice examples of a good fit between media and subject matter are given by Bett, French, Farr, and Hooks (1999). The virtual cell online tutorial in the webpage of Integrative Biology 100 and 101 at the University of Illinois at Urbana–Champaign (*www.life. uiuc.edu/bio100/*) is a good example of an Internet-based textbook. Biology 1410 learners at Southwest Texas State University (*www.study.swt.edu*) receive web-based lecture slides to take home to review after a lecture. Communication 201, a public speaking course at Cornell University, uses Netscape sound files to make audio examples of famous speeches available to all students to replay as often as they wish, thereby providing concrete examples of a variety of communication styles (*instruct1.cit.cornell.edu/ courses/comm201e*).

However, evaluators should not assume that the fit between media and the subject is always optimal. With its sound capabilities, multimedia is a good fit with a second-language listening comprehension curriculum. However, multimedia is a poor fit and, moreover, needlessly expensive, with a curriculum in reading a foreign language (Ruhe, 2002a). The fit problem is exacerbated by the proliferation of new technologies in various combinations or hybrids (Ljosa, 1993), which increase the chance of mismatched technologies, redundancy, and wasted expenditure (Bourdeau & Bates, 1997). The media or subject matter may also be a poor fit with the class size, geographical location, or interactivity (Belanger & Jordan, 2000). In sum, media need to be chosen to fit the subject matter, and if the fit is not good, then this mismatch needs to be brought forward, along with recommendations for course improvement, in the final course evaluation report.

Fit between Learners and the Course

"The importance of understanding the learners' goals, needs and motivation in taking a course is a basic tenet of instructional design (Tallent-Runnels et al., 2006). Evaluators need to consider the fit between the age and demographics of the target learner group and the media and course activities. An *adult learner* is defined as any learner over the age of 20 years (Ruhe et al., 1999). Adult learners "are not looking for a residential experience," "have limited patience with a 'talking head' approach," and value convenient schedules and proximity to home (Blustein et al., 1999, p. 57). Traditional learners are young people between the ages of 18 and 25 years, who make up the residential postsecondary population. Farrington (1999) believes that "most traditional undergraduates between the ages of 18 and 25 are not sufficiently self-directed to manage an educational program like that of the University of Phoenix" (p. 83). High school students may lack the motivation or prior experience with complex technology (Clark, 1994a) or the discipline of staying focused without weekly class meetings.

There are considerable differences of opinions about the characteristics of young high school or college students. Some authors see today's high school and college students as members of the *digital generation* (Duderstat, 1999). According to Duderstat, interactive and collaborative learning approaches are appropriate for the digital age, the plug-and-play generation. Raised on highly visual and interactive technologies, today's learners would seem to be well suited to constructivist approaches. These learners may need training in self-regulation, which is a complex set of skills involving articulation, planning, better self-discipline, research and problem solution, and self-evaluation skills.

The promise of technology is to create learning environments customized to individual needs. Instead of a standardized approach, a postindustrial model is adaptive and responsive to learners' abilities. Instructional design must consider several learner segments, with different needs and preferences, of which the most fundamental contrast is that of adult learners and traditional learners. The evaluator will need to identify the demographics of the learner group and determine whether there is a fit among the needs of these learners, the technology, the goals in the course outline, the underlying values expressed in the course outline, and the course activities.

Fit between Relevance and the Course Activities

Evaluators of distance/e-learning courses also need to assess the fit between underlying theories around relevance and the course design, implementation, and activities. For example, the course goals and objectives may emphasize that the course activities are based on an Information Age paradigm. As an evaluator, you need to compare this statement with the actual course implementation to determine the extent to which this is the case. Peters (1993), for example, found that, although Britain's Open University espoused open and customized learning in its early history, they continued to deliver large-scale, standardized programs designed to meet general needs for knowledge transmission, "with closed and rigid systems and inflexible deadlines, learning materials that narrow the curriculum and leave little room for interpretation outside the direction of the course designers" (p. 24). Because distance education challenges linear sequencing of content and standardized measures of assessing student learning (Seel & Winn, 1997), you need to determine the extent to which learning is customized for different individuals and the degree of departure from traditional, linear course designs.

In your recommendations, you might mention that innovative instructional design models represent a departure from the traditional, linear models of instructional design. Would complexity theory provide a better foundation for a complex, adaptive, nonlinear problem-solving models of instructional design (Tennyson, 1997) for this particular course? If so, how would you use this approach to redesign the course? There are also many different approaches to instructional design that are based on the learning theory of constructivism (e.g., Gardner, 1999; Schwartz, Lin, Brophy, & Bransford, 1999; Mayer, 1999). For example, you might recommend an instructional model based on divergent learning, in which multiple perspectives are more highly valued than discrete answers (Hannafin et al., 1999). You might want to introduce activities based on tools such as spreadsheets, graphing programs, web browsers, or intelligent tutors, which diagnose and respond to learners' ability levels, and use discovery approaches that give learners "primary control" (Snow, 1997).

For example, at the University of Minnesota, an undergraduate family social sciences course in personal finances was evaluated by a team that included the professor, a graduate and an undergraduate student, an evaluation consultant, and an instructional design consultant. The course outline and textbook emphasized relevance and transfer as course goals. Students were expected to learn how to do household budgets, and it was hoped they would apply these skills after they graduated. The evaluation report, however, showed that the textbook contained examples of case studies with characters who not only appeared "canned" but also outdated. This inauthentic nuclear family had an image, goals, and values from the 1950s, even though nuclear households are now a minority of households across the United States, and certainly did not reflect the daily lives of most of the students in this family sciences class. In response to this evaluation finding, the textbook was replaced by webpages with a case study of a young undergraduate in a family sciences class who later gets married and starts a family. The new online case studies were vastly more contemporary and relevant to the lives of these young adult learners. In sum, the whole point of evaluating the fit between the rhetoric of the course outline and the course activities is to generate specific strategies to improve the course for your learners.

Fit between Underlying Theories and the Course Activities

Constructivist theories are reflected "in the design of learning environments to facilitate exploration and reinforce context, expand learner control and facilitate integration" (Tennyson & Elmore, 1997, p. 56). There are several examples of constructivist learning environments that provide excellent applications of constructivist theories. Jonassen et al. (1996) also gives several examples of highly effective constructivist learning environments: (1) multimedia or CD-ROM production projects such as Astonomy Village, where students are astronomers and map out a plan of exploration of the galaxy, (2) hypermedia authoring projects such as exploring the Nardoo River in Australia, and (3) Goldman-Segall's (1995) Constellations, where students use multimedia to create digitized video and text story chunks, or "stars," which represent different viewpoints—"multi-loging" instead of "dialoging"—and assembled into "constellations." Similarly, Joan Fleitas's (1999) award-winning Band-Aides is a child-centered webpage where teenagers give their perspectives on growing up with medical problems. In all these examples, students are at the center of everyday activities based on constructivist theory-based approaches to multimedia (Hannafin, Hall, Land, & Hill, 1994). In these examples, technology is used to the best advantage because the activities are designed creatively to fit closely with the underlying theory of constructivism.

Evaluators should be aware that, despite the rhetoric, teaching practices are sometimes painfully slow to change (Sandholtz et al., 1997), and some teachers may not shift from traditional roles with ease (Kent & McNergney, 1999). Even with greater access to technology, the underlying constructivist theory may not be fully reflected in the daily course activities. In the courses they investigated, for example, Kanuka and Anderson (1998) raised concerns that online conversations tended to "lack fluidity" and generated "inconsistent and unchallenged ideas" and "little negotiated meaning or new knowledge construction" (p. 96). You should try to determine to what extent learners have control, or the effectiveness of the instructor's role. You might consider whether instructivist activities are blended with constructivist activities and, if so, to what extent (French,

1999). Such findings are important to bring forward, so that the evaluator can then do some detective work to identify the cause of problems and make recommendations to redesign this component, select learners more rigorously, or provide some modeling or training regarding participation in online discussions. Of course, if there is a good fit between the underlying theory and the course activities, this finding is very important to emphasize in your report.

How to Enhance the Validity of Your Findings

There are several strategies for enhancing the validity of your findings (Figure 7.13).

Use Random/Stratified Sampling

One of the best ways to enhance credibility for your qualitative findings is random and stratified sampling of interviewees. You should select interviewees at random, and take steps during the interview and analysis to control for your own biases. We recommend you ask another independent researcher to triangulate your data. You should also be aware of novelty effects, such as Hawthorne effects (i.e., individuals react differently because of the interest that significant others show in them), which are probably common but seldom acknowledged (Suen & Stevens, 1993).

Write "Good" Survey Items

One way to increase the credibility of your findings is to write good survey items. Each item should measure one and only one construct and

---

- Use random or stratified sampling.
- Write "good" survey items.
- Control for your own biases with member checks and memos to yourself (memoing).
- Use triangulation.
- Keep audit trails.

FIGURE 7.13. How to enhance the credibility of your findings.

should not include complex or compound sentences or sentences that could be interpreted differently by respondents. In their review of quantitative evaluation studies in distance education, Suen and Stevens (1993) noted that most evaluation studies in distance education do not report reliability or validity coefficients or that reported values are often incomplete. Therefore, whenever possible, you should report the validity and reliability coefficients of surveys (Design-Based Research Collective, 2003), especially if you have written the survey yourself. Calculating and reporting these values will give your findings more credibility (Meier & Davis, 1990; Suen & Stevens, 1993).

Control for Your Own Biases

You need to be aware that the greatest threat to the credibility of qualitative findings is coding bias. As an evaluator, your own values and beliefs will enter into the evaluation process at every stage. You must be careful to identify your own values and not let your own preferences lead to poorly supported conclusions (Davidson, 2005). On the one hand, you should be alert to letting personal feelings about individuals influence your results (Fitzpatrick et al., 2004). On the other hand, you must be careful not to "go native," that is, unconsciously adopt stakeholders' values and downplay disappointing findings (Fitzpatrick et al., 2004). To control for your own biases, you should ask an independent researcher to code the data or confirm your codes and then negotiate any disagreements. Other strategies include daily or weekly reflection logs, peer debriefing, and an audit trail of files kept by an external evaluator (Fitzpatrick et al., 2004).

Memoing

One strategy to control for bias is memoing, that is, writing notes about what the data meant and how they were linked to other data segments. You can write down marginal notes, "a stream-of-consciousness commentary consisting of hunches, observations, questions and critical self-checking" (Van Maanen, 1988, p. 150). As recommended by Stake (1995), you search for additional interpretations rather than confirmation of a single meaning. Memoing is a record of your assumptions, reflections, and biases that surface during the process of coding the data (Lecompte & Preissle, 1993) and a strategy for being aware of those biases and controlling for them. Note that these memos are private, for your own records, and are not sent to colleagues or administrators! Figure 7.14 provides an example of a

February 24, 8:44 P.M.: After going through the data
today, I drew a model of the course implementation
environment. Realized that there may be no "true"
model. I've also caught myself looking for proof of my
current favorite model and ignoring other evidence when
going through the data. Must be careful to be aware of
this kind of bias and keep checking for it!
    Reread Modern Languages report and transcripts
today. Noticed new things (e.g., student line-ups outside
the university computer labs). One student said that
she "didn't really see the point of the highlighting"
and she believed the CD-ROM had sound, but my other
interviewees said it had no sound. The same student,
whose views represented the views of the satisfied
group, said she missed the lecture format. Why had I not
picked up on this in my first analysis of the data?

FIGURE 7.14. A sample memo.

memo written to yourself for the purpose of reflecting on, identifying, and controlling for your own biases.

Use Triangulation

Triangulation is very important for enhancing the trustworthiness, or credibility, of case studies (Flick, 1992; Merriam, 2002; U.S. General Accounting Office, Program Evaluation and Methodology Division, 1990). You can triangulate data across respondents and across methods (quantitative and qualitative) or data sources (Lincoln & Guba, 1985). When you compare data across respondents, the convergence of multiple perspectives increases the confidence of your interpretations. Triangulating within data sources is when you compare closed- and open-ended survey responses. Triangulating across data sources is when you compare survey with interview data or when you compare findings across multiple sources such as documents, course outlines, webpages, interviews, and open-ended survey items for convergence. Finally, your findings can also triangulated with the literature, as recommended by Eisenhardt (1989). In sum, triangulation across sources, participants, methods, and theory provides the required checks and balances, which enhances the validity and generalizability of your research. When findings converge toward the same conclusions, your findings have more credibility. When they do not converge, you may find unintended consequences at work.

Keep Audit Trails

Other strategies such as member checks (Guba & Lincoln, 1985), audit trails, and appropriate random sampling methods are also helpful in lending credibility to your conclusions. Trustworthiness can also be earned by using an audit trail to create a chain of evidence (U.S. General Accounting Office, Program Evaluation and Methodology Division, 1990). Coded transcripts, documents, and memos should be filed in a sound organizational system. All filed items are critical components of an audit trail that allows an auditor to determine whether conclusions are warranted by the findings (Merriam, 2002).

Conclusion

This methodological logic-in-use struck a balance between control and creativity, as recommended by Eisenhardt (1989). That is, attempts to reconcile evidence across cases, types of cases, and different investigators and between cases and literature increase the likelihood of creative reframing (Eisenhardt, 1989). Moreover, the use of unintended consequences as a coding category enhances credibility by reducing selectivity or bias toward programs that work (U.S. General Accounting Office, Program Evaluation and Methodology Division, 1990).

Recommendations for Course Improvement

Course Implementation

The course implementation refers to the day-to-day operations of the course. To determine how well the course is actually working, you need to blend all of your findings and make connections among them. Your interview and survey data can help you to understand how satisfied learners were with the course. Quantitative data such as the frequency of interaction among learners, or between learners and the instructor, or scores on a rubric of online discussions can be used to determine how much activity learners actually engaged in. Outcomes are used to measure how much learning actually occurred. We recommend that both qualitative and quantitative evidence be analyzed and compared to understand how the course works as a complete system. This analysis shows how the course works as a complete system; therefore, we have used the term *course implementation* instead of course environment to emphasize the dynamic nature of the course as a system.

After you have immersed yourself in the data and user reactions, you wait for and make a list of any problems that emerge. Because unintended consequences can be either positive or negative, you need to weigh the unintended negative effects against all of the beneficial effects such as the currency and relevance of computer-based learning to a generation growing up in the digital age. One positive unintended effect is enhanced internationalization of the university, as distance/e-learning courses pick up foreign enrollments.

You then use your findings to make tentative recommendations for course redesign and improvement. These recommendations should include a mix of both general and specific actions to be taken by named individuals by a deadline (Hendricks, 1994). Your recommendations may include eliminating or adding a technology, changing a course component, identifying a need for changes in enrollment policies, or migrating materials onto the web. If you found that students experienced isolation or lack of socialization, you might recommend creating online clubs or adding "real-time web conferencing tools that integrate chat, voice, webcam and whiteboard or occasional in-person meetings" (Watson, 2007, p. 27). In Chapter 8, we provide specific recommendations for improving two authentic postsecondary courses evaluated with our framework. We show that the documentation of unintended consequences by program evaluators is actually beneficial because it provides specific direction for course improvement.

Consulting with Stakeholders

Sometimes recommendations in program evaluation reports can generate considerable controversy or political fall out. Therefore, it is imperative that you consult key stakeholders about your findings and their expectations for how these findings will be used *before* you release the final version of your report. There are more issues at stake than the trade-offs between quality and cost. For example, a cost–benefit study might show that the most efficient delivery method is to simply deliver the facts and minimize interaction with the instructor or simply eliminate the instructor altogether. For another example, if you conclude that multimedia simulations provide more educational value than is provided by content transmission but these simulations are considerably more expensive and difficult to design and develop, should you recommend that funding be terminated? Before making your final recommendation, you need to obtain the input of stakeholders, perhaps by inviting them to a meeting, so that when you release your final report, there will be no surprises.

Writing the Evaluation Report

In our approach, each distance course is a case; therefore, you should write one case report for each course. Because a case study report presents a true-to-life "big picture," your report should be easier to understand and more persuasive than the typical report (Fitzpatrick et al., 2004). In the report, you must integrate empirical data with values into an evaluative claim, which is the conclusion (Scriven, 2003). An evaluation report must, almost by definition, lead to a conclusion about merit or worth, usually expressed with language like "good/bad" or "better/worse" (Scriven, 2003). "Facts and value claims are not totally different types of claims, but rather blend into one another" (Scriven, 2003, p. 11). The idea that evaluators should not draw evaluative conclusions is "evaluation-free evaluation," which is a contradiction in terms (Scriven, 2003, p. 19). However, an evaluative claim can be little more than a simple sentence about the course, which blends or fuses both facts and value claims (Scriven, 2003). Your purpose is to "make a splash, to have that impact, to change situations in a desired direction . . . [and] how we report our results is often the difference between creating a tiny ripple or making a proper splash" (Hendricks, 1994, p. 549).

Know Your Audience

The most important consideration in writing evaluation reports is to know your audience and to write your report in a way that responds to their particular needs (Fitzpatrick et al., 2004). You should be familiar with your audience's background, biases, and preferences and ask them for their input, perspectives, and concerns. It is also wise to involve your audience by holding meetings, giving them responsibilities and training, showing respect, and consulting with them on the report's format or timing (Fitzpatrick et al., 2004). Although you need to ask stakeholders to sign off on the report, they should not be allowed to influence the findings (Fitzpatrick et al., 2004). You might consider writing a longer report for internal use and a shorter one for external audiences. The longer version could be used to provide direction for course improvement, and the shorter version could be uploaded on the web and distributed to a wider audience or used to market the course.

Organization

Communicating effectively is essential if the report is to have its intended impact (Fitzpatrick et al., 2004). Your report should begin with a title page followed by a one-page executive summary, with the course description, methodology, number of participants, key findings, and recommendations. Your complete evaluation report should include all of the following elements:

- Title page
- Executive summary
- Introduction
- Course overview: subject, materials, interaction, learner characteristics, assessment/feedback, course implementation
- Underlying values: goals, objectives, philosophy, theory, ideology
- Evaluation design: mixed methods, procedures for data collection and analysis
- Findings: learner satisfaction, materials, learning, flexibility, support services
- Costs and benefits, relevance
- Unintended instructional and social consequences: lack of fit across the facets of the unfolding model
- Problems, issues, and recommendations for course redesign or improvement
- Conclusions
- Appendix: survey and interview protocols

The body of your course evaluation report should begin with a paragraph identifying the values, theory, and ideology on which the course is based. Your survey and interview data should be organized around the categories of the framework and themes that emerged within each category of value. Your report should include both the strengths and weaknesses of the course. Presenting the strengths first will make it easier for your audience to accept the weaknesses (Fitzpatrick et al., 2004). Your recommendations should include a mix of general and specific actions (Hendricks, 1994) for course improvement. Write your report in lay language, avoid jargon, and use correct grammar and punctuation as well as headings, boxes, and other visual displays (Fitzpatrick et al., 2004).

Enhancing the Credibility of Your Findings

The fundamental challenge for all evaluators is to demonstrate a warrant, or a basis, for the conclusions of your report. For this reason, you should report the steps taken to enhance the credibility of your findings in your final report. Credibility for quantitative findings is enhanced with random sampling, a large sample size, and large response rates. Random sampling builds credibility because your respondents were not selected based on their perceptions of the course. However, you will be working with intact classes, so you want as large a response rate as possible. Another way to build credibility is to report your response rates (i.e., the number of survey respondents divided by the total number of course participants). A high response rate bolsters the credibility of your findings because it reflects the opinions of a larger number of individuals rather than just a few.

A third way to increase the credibility of your findings is to attach the survey items in an appendix so that your readers can see that you have written good items. That is, each item should measure one and only one construct and should not include complex or compound sentences or sentences that could be interpreted differently by respondents. You should also calculate and report reliability and validity coefficients (Design-Based Research Collective, 2003), especially if you have written the survey yourself. Calculating and reporting these values will give your findings more credibility (Meier & Davis, 1990; Suen & Stevens, 1993). To enhance the credibility of qualitative findings, you need to show that you have controlled for researcher bias with strategies such as selecting interviewees at random, controlling for your own biases during data collection and coding, memoing, and asking an independent researcher to triangulate your data. You also want to triangulate not only within and across respondent groups but also within and across quantitative and qualitative research methods.

How Much Detail Should You Include?

As for how much detail to include, the answer is "only as much as your audience needs" (Fitzpatrick et al., 2004). When presenting charts and graphs, you need to select graphs that best convey your message. For example, pie charts are used to convey parts of a whole, bar graphs to compare different units, line graphs for different points in time, and scatter plots for relationships between two variables (Hendricks, 1994). If your final evaluation report is not very flattering, you may have to disguise the name of the course to provide anonymity for the course developers and instructors. You will also need to follow your university's policies for public documents, which may include the university logo and disclaimer statements.

Avoiding Damaging Conclusions

In your evaluation report, you need to exercise caution in reporting findings that might "damage interventions or innovations and poison the well for new settings or users of technology" (Baker & O'Neil, 2006, p. 10). When systems are unstable, you may prefer to focus on "interim goals, or quality of the instructional science underlying the implementation" (p. 10). When the system is "medium mature," you should select outcome measures "that are consistent with realistic expectations of the Web-based system (rather than relying on rhetorical claims)" (p. 11). You need to be friendly with the designer and show how you can add value, but also want to avoid perceptions that you have been co-opted or that your study is biased. You want to "use words to modify descriptions of negative or absent functions such as 'as yet,' 'not that we could find' and 'apparently' to illustrate both . . . that things can be fixed [and to avoid a] confrontation with the developer" (p. 11). Finally, you might also want to focus on why positive and negative effects occurred.

Maximizing the Use of Your Findings

The extent to which your findings will be used may depend on the decisions of the grant administrators or department heads. You can increase the chances that your findings will be used if you (1) write a report with high technical quality, (2) recommend specific, practical course improvements (Fitzpatrick et al., 2004), (3) include an estimate of the cost and consequences of your recommendations (Hendricks, 1994), and (4) earned the confidence of faculty and other stakeholders. If you are proposing major changes, you may require some sophisticated political and communicative skills (Hendricks, 1994). As a final word, you must also remember that your evaluation report is only one piece of information in a process of change (Hendricks, 1994) and not be too downhearted if your recommendations are not fully implemented. For more information on writing evaluation reports, see Fitzpatrick et al. (2004).

Sample Model Reports

The Online Evaluation Resource Library is a warehouse of "evaluation plans, instruments, and reports for NSF [National Science Foundation] projects that can be used as examples by Principal Investigators, project evaluators, and others outside the NSF community as they design proposals and projects" (National Science Foundation, Division of Research, Evaluation and Communication, Directorate for Education and Human Resources, 2007, p. 1). Model evaluation plans and reports, as well as guidelines for improving evaluation practice for a range of educational interventions, including postsecondary and technology-based courses, are available free of charge at *oerl.sri.com/home.html*.

The NSF also has online evaluation reports that can be used as examples or models of good practices. One such report is the final evaluation report of the initial impacts of the NSF's Integrative Graduate Education and Research Traineeship Program (Abt Associates, Inc., 2006), an innovative program aimed at transforming the postsecondary culture of science teaching. This report is available at *www.nsf.gov/pubs/2006/nsf0617/nsf0617.pdf*.

Finally, the American Evaluation Association has a list of online resources and links to websites for evaluators. The list is organized by topic (e.g., qualitative data analysis software, survey design, administration, scanning and analysis products, and university and college programs). This information is also available free of charge from *www.eval.org/resources.asp*. The American Educational Research Association also has information available to members of Division H: School Evaluation and Program Development: *www.aera.net/Default.aspx?id=26*.

Conclusions

In this chapter, we reviewed the lower two boxes of the unfolding model— underlying values and unintended consequences—as well as the fit among the various facets of value. You can identify the ideologies, values, and theories underlying your course by analyzing the course documents or interviewing course designers. Once you have a clear sense of the intended implementation, you can then write your survey and interview items to determine how well these goals were met. You can identify unintended consequences by reviewing the course history, interviewing participants about the process, and comparing the course objectives with the actual course implementation. Comparing data for convergence across different participant groups and across methods is another way to bring unintended consequences out of the shadows and into the foreground. These findings, often completely unexpected, will provide specific directions for course improvement. To increase the credibility of your findings, you should use appropriate random sampling methods, large response rates, triangulation, and audit trails. Finally, the evaluation report can be written for either an internal or an external audience; in both cases, the report should not include more information than the audience needs. In Chapter 8, we show our unfolding model in action by presenting the rich findings and recommendations for improvement that resulted from using our framework to guide evaluation studies of two authentic, postsecondary, distance/e-learning courses, one in North America and the other globally.

CHAPTER 8

■ ■ ■ ■ ■ ■ ■ ■

Findings from Two Authentic Case Studies

In this chapter, we report on our findings from using the unfolding model to guide two evaluation studies of authentic postsecondary courses, one a distance course and the other an e-learning course. Our purpose is to show how our framework performs when used to guide an evaluation study of authentic evaluation data from two real courses: (1) Computing Science 200 (CPSC 200), a continuous-enrollment computer training course; and (2) Professional Writing 110 (PWRIT 110), a globally delivered e-learning course (Ruhe & Zumbo, 2006). The first course was delivered by a private sector provider to learners in the Pacific Northwest and the second was delivered globally by an international, nonprofit organization. The findings in this chapter are taken from the data used in Ruhe (2002a, 2003), and Qayyum and Bates (1999).

Because each course brings a different emphasis to the four facets of value in our framework, the report outline in the previous chapter may not always be applied lockstep to all courses. Instead, there may be minor variations in the reporting format so that the unique findings of each course can be given appropriate emphasis. We believe that reporting findings from different types of educational institutions, with different goals and mandates, demonstrates the generalizability of our framework. Finally, the names of the courses and universities have been disguised to protect anonymity.

TWO AUTHENTIC CASE STUDIES			
Course	Method	Scope	Type
Computing Science 200	CD-ROM	North America	Distance education
Professional Writing 110	E-mail	Global	E-learning

Methods and Procedures for Both Studies

For both courses, documents, survey, and interview data were collected. The course outline, webpages, and course materials were reviewed, surveys on learner satisfaction were written, and telephone interviews of learners, tutors, and course designers were tape-recorded. Data were collected on learner satisfaction with the course components (i.e., delivery method, instructors, interaction, student support, feedback, and assessment).

The same survey and interview protocols were not used for both courses. For the second course, a survey and interview protocol written by course administrators was used. For both courses, frequencies, means, standard deviations, total number of respondents, and response rates for each survey item were calculated. Using qualitative data analysis procedures, we coded all interview data for evidence, values, and consequences. These findings were then analyzed to determine how well the courses worked, the extent of the gap between the intended and the actual course implementation, and recommendations for course improvements. We now provide a summary of the evaluation findings from both courses.

Distance Learning: Computing Science 200 (CPSC 200)

Course Overview

Computing Science 200 (CPSC 200) is computer-based vocational training course offered by an American private-sector provider and delivered across North America. There was a rigorous screening program for admission and a long waiting list. The module-based course was held at a local vocational training center and had been running for 2 years when these data were collected. In the scheduled section, course fees were paid by various government agencies, and learners were required to be in the computer lab every day. The continuous-enrollment students paid for the course themselves and set their own hours. The 14 student participants in this research were mature learners, ages 24 to 55 years.

Ideology, Philosophy, and Goals

EduComp is a private-sector company dedicated to maximizing returns to shareholders, increasing profits, lowering costs, and market expansion. As a private-sector institution, EduComp's goal was to provide high-quality, cost-effective training. The course manual reflected an underlying belief in the benefits of using technology in a self-study format. The goal was to develop high-demand skills for the computer industry as well as job search and professional interpersonal skills so that learners can find jobs. With this approach, learning is customized to the needs of the individual. The underlying theory is that computers ensure a high-quality pedagogy and are a superior training method because of their flexibility. The vision of education is a self-study technology-based model with frequent tests and a facilitating role for instructors. The core of the teaching philosophy is that learner self-reliance is highly beneficial for mature learners whose goal is job retraining and employment.

CPSC 200: UNDERLYING VALUES

- Belief in technology
- Learner-centered philosophy
- Testing requirements
- Relevance: job training in computer engineering
- "Hard" and "soft" skills
- Cost savings

Course Materials

The course materials were Shalinsky's (1998) orientation manual, computer training materials on the hard drive, required textbooks, and online resources. The computer lab is an enhanced self-study environment, with books and computers, computer-based tests (CBTs), CD-ROMs, and instructional videos. Students were not permitted to copy any course material or take CD-ROMs or instructional videos home because of licensing restrictions, and there was no remote access from home. Students work through the course materials at their own pace with two instructors available for support and are also encouraged to collaborate with their peers to clarify the course material. A series of computer-based practice exams, preparatory exams, and a final exam are provided by a private tutoring company. Learners are required to pass each test in order to become certified, and repeat trials are permitted for an additional fee. However, interaction with the technology and passing the tests, not interaction with the instructor or other learners, occupies center stage.

Learner Satisfaction

Sixty percent of respondents said they liked the delivery mode because it gave them flexibility, 33% were neutral, and 7% did not like it. Among the students, 67% rated the materials as good, 7% as average, 20% as fair, and 7% as poor. Ninety-three percent were satisfied with the opportunities for student interaction, and only one person was dissatisfied. Forty percent felt they were satisfied with the support services, 13% were neutral, and 40% were unsatisfactory. Recommendations for improving support services include access, more instructor contact, scheduled lab assignments with instructors, regular review of student progress, and better certification of trainers.

Relevance

CPSC 200 is perceived as relevant to these unemployed adult learners because it certifies them for future employment. Sixty-seven percent felt the materials were relevant to their personal or professional needs, 20% were neutral, and 13% disagreed. Similar numbers felt the technology in this course helped them learn with greater depth of understanding. Half of all respondents felt that interaction with the instructor was relevant to their learning compared with 63% for interaction with other learners. Sixty-seven percent of respondents felt that the technology helped them learn more relevant information, 20% were neutral, and 13% disagreed. Sixty-eight percent agreed that the technology helped them learn with greater understanding, 13% were neutral, and 20% disagreed. Fifty percent saw the interaction with the instructor as relevant to their learning, 14% were neutral, and 34% disagreed. Finally, 80% of respondents disagreed that interaction with other students was relevant to their learning. In sum, these findings show that learner response to the CPSC 200 course was mixed.

Cost–Benefit

According to the respondents, the average amount spent on tuition was $10,200 ($SD$ = $1,476, N = 10). The government paid tuition fees for some students, but the continuous-enrollment students paid for their own tuition, books, and tests. The average amount spent on books was $354 ($SD$ = 19.15, N = 6). The six required exams cost $600. Thirty-four percent of learners felt that the course was not worth the money, 41% were neutral, and 25% felt it was worth the money.

One important benefit of the course, mentioned by 10 of 13 learners, is self-pacing. For funded learners, the course has a quick, flexible time frame of 26 weeks, which minimizes the transition to their new careers as systems engineers. The sole continuous-enrollment learner had been in the course for 1½ years! The most frequently mentioned drawbacks were that it was not instructor led, that there was insufficient structure, and that there were computer glitches and errors in the materials. Even with a weekly lecture, student interviewees said they wanted more instructor-led sessions, including overviews and exercises. In response to the question about problems, there were 17 comments covering a wide range of issues. The most frequently mentioned problems were computer glitches and downtime, errors in materials, lack of formal instruction and unqualified instructors, and a long waiting period. Data on the costs of delivering the CPSC 200 course were not collected, so a cost–benefit ratio cannot be calculated.

CPSC 200: SCIENTIFIC EVIDENCE

Mixed methods: Surveys and interviews with learners and tutors on the following topics:

- Learner satisfaction with course components (e.g., materials, instructor, system support, opportunities for interaction).
- Relevance with job training needs of workplace.
- Cost–benefit (cost savings): costs to learners, funding agency, and EduComp.

Unintended Consequences

Fit with Employment Needs

The orientation manual promises that graduates will be highly market-able, yet at the time this course was offered, the program coordinator said it had become more difficult to get a job because the market was shifting in favor of "soft skills" (i.e., interpersonal and communications skills). There was, therefore, a mismatch with the underlying ideology that students learn best in technology-based self-study format and the needs of the job market. Moreover, using the "boot camp" approach to pedagogy favored by the American military is hardly an appropriate way of modeling these soft skills. A better method might be a field-tested team skills training program (Hartley & Robson, 1998a, 1998b).

Access and Flexibility

The kinds of technologies used in this course are often used elsewhere to provide learners with the means for studying from home. Some CPSC 200 students buy a computer, set up their own local area networks at home, and experiment, which is considered "value added" by the program administrator. In fact, however, the funding agency's and EduComp's policies and regulations intervened, making the CPSC 200 course "place bound." First, learners are not permitted to take course materials home because of licensing agreements. For the same reason, there is no remote access. As a result, the potential of the technologies to provide remote access is not realized. In sum, policies and regulations intervene in the course implementation, and learners are required to travel to local training and testing centers, where they work through the materials.

Adding Lectures

Instructor lectures were added on to the course after learners in a previous section demanded it. The orientation manual stresses a model of instruction in which a range of technologies in a self-study format is optimum. In fact, instructors were added on when learners complained that the self-study format was not working. Students in a previous offering of the program had asked for more formal instruction from the instructor. In this offering, the instructors gave weekly lectures that CNS and CPSC 200 (continuous-enrollment) students had the option of attending. As one instructor explains:

"So those courses ... should be learner-centered, not instructor-centered or, you know, institution-centered. And so toward that end ... we offer here the computer-based training coupled or complemented with the instructor-led training, which actually ... work very well together."

Over the 2 years that the CPSC 200 course has been running, the program administrator has added several face-to-face components to meet the needs of learners. He visited industry people at their work sites, assessed their employment needs, and reported back to the group at face-to-face orientation sessions. On the basis of his findings, he redesigned the lectures and activities to include a new focus on soft skills, which are in demand by the industry.

To provide learners with these soft skills, the instructors give face-to-face motivational lectures and require learners to do two face-to-face job interviews with managers as a practice job search at the beginning of the program. As one instructor said:

"They have to go out into industry, speak with and find out some key questions."

Students are also required to do a practicum and are monitored by instructors for "negative attitudes." These negative attitudes are shaped using strategies based on the methods used by American military academies. To quote one instructor:

"In basic training ... In military academies, like in the Armed Forces in the United States, they really give them a rough time or give them a kick and just yell and scream at them. It's like a boot camp initially. That's what we do to these people who come in here for project-based-training. ... We're trying to, in a sense, change their attitude right from the beginning and shape their behavior."

Frequent Updates of Curriculum and Tests

Because specifications in the industry are constantly changing, there is a need for almost constant updating of the course materials. Instructors struggle to keep up with these changes by updating the CBTs and keeping up with new materials. As one instructor said:

"I have been in the industry for three years. The industry actually tilted so much I had to retrain myself. There is a lot of uncertainty.

... Everything is constantly changing ... the curriculum is very, very dynamic."

Presumably, materials designers and test developers are also struggling to respond to short product cycles. The orientation manual admits to the presence of errors in the tests and gives students advice on how to deal with them. Both a student and an instructor interviewee mentioned that there were sometimes wrong answers in the answer keys, and the instructor described the tests as "nebulous," with the exams not closely tailored to the material (Qayyum & Bates, 1999). The short product cycles may explain the presence of errors in the testing materials and the nebulous nature of the course materials. In sum, because short product cycles leave the developers and instructors struggling to stay current, the curriculum is nebulous and the tests sometimes contain incorrect answers.

Lower Cost Savings

One would think that the dynamic nature of the curriculum and the presence of testing errors would make it important to have an on-site instructor who is an expert in the material and who can assist the students with these problems. One imagines that resolving these problems is important for sustaining the motivation of learners, especially those in continuous enrollment. The program administrator acknowledges that students need to ask someone, such as an instructor, for clarification when they are struggling, yet the core of the course is self-study. Interviewees said that the only thing that worked was interaction with the other students and that interaction with the teacher did not help "because I kept getting the wrong answers, or because the instructor was working on the lessons just ahead of the students, or lacked certification."
According to another student,

"[You] didn't find out it was wrong until [you] write your test, fail it .... One of the things that really upset me, actually, was two of the test questions were wrong and every time I went to the instructor [he] said they were right. Yeah, going through all that material I found out it was wrong to begin with ... so that was quite frustrating."

This may explain why learners depend on each other for support with their learning. This also has an unintended consequence regarding exam preparation. For those who engage in discussion groups on the web, answers to the exam questions are sometimes shared, a practice not encouraged by EduComp. As one of the learners said:

"People who've written exams and stuff share concepts and they discuss them, and this is all through the Internet. The students often access that on their own."

There is no information on how widespread this practice is, but it raises questions about the validity of the tests and the certification. In a previous course offering, EduComp had attempted to eliminate instructors, but student complaints forced them to bring the instructors back as facilitators.

Continuous Enrollment

The individual needs of the CPSC 200 (continuous-enrollment) learners are especially hard to meet because each one is at a different place in the curriculum at any given time. To make the lectures relevant for these learners, the instructor has to design each lecture so that it includes concepts from all six modules. For continuous-enrollment learners, obtaining help from other students who are in the classroom at the same time is not always a viable option. As one learner said:

"Because everybody's on different schedules . . . like for me, I sort of need someone with a gun to my head, so [laughter]. No, but you know what I mean . . . basically, motivation."

This learner, who was off work because of a work-related disability, took 1½ years to work through five of six modules. He was not happy with continuous enrollment and wanted more in-class training and set goals instead of self-pacing. Although an interview with one learner does not allow for generalizations, it does show that the continuous-enrollment model does not work for everyone.

CPSC 200: UNINTENDED CONSEQUENCES

- Fit with employment needs
- Access and flexibility
- Adding lectures
- Frequent updates of curriculum and tests
- Lower cost savings
- Continuous enrollment

Recommendations

In this case study, the recommendations include better alignment of the course and teaching materials and more remote access. EduComp was already aware of and improving these areas when this evaluation study was in process. EduComp responded to learner concerns by providing more and better technology and redesigned the course with many improvements. We have learned that the course has since been redesigned with technology as the centerpiece of a world-class true remote-access course, with web- and video-based technologies.

CPSC 200: RECOMMENDATIONS FOR COURSE IMPROVEMENT

- Revise testing materials
- More web-and video-based training

Note: EduComp was redesigning the course along these lines as our evaluation study was underway.

Summary

In conclusion, EduComp's belief in technology and mandate to cut costs led to a course implementation to which the response of learners to the CPSC 200 course is mixed. In an industry with short product cycles, materials require such frequent updating that it is difficult to keep up with change. As we have shown, a few unintended consequences surfaced in this course. First, licensing restrictions prevent learners from using the technology to work from home. Face-to-face components were reluctantly added in to satisfy learners, who needed help with the errors in the course tests. Instructors are perceived as poorly qualified, so students rely on each other for assistance and sometimes even for the answers to exams. Learners take on the instructor's role, even though they are not being paid for this work.

Next, information should be provided on the frequency with which the course materials and tests are updated and the kind of quality control that is done on the student tests. Third, data on salaries and employment rates of new graduates would address the criteria of relevance. A better estimate of costs to learners and the institution is needed. Only the cost items for tuition, books, exams parking, travel, and Internet rates were analyzed because of low response rates and missing data on other items (e.g., software, Internet connections). Finally, we were unable to collect data on program impact (i.e., how many of these learners found employment). Capturing these "downstream" effects are almost always difficult because of learner attrition and the difficulties in contacting graduates, who may have moved in search of employment. Nevertheless, if time and resources are available, these studies can sometimes yield highly worthwhile scientific evidence of the impact of the course on learners.

E-Learning: Professional Writing 110 (PWRIT 110)

Course Overview

Professional Writing 110 (PWRIT 110) is a print/online course in professional writing delivered to the supervisors and staff of a highly respected international, nonprofit organization. The course provider is dedicated to global distance education and e-learning. The course is supported by one-on-one tutoring via e-mail, and assignments are submitted and graded electronically. Operating on a cohort model, there are fixed starting dates for each cohort. Eight hundred staff members in field and regional offices in up to 70 countries had participated in the course when these data were collected for an internal evaluation study. Learners are expected to complete the course within 6 months, but extensions are granted where justified. When this evaluation was conducted, the course was in its first 2 years of operation.

Learner and Tutor Characteristics

To assess learner characteristics, we used data from a random sample of 39 learners drawn from the three cohorts for which data were available for this study. Thirty-six percent of learners were located in Africa, 20% in Eastern Europe, 15% in Western Asia, and the remainder in North America, Western Europe, and Eastern Asia. Together, these 39 students speak 26 different native languages.

The tutors were highly qualified: 28% had diplomas, 40% had bachelor's degrees, 24% had master's degrees, and 7% had PhDs. Each tutor had between seven and nine learners per cohort. The tutors' role is to comment on and evaluate learners' assignments electronically. Teaching takes place through tracked changes on student papers and tutors' notes or referrals to web-based resources. Tutors are hired on the basis of qualifications and are provided with three kinds of professional development: (1) semiannual workshops, (2) tutor toolbox, an electronic file of information, including tutor-marked assignments (TMAs), and (3) the monthly electronic discussion group. Learners are assessed on one assignment for Module 1 and one assignment for either Module 2 or 3. The tutors read and comment on these assignments and send them back to the learners with either a grade of Pass or a request to revise and resubmit. Scoring rubrics and sample student assignments set the standards for achievement. Learners have three chances to submit their assignments to earn a grade of Pass.

Course Objectives

The survey and interview findings showed that the course design has many strengths and that the objectives were clear to the learners: 95% of participants across four cohorts felt that the learning objectives were explicit and clear all or most of the time, over 95% could find course information in the course guide all or most of the time; and 96% felt that the course curriculum helped them understand what was expected from them.

The individualized nature of the course design is another major strength. The course is a "postmodern" course, where improvement is individualized and learners of widely different English writing skill levels can draw from the course whatever they need to meet their needs. The Pass/Incomplete grading system complements this focus by accommodating learners with a wide range of skill levels.

PWRIT 110: UNDERLYING VALUES

- Geographical reach
- Flexible access
- "Standard" English writing
- Respect for diversity

Course Materials

The manual consists of three modules, all of which focus on the "principles and strategies of successful workplace communication" (Ruhe, 2002a, p. 1). The objectives of Module 1 are to "solve problems requiring the application of written communication skills" (p. 1). Module 2 focuses on how to write general office correspondence such as memos, faxes, notes verbales, minutes, letters, and e-mails, while Module 3 focuses on writing reports. All participants are required to study Module 1 and then choose either Module 2 or Module 3.

Learner Satisfaction

The response of learners to the course was very positive: 95% of course participants across four cohorts felt that the organization and progression of the topics in this course were sensible and coherent; 96% across four cohorts felt that the sequencing of topics was coherent and logical; 96% across four cohorts felt that the assignments were specified sufficiently for them to know what to do for the assignment; 96% across four cohorts felt that the way this course is taught is appropriate for the material; and 92% across three cohorts felt each topic contained examples or activities that prompted them to use their own knowledge and experiences to understand the material.

As one learner said:

> "The manual is well-written, edited, formatted, the same for everyone."

The course materials are highly relevant to the workplace, which makes the activities and assignments meaningful. In their interviews, the learners said they appreciated the lessons on professional terminology, discriminatory language, grammatical structures such as parallelism, and concise language. One learner had this to say about the course manual:

> "It is 'really up to standard.' The ideas are well organized and . . . not much consultation with the dictionary. It was 'within reach.'"

Another said:

> "The course materials are good. The level of English and the workload were appropriate. The tutor's comments were helpful. I thought I did everything right on the first submission, but the tutor's comments drew my attention to things I didn't know. I learned a lot from the tutor's comments."

Ninety-seven percent said their course materials arrived well ahead of time or just in time, except for the September 2001 cohort, when only 73% said their course arrived early or just in time; 90% of course participants across four cohorts felt that the content materials for each topic were clear and easy to follow.

Geographical Reach

The course provides access to professional development for staff and supervisors in 70 countries as well as the flexibility they need to fit the course into their busy lives. One student interviewee said that there was a location near him where he could have taken a writing course in a face-to-face mode, but another stressed that, for staff on field missions, a globally delivered course is the only possible means of access. One learner said there were no writing courses available in the field offices. Another said:

> "The print/e-mail delivery method for the distance learning is very useful for developing the staff in the remote field office. It widens the eyes of the staff and it encourages participating in such courses. . . . In the remote field office there are neither writing courses nor good books for reference. In addition, some tutors recommended referring some books in the Internet . . . but in OCM Yangon, the Internet is not accessible."

Over 95% of course participants across the four cohorts felt that the communication modes enabled them to express their queries to the tutor and to submit and receive assignments all or almost all of the time. This figure fell to 87% for the September 2001 cohort, which reflects a decrease in e-mail connectivity experienced by tutors and learners after 9/11. On rare occasions, e-mails were not received by tutors or by course participants. One course administrator who was interviewed said that the problem affects less than 5% of e-mails. The course administrators identified three main reasons for this problem: (1) a hub address, (2) a bad connection, or (3) the line being down. A hub remote is a single machine that dials and sends and retrieves e-mails that are not distributed to individual e-mail IDs through the system. Course participants have to look them up on that particular machine or be sent a printed version of the message. It is conceivable that messages may be misdirected or deleted by mistake without the recipients' knowledge. In the countries in which the students are located, line connections may be slow and the quality unreliable. If the e-mail does not go through, a message to that effect will normally be received by the sender. However, this may not happen if there is a problem with the line, and tutors cannot always rely on a Failure notice being generated.

Completion Rates

Between December 2000 and April 2002, the average Pass rate was 75%. These rates are lower than the real Pass rates because learners on extensions were not counted, and these figures need to be adjusted to include their final grades.

Record Keeping

A broad range of formats were used for the management of student records, including both the filing of student assignments, copies of e-mails sent and received, and monthly progress reports (MPRs). Interviews with tutors revealed that most student records are paperless. Some who began with extensive paper records later moved mostly to an electronic format. Two course administrators, in North America and Europe, are linked by e-mail.

Two course advisors perform a quality control review of instructor-marked assignments at least once per cohort. All assignments marked by tutors for all course participants are submitted to the course administrator, who selects randomly for quality control checks. Tutors keep a detailed record of the work of course participants in their MPRs, which they are required to submit to the administration each month. The template for these reports was a 6-month calendar with space to track the dates of learners' e-mails and assignment submission and their grades. The MPRs record the dates of learners' assignment submissions, the parts submitted, grades, dates of e-mails, and feedback notes. The MPRs allow tutors to identify students who do not submit work or respond to e-mails in a timely manner. Tutors are expected to send learners a reminder letter once a week.

Assessment

Ninety-five percent of course participants across four cohorts felt that the assessment tasks helped them to develop knowledge and skills identified in the learning objectives; 92% across four cohorts felt that each topic provided activities for testing or self-monitoring their own learning. The responses to the item about course workload show more variation than the responses to the previous survey items. Between 50% and 60% of course participants across the four cohorts felt that the workload was too great all or most of the time, whereas a minority (between 13% and 33% across the four cohorts) felt it was too great very little or none of the time. All course participants across the four cohorts felt that (1) the tutor was interested in helping them to learn, (2) the feedback was helpful to their learning, and (3) the feedback on their work was provided promptly and normally not later than 2 weeks. Ninety-two percent of course participants across four cohorts felt that the tutor gave them individual help. All course participants across four cohorts felt that marked work was returned promptly, 92% felt that comments on their marked work indicated things they had done correctly or well, and 97% felt that comments on their marked work indicated the sorts of things they could do to improve.

Quality Assurance: TMAs

The course providers hired external course advisors to review TMAs to ensure that the tutors' comments on students' papers meet their high standards. First, tutors send a copy of all marked assignments for filing to the course administrator in Vancouver. At least once per cohort, the course administrator then selects two marked assignments at random and evaluates them for convergence with the ideal TMA. The ideal TMA is marked electronically using the tracking facility in MS Word and has footnoted comments that reflect a balance between language and communications skills. TMAs that are close to the model marked assignment receive higher scores, while others receive lower scores. Of a maximum score of 10, average scores range from 6.65 to 7.1.

Relevance

Ninety-five percent of course participants across four cohorts felt that the content of each topic was deliberately related to the workplace; 96% of course participants across four cohorts felt that the assigned written work improved their writing and analytical skills. As one learner said:

> "It was very, very relevant. It was really, really relevant. When I went through the course, it gave me a lot of opportunity to make progression on documents I've been working on. . . . Like it provided a general framework for how to write a report."

Interviewees said they appreciated receiving instruction in strategies for clear and simple writing, in contrast to the more traditional, formal style of workplace communication. One tutor said:

"Students become more aware of expressing themselves in a concise way. Of everything, that seems to be what they get the most. The biggest improvement is clarity . . . [and] better paragraphing and major and minor points."

Another tutor said that all of her feedback indicated that the students "felt gratitude about the course and this was really worthwhile." Students who completed persisted because of their interest in the subject matter, to obtain the certificate for which the study costs were paid by the organization, and to earn promotions. One participant mentioned that the course enhanced his motivation because his employer recognizes professional development efforts in their promotion decisions: "It's a feather in my cap."

PWRIT 110: SCIENTIFIC EVIDENCE

Surveys and interviews with learners and instructors on these topics:
- Learner satisfaction: course materials, tutor feedback, etc.
- Relevance to professional needs

Counts and percentages:
- Count of learners by staff ranks and tutors by educational credentials
- Geographical reach: numbers of countries
- Completion rates: numbers of learners by number of months to complete
- Quality assurance: average TMA scores

Negative Unintended Consequences

Course Noncompletion

Learners who did not complete the course did so because of circumstances beyond their control (e.g., war, floods, pregnancy, illness, surgery, transfer). In Afghanistan, some learners continued to study "even as the bombs were falling around them" but were eventually overwhelmed. According to one tutor, several students caught in the aftermath of 9/11 received 6-month extensions but did not complete the course because of time pressures and stress from "the kind of work they do." One of the students was transferred from Tanzania to Pakistan to deal with the refugee crisis. In the MPRs, it was difficult to find even a single case of noncompletion that could not be explained by events beyond the learner's control.

Although some interviewees perceived the course as flexible because of the Pass/Fail grading and the 6-month completion time, two perceived the course as stressful. Their profession brings heavy and often erratic schedules, transfers to remote locations, and the need for stress leave. Two student interviewees said that they did not receive any release time at work to study the course. One said that in Africa there is the cultural expectation that time must given to family commitments, which cannot be set aside to work on a course.

> "Because of the intensity of the job, . . . I get up at 5:30 A.M. . . . and don't get home until 8:00 P.M. every day. What time will you have to study? I'm living in Africa and have other family commitments."

Another student in Georgia said:

> "I never had time to work on the course during my working hours. I was daily working at home. In Georgia we have a terrible problems with electricity. Even now I don't have electricity and water but I managed to do it because I want to."

Learner Nonresponse

The tutors provide students with the motivation to persist in learning at a distance. As one tutor said:

> "With e-mail, you're working in the dark. They haven't responded. Should I be indignant, concerned? If someone confesses they're lacking confidence and don't have time, then I'll go into high support mode. My role is support and feedback and maintaining motivation."

Another tutor said she teaches grammar more than is recommended in the course because her students have said they appreciated it. Two tutors said they supplemented material in the course manual with materials they had designed themselves.

Positive Unintended Consequences

Quality Assurance

There were several unexpected positive unintended consequences. First, the TMA review process functions as a professional development opportunity for tutors. Tutors are given samples of marked student assignments with tutor comments that represent the ideal in terms of tone, focus, and relative emphasis on language versus communication skills and format (footnotes in the text, with comments underneath the student's work). All of the tutor interviewees felt that a quality assurance mechanism was a major strength of the course. Although one tutor said he found it "disconcerting" that he was "being observed"—"It's like a face-to-face classroom visit"—he acknowledged that it was important to establish consistency and to ensure that tutors' comments were not "all over the place."

Rejuvenating Effects of the Tutor Listserv

Finally, the monthly tutor discussion group provided not only regular professional development opportunity for tutors but also "a community." With predetermined time boundaries, it did not "drag on indefinitely" but "rejuvenated itself" during the last week of each month, which made the discussions especially effective. There was also considerable linking among postings, making the discussions a "multi-logue" among tutors for the purpose of improving their tutoring practice.

PWRIT 110: UNINTENDED CONSEQUENCES

Negative:
- Course noncompletion
- Learner nonresponse

Positive:
- Quality assurance
- Rejuvenating effects of the tutor listserv

Recommendations

Revise the Course

Comments from tutors and learners show that Module 1 works well for most learners, but some needed more clarification about the instructions and activities for Module 1. A few seem to be confused about the requirements. One learner said:

> "From the beginning it was difficult to know what to do."

A few learners wrote the answers to all the activities, sent them to tutors, and were told that they were not required. Another learner said some activities "distracted from the main point." Finally, more sample or model compositions might help learners who were confused by unfamiliar cultural assumptions and expectations.

One learner suggested that the course have two levels: one for intermediate-level English writers and a second for those who already have advanced writing skills. According to one of the course administrators, this approach would require a more rigorous method of testing learners and may create unanticipated effects such as challenging by students of their assigned levels. As it is, the course was designed in a way to meet the needs of all learners, who can draw from it the teaching points that meet their individual needs. Finally, one learner suggested that the course expand its scope to include more documents from other units in the organization to provide a more complete coverage of the kind of content found in correspondence and reports.

Create a Pool of Reminder Letters

The importance of regular and frequent contact with tutors was a recurring theme throughout the interviews. Because so many learners are juggling multiple and often unexpected responsibilities and stressful workloads, tutors need to send out frequent reminder letters to students, and course administrators should ask tutors to do this. Otherwise, a few learners may forget the deadline for course submissions and find that they cannot complete the work because the deadline has passed. One recommendation is to create a pool of reminder letters from which tutors could draw to send out reminders. This suggestion found its way into a tutor listserv, which generated a discussion about reminder notes. The listserv provided a valuable mechanism to implement tutors' suggestions, thereby enhancing the quality of the course.

Grant More Extensions

A recommendation for greater approval of extensions was a common theme in the interviews with learners. One learner said that the main weakness of the course was the 6-month duration, and he recommended an 8-month duration. Learners felt that extensions should be granted to those who cannot complete the course in time because of heavy workloads. This would allow them to complete at their own convenience and to write a better product.

PWRIT 110: RECOMMENDATIONS FOR COURSE IMPROVEMENT

- Revise the course.
- Create a pool of reminder letters.
- Grant more extensions.
- Have face-to-face follow-up meetings.

Have Face-to-Face Follow-Up Meetings

Another recommendation is for the learners in the same geographical location to meet at a central place to debrief and to plan a strategy and activities for the group to continue working on the course. The reader should note that the course was designed to achieve better cost efficiency than face-to-face courses. However, there were cases in which learners in the same office formed study groups. Attempts by learners to create online learning communities appear to have been less successful, most likely because of cultural preferences for e-mailing the tutor, who is the "expert."

Summary

In conclusion, participants were very satisfied with PWRIT 110. The high satisfaction ratings on almost all items on the survey of course participants indicate that learners perceive the course to be highly successful in delivering high-quality instructional materials and feedback to learners in remote locations in 70 countries around the world. There was an enthusiastic consensus among tutors, administrators, and participants that the course is highly successful. As a system, the course functions remarkably smoothly, with almost no unintended consequence. Noncompletion rates are low, and in almost all cases, noncompletion resulted from the interference of factors beyond the students' control, including war, floods, abrupt and overwhelming changes in staff workloads, reassignment, pregnancy, illness, and surgery.

In sum, the high quality of PWRIT 110 rests on simple technology, a highly relevant and situation-specific course manual, highly qualified and dedicated course administrators, designers and tutors, dedicated learners, and a supportive culture of writing within the organization. By providing instruction and feedback to learners who are often in remote field offices in 70 countries, the course achieves its goal of geographical reach, presumably at considerable cost savings over face-to-face delivery. Finally, there is a very nearly paperless record-keeping system on the part of both course administrators and tutors.

Conclusions

In this chapter, we took the unfolding model on a "test drive" and showed how it was used to evaluate Computing Science 200, a distance learning course, and Professional Writing 110, an e-learning course. In this overview, we used the unfolding model to evaluate two very different courses. The first was a CD-ROM course delivered to learners in North America and the second an e-mail-based course delivered across 10 time zones. For both courses, we presented scientific evidence in the form of learner satisfaction surveys and interviews about the course components. We have also shown how differently underlying values and unintended consequences played themselves out in the two courses. In Computing Science 200, learners needed more technology to provide better remote access and help with the mandated tests in order to pass the course. As the evaluation study was in progress, this course was already being redesigned to incorporate these improvements. In Professional Writing 110, there were almost no unintended negative consequences, but a few positive unintended consequences did emerge. We believe that this outcome was a result of using e-mail, which is a mature and simple technology, as well as very careful course design and implementation procedures by professional course designers.

The Dynamic, Adaptive Nature of the Unfolding Model

By applying the unfolding model, we produced two comprehensive evaluation reports. Both reports included survey and interview findings, as well as an analysis of values (course objectives and underlying theories) and unintended consequences. The dynamic nature of the unfolding model is shown in the overlap among the four boxes; for example, the type of scientific evidence collected varied in response to the different needs and interests of stakeholders. The PWRIT 100 report included a summary of tutor qualifications, quality assurance procedures, and criteria for evaluating tutors, which were not needed in CPSC 200. We reported completion rates and average TMA quality scores for PWRIT 100, but these data were not reported in the evaluation study of CPSC 200 where the focus was on learner satisfaction. Second, the differences in these two case reports show how you can tailor the unfolding model to collect diverse kinds of scientific evidence that meets the diverse needs of stakeholders and still provides a comprehensive assessment of merit and worth.

CHAPTER 9

■ ■ ■ ■ ■ ■ ■ ■ ■

Bringing It All Together

In the first two chapters, we discussed the need for a comprehensive, professional model of program evaluation in distance education. In Chapter 2, we showed that Messick's (1989) framework is a comprehensive, unifying omnibus model for classifying professional program evaluation approaches, all of which are based on scientific evidence, values, and consequences but that differ in their relative emphasis. With this common conceptual core, assessment and program evaluation overlap and are not really distinct fields. Both fields deal with the determination of merit, worth, or value, and both tests and programs are sets of educational activities oriented toward a goal, which is Wholey's (1987) definition of a program.

In Chapter 3, we provided an overview of evaluation theory and practice in distance education. We also showed that some evaluation models in distance education and e-learning have been based on scientific evidence, values, and consequences. We also showed that many authentic distance education evaluation studies have identified a surprising array of unintended consequences.

In Chapter 4, we discussed Messick's (1989) very insightful theoretical analysis of evidence, values, and unintended consequences. We then took his framework from the field of assessment and applied it to a new area: program evaluation. To adapt his framework to distance education, we offered the unfolding model as a conceptual bridge between professional program evaluation and distance education. In Chapters 5 to 7, we discussed the practice of evaluation and ways to use the unfolding model to conduct evaluation studies. In Chapter 8, we showed how our model performed in a "test drive" by applying it to an authentic distance course and an authentic e-learning course, presenting our empirical findings and making specific recommendations for course improvement. In this final chapter, we summarize key points and discuss future directions for distance education and e-learning and the implications for the unfolding model.

Using Messick's Framework to Evaluate Distance and E-Learning Courses

In this book, we have revised Messick's framework into an adaptive, dynamic framework for the evaluation of distance and e-learning courses. Messick's (1989) framework is a four-faceted conception of the validity, or merit and worth, of standardized tests. As such, his framework is within the realm of assessment, a field focused on student achievement, tests of attitude and performance, and psychometrics. Messick's framework was devised to guide the test validation process, that is, to guide studies conducted to determine the merit and worth of educational and psychological tests. Even so, there has been increasing interest in its application to distance education (Bunderson, 2003; Chapelle, Jamieson, & Hegelheimer, 2003; Ruhe, 2002b; Ruhe & Zumbo, 2006). In this book, we have shown that scientific evidence, values, and consequences are overarching criteria of merit and worth in both professional test validation and program evaluation models. Therefore, Messick's model provides us with a conceptual bridge between assessment and program evaluation. We have also shown that distance and e-learning courses consist of various components and can be evaluated as though they were programs. We believe that Messick's (1989) framework may be suited more to program evaluation than to the context from which it emerged, that is, assessment, where practical difficulties in using the framework in evaluation practice can occasionally be encountered (e.g., Green, 1998).

> Evidence, values, and consequences are the three corners of assessment that recur in program evaluation, and a comprehensive evaluation of distance courses requires an investigation of all three areas.

Using the Unfolding Model to Evaluate Your Courses

The unfolding model is an adaptive, dynamic framework that provides a conceptual road map to guide evaluation studies in distance education and e-learning. In this book, we have shown that an investigation of scientific evidence, values, and consequences is essential to our approach, but you are free to choose from among the many tools provided within each of these areas of merit and worth. Mixed methods is essential to our approach because survey data provide breadth and credibility while qualitative data provide richness and depth. Surveys and interviews on learner satisfaction are the most basic scientific evidence, whereas other types of evidence such as grades and completion rates should be collected only if you and the stakeholders feel they can be obtained. The facet of relevance encompasses (1) alignment between the course and the needs of society, (2) meaningfulness of the course to learners, and (3) the transfer of learning to authentic contexts. A cost–benefit analysis, which can focus on costs to learners or costs to the university, is recommended but not essential to our approach. Some investigation of values and consequences, however, *is* essential to our approach. Values can be found in the course outline, course textbook, and other documents that lay out the goals and objectives of the course, that is, the *intended* course implementation. Unintended consequences tend to emerge mostly in the analysis stage, as you compare quantitative with qualitative data and analyze "fit" across the four aspects

> In the unfolding model, each facet expands to show diverse data sources, which are not essential, but optional, depending on your course. Beyond surveys and interviews of learner satisfaction, you have considerable latitude in choosing which kind of scientific evidence to collect. Your choice depends on your technologies, course design, purpose of your evaluation study, and the needs and interests of stakeholders.

of value. Unintended consequences can be instructional or social, negative or positive, and are important because they lead to recommendations for course improvement.

Conducting Your Evaluation Study

In our approach, a distance course is a "stand-alone" case study, and mixed methods are used to obtain a comprehensive assessment of merit and worth. Before you begin your study, you need to make some planning decisions, obtain written approval or exemption from your university's Institutional Review Board for the Protection of Human Subjects, and align your procedures with the Joint Standards for Program Evaluation. You will be using mixed methods as equal and parallel methods but will also need to select the data sources that are most appropriate for your course. To enhance credibility, you should use random and stratified sampling, write good survey items, control for researcher bias, and use triangulation, memo-ing, and audit trails. Your analysis of fit will lead to recommendations for course improvement, which you should discuss with stakeholders before writing up your final report based on the outline in Chapter 7.

WHAT ARE THE BENEFITS OF USING THE UNFOLDING MODEL?

- Brings Messick's (1989, 1998) keen theoretical insights into distance education.
- Organizes and connects empirical findings in a coherent way.
- Brings forward rich findings that might otherwise have been dispersed, hidden, or in the background.
- Offers a contemporary approach to values, that is, value pluralism.
- Easy to use to guide evaluation practice in distance education and e-learning.
- An adaptive and dynamic approach applicable to any course or technology.

What Have We Learned from Two Case Studies?

When we used the unfolding model to guide evaluation studies of two authentic courses, surprising findings emerged, providing a comprehensive assessment of merit and worth. We now weave our theoretical insights into our empirical findings to provide an overview of the contribution of the unfolding model.

Underlying Values

In our two case studies, underlying values emerged into the foreground where they could be carefully scrutinized. As our findings have shown, values permeate meaning and consequences in subtle ways (Messick, 1989). Distance/e-learning courses reflect both underlying learning theories and theories about the use of technology and institutional missions. Some courses may not rest on a singular value basis but on multiple value bases. In distance education, multiple and diverse sets of values underlie the theories and use of technology, learning theories, course objectives, choices made by course designers, and motives for developing postsecondary courses. Comparing the very different value bases underlying our two case studies in Chapter 8 provides us with a better understanding of the diversity of values underlying distance/e-learning courses.

In PWRIT 110, there was an absence of rhetoric, although the course was highly successful. Investigating underlying values in the evaluation of distance/e-learning courses brings the contrast between the vision and the reality to the foreground. Armed with this knowledge, course designers can identify and implement changes to bring the reality closer to the vision or perhaps extend the vision in response to new technological developments.

CPCS 200 is based on an ideology of service to learners but also on unrealized potential of the benefits of technology. Underlying this course is the value of cost relative to benefit, with the balance tilted in favor of the former. PWRIT 110 was based on an ideology of a single common standard of correct English and the importance of clear, concise communication in a diverse, global workplace. Yet there was a need to balance this goal with respect for local variations of English from learners from diverse linguistic and cultural backgrounds. The solution was a postmodern approach to grading, that is, a system-based value pluralism, where learners were graded relative to where they began, not to each other, and where the emphasis was on organization and concise language, not on the details of grammar. Finally, as evaluators, we do not need to camouflage, dismiss, or "force" a kind of consistency on programs that reflect these kinds of underlying tensions. Instead, we can be sensitive enough to recognize them, allow them to emerge, and document their emergence.

The Tension between Facts and Values

Finally, we need to see how conflicts among facts and values play themselves out, how these tensions pull the course in different directions, and what adjustments need to be made to the course. With CPCS 200, there was a tension between EduComp's goal to cut costs and the learners' preferences for an instructor. The values underlying CPCS 200 came into conflict with the rapid updating of materials and tests and the needs of learners, a tension that was likely resolved in the subsequent course design.

Unintended Consequences

With CPCS 200, we found lack of flexibility because of licensing arrangements, the reluctant addition of face-to-face components in response to learner complaints, learner dissatisfaction with the errors in the tests, and the elimination of qualified instructors. These unintended consequences appear to have had compounding effects. With PWRIT 110, no substantive negative consequences were identified, except for interruptions in e-mail delivery after 9/11 and resistance to European cultural expectations around workload. One positive unintended consequence was that some learners formed online study groups with others on their own initiative.

> In our evaluation of two authentic postsecondary courses, the unfolding model brought forward several unintended consequences. These effects were not trivial and did not result from a mistaken *implementation* of these courses but from implementing these courses *exactly* as they were supposed to be implemented.

Recommendations for Course Improvement

With CPCS 200, the course provider was already redesigning the course to address the same issues raised by the evaluation study and to maximize the learning opportunities provided by technology. With PWRIT 110, we recommended biweekly e-mail reminder messages, drawn from a pool of such letters, to keep learners on track, and reduce the number of noncompleters.

E-Learning and Beyond:
Is the Unfolding Model the Last Word?

The Dynamic Nature of the Unfolding Model

In response to the question, "Is the unfolding model the last word?," the answer is "no." First, it is generally accepted wisdom among program evaluators that "there is no single best model or method to carry out evaluations" (Stufflebeam & Shinkfield, 2007, p. 7). Second, before this book appeared in print, our adapted framework had already undergone three prior design iterations. Ruhe's (2002b, 2003) models, for example, are "bare-bones" one-level adaptations of Messick's (1989) model. The first was developed to validate technology-based assessment tasks, whereas the second was developed to evaluate instructional programs. Both of these early models relied heavily on Messick's (1989) terminology. Ruhe and Zumbo's (2006) model was also developed to validate technology-based assessment tasks in a globally delivered online course. All of these prior iterations culminated in our unfolding model, which could be used either to validate assessment tasks or evaluate instructional programs. Similarly, evaluators may wish to add categories to the unfolding model that meet their particular evaluation needs. For example, blended learning can foster a greater sense of "localness" on the part of colleges and universities (Mayadas, Alfred P. Sloan Foundation, & Picciano, 2007). *Localness* is a term used at the Alfred P. Sloan Foundation as part of a new funding initiative to support academic programs designed to strengthen a college or university connection to its core constituencies. Therefore, some measure of localness could be a criteria of merit and worth that an evaluator might wish to add to the unfolding model.

Variations of the Unfolding Model

As various iterations of our framework emerged, so did more questions. For example, does scientific evidence belong under only one category or could it belong under more than one category? Does the category or categories in which overlapping concepts are placed matter? What are the strengths and limitations of placing any term in one box instead of another? Which boxes should one choose, and does it matter? Can the framework be used to evaluate interventions as well as courses? Would the model perform equally well? Would the findings be as rich? Future applications of our framework in diverse technological and pedagogical contexts are needed to address these kinds of questions and to validate or extend our model.

In sum, the power of our unfolding model is that it is dynamic and will continue to evolve in response to new technologies.

The Future of Distance Education and E-Learning

Messick (1988) predicted that the curriculum of the future would be learner centered and that course content would be "personalized," "adaptive," and "dynamic." Although these trends have been ushered in by Web 1.0, they will accelerate considerably under Web 2.0. Today, the web is moving away from an architecture of presentation to an architecture of participation, as learners upload their videos to "very popular and massively distributed websites such as Amazon, Wikipedia, My Space, You Tube, and a rapidly growing number of personal weblogs, or blogs, as well as downloadable video and audio podcasts" (Sinclair et al., 2006, p. 6). The cost of broadband will continue to fall, broadband penetration will increase, and "there will be an increase in devices that can access the Internet and a convergence of capabilities" (Watson, 2007, p. 23). New applications are evolving, including professional development for teachers (Watson, 2007), corporate training (Bendus, 2005), and opportunities for senior citizens (Awalt, 2007).

> Just as learners modify content in Wikipedia, course developers may find they need to select from, tailor, or even modify the unfolding model in response to new technological learning environments. We support and encourage this practice and look forward to ever evolving modifications of our framework.

The Future of the Unfolding Model

The power of our unfolding model is precisely its adaptive and dynamic nature, which means that it can continue to be applied to new e-learning course designs from "Web 1.0 and Learning Environments 1.0 to Web 2.0 and Learning Environments 2.0" (Sinclair et al., 2006, p. 6). In the future, we expect to see the unfolding model adapted to new and diverse contexts. In the new environments of Web 2.0, we expect to see new iterations and multiple variations of the unfolding model. New technologies, roles, and categories keep evolving, requiring us to continuously reconceptualize even the most robust constructs such as learner satisfaction or peer interaction. For example, Sener and Humbert (2003) reconceptualized learner satisfaction as two distinct constructs, one for online and one for blended learning environments; these constructs are distinct just as wilderness camping is distinct from car camping. Another future development is more longitudinal studies to evaluate the long-term results of online learning, more large-scale studies (Sener & Humbert, 2003), and more longitudinal, multilevel studies (Rumberger, 2003). The future may also see more work on setting quality standards and on the alignment of standards across universities at the level of tests (Cizek & Bunch, 2007), curricula, and programs. This trend is already underway with the U.S. Department of Education and the Spellings Commission. Finally, we believe the unfolding model would also be useful at the program level, where a blending of technologies and delivery methods frequently occurs. The point we want to make is that evaluators can continuously adapt the unfolding model in response to these new evaluation needs and continue to use insights from current literature to inform and advance the use of the unfolding model.

Conclusions

As distance education evolves into e-learning, there is a need for a dynamic evaluation framework that provides a comprehensive assessment of the merit and worth of innovative educational experiences. Our framework responds to recurring calls (e.g., Rumble, 1981) to adopt a professional approach to evaluation in distance education. Messick's (1989) framework, consisting of fewer than 20 words, can be used as a professional omnibus model to classify professional program evaluation theories. Based on Messick's (1989) framework, the unfolding model brings these same theoretical insights into distance education. First, our framework brings learner response, costs, relevance, unintended consequences, underlying values, and unintended consequences (and their interaction) into the foreground. The plurality of values resonates with the approach to values and consequences in the contemporary approaches to program evaluation based on impact and value pluralism. In this way, our framework provides a comprehensive and adaptive assessment of the merit and worth of distance instructional programs.

Our findings from using our framework to guide two authentic postsecondary courses have demonstrated the benefits of our framework as a model to guide the evaluation of distance programs. The unfolding model merges the fields of distance education and program evaluation and brings the insights of the latter into the former, with a view to improving the quality of evaluation practice. With our framework, we can be advocates for consumers and provide them with engaging, "world-class" educational experiences.

Finally, the real power of the unfolding model lies in its unfolding or dynamic nature. Our model is not only comprehensive but also flexible because it can be tailored to specific evaluation contexts, as recommended by Rossi et al. (1999). As distance learning evolves into the next wave of technological development, e-learning is shifting from an architecture of presentation to an architecture of participation, which takes the culture of collaboration far beyond our current educational models (Sinclair et al., 2006). Just as registered users modify and adapt encyclopedia entries in Wikipedia, so we expect and encourage evaluators to adapt our unfolding model to accommodate relentless and unprecedented changes expected in distance education, "e-learning and beyond" (Sinclair et al., 2006, p. 1).

APPENDIX A

■ ■ ■ ■ ■ ■ ■ ■ ■

Summary of the 1994
Program Evaluation Standards

Utility Standards

The utility standards are intended to ensure that an evaluation will serve the information needs of intended users.

U1 Stakeholder Identification   Persons involved in or affected by the evaluation should be identified, so that their needs can be addressed.

U2 Evaluator Credibility   The persons conducting the evaluation should be both trustworthy and competent to perform the evaluation, so that the evaluation findings achieve maximum credibility and acceptance.

U3 Information Scope and Selection   Information collected should be broadly selected to address pertinent questions about the program and be responsive to the needs and interests of clients and other specified stakeholders.

U4 Values Identification   The perspectives, procedures, and rationale used to interpret the findings should be carefully described, so that the bases for value judgments are clear.

Source: Joint Committee on Standards for Educational Evaluation (*www.wmich.edu/evalctr/ jc*). These standards are currently under revision, and the third edition is expected in 2009. The draft version of the revised standards is available at: *www.wmich.edu/evalctr/jc*, the website of the Joint Committee on Standards for Educational Evaluation.

U5 Report Clarity Evaluation reports should clearly describe the program being evaluated, including its context, and the purposes, procedures, and findings of the evaluation, so that essential information is provided and easily understood.

U6 Report Timeliness and Dissemination Significant interim findings and evaluation reports should be disseminated to intended users, so that they can be used in a timely fashion.

U7 Evaluation Impact Evaluations should be planned, conducted, and reported in ways that encourage follow-through by stakeholders, so that the likelihood that the evaluation will be used is increased.

Feasibility Standards

The feasibility standards are intended to ensure that an evaluation will be realistic, prudent, diplomatic, and frugal.

F1 Practical Procedures The evaluation procedures should be practical, to keep disruption to a minimum while needed information is obtained.

F2 Political Viability The evaluation should be planned and conducted with anticipation of the different positions of various interest groups, so that their cooperation may be obtained, and so that possible attempts by any of these groups to curtail evaluation operations or to bias or misapply the results can be averted or counteracted.

F3 Cost Effectiveness The evaluation should be efficient and produce information of sufficient value, so that the resources expended can be justified.

Propriety Standards

The propriety standards are intended to ensure that an evaluation will be conducted legally, ethically, and with due regard for the welfare of those involved in the evaluation, as well as those affected by its results.

P1 Service Orientation Evaluations should be designed to assist organizations to address and effectively serve the needs of the full range of targeted participants.

P2 Formal Agreements Obligations of the formal parties to an evaluation (what is to be done, how, by whom, when) should be agreed to in writing, so that these parties are obligated to adhere to all conditions of the agreement or formally to renegotiate it.

P3 Rights of Human Subjects   Evaluations should be designed and conducted to respect and protect the rights and welfare of human subjects.

P4 Human Interactions   Evaluators should respect human dignity and worth in their interactions with other persons associated with an evaluation, so that participants are not threatened or harmed.

P5 Complete and Fair Assessment   The evaluation should be complete and fair in its examination and recording of strengths and weaknesses of the program being evaluated, so that strengths can be built upon and problem areas addressed.

P6 Disclosure of Findings   The formal parties to an evaluation should ensure that the full set of evaluation findings along with pertinent limitations are made accessible to the persons affected by the evaluation and any others with expressed legal rights to receive the results.

P7 Conflict of Interest   Conflict of interest should be dealt with openly and honestly, so that it does not compromise the evaluation processes and results.

P8 Fiscal Responsibility   The evaluator's allocation and expenditure of resources should reflect sound accountability procedures and otherwise be prudent and ethically responsible, so that expenditures are accounted for and appropriate.

Accuracy Standards

The accuracy standards are intended to ensure that an evaluation will reveal and convey technically adequate information about the features that determine worth or merit of the program being evaluated.

A1 Program Documentation   The program being evaluated should be described and documented clearly and accurately, so that the program is clearly identified.

A2 Context Analysis   The context in which the program exists should be examined in enough detail, so that its likely influences on the program can be identified.

A3 Described Purposes and Procedures   The purposes and procedures of the evaluation should be monitored and described in enough detail, so that they can be identified and assessed.

A4 Defensible Information Sources   The sources of information used in a program evaluation should be described in enough detail, so that the adequacy of the information can be assessed.

A5 Valid Information   The information-gathering procedures should be chosen or developed and then implemented so that they will assure that the interpretation arrived at is valid for the intended use.

A6 Reliable Information   The information-gathering procedures should be chosen or developed and then implemented so that they will assure that the information obtained is sufficiently reliable for the intended use.

A7 Systematic Information   The information collected, processed, and reported in an evaluation should be systematically reviewed, and any errors found should be corrected.

A8 Analysis of Quantitative Information   Quantitative information in an evaluation should be appropriately and systematically analyzed so that evaluation questions are effectively answered.

A9 Analysis of Qualitative Information   Qualitative information in an evaluation should be appropriately and systematically analyzed so that evaluation questions are effectively answered.

A10 Justified Conclusions   The conclusions reached in an evaluation should be explicitly justified, so that stakeholders can assess them.

A11 Impartial Reporting   Reporting procedures should guard against distortion caused by personal feelings and biases of any party to the evaluation, so that evaluation reports fairly reflect the evaluation findings.

A12 Metaevaluation   The evaluation itself should be formatively and summatively evaluated against these and other pertinent standards, so that its conduct is appropriately guided and, on completion, stakeholders can closely examine its strengths and weaknesses.

APPENDIX B
■ ■ ■ ■ ■ ■ ■ ■ ■ ■

Glossary

Accreditation: "the process by which an organization grants approval of institutions such as schools, universities and hospitals" (Fitzpatrick et al., 2004, p. 214).

Applets: mini-software web-based applications, written in Java, for example, animations such as a moving ticker tape of stock prices (Helicon Publishing, 2008).

Approach: theoretical conceptions or models to guide evaluation studies.

Architecture of participation: a major characteristic of Web 2.0. Web users contribute to growing pools of information, becoming codevelopers of websites and citizen-producers and publishers, working in a range of media (Sinclair, McClaren, & Griffin, 2006).

Architecture of presentation: a major characteristic of Web 1.0. Learners find information on the web and download it without changing anything at the website (Sinclair, McClaren, & Griffin, 2006).

Assessment: a formal, systematic attempt using instruments such as paper-and-pencil tests, portfolios, or checklists to determine the status of students with respect to knowledge, skills, or attitudes (Popham, 1995).

Asynchronous: "used to describe a situation where learners and instructor are not in communication at the same time (e.g., Internet-based or videotaped courses" (South Central Regional Library Council Distance Learning Glossary, 2002, p. 1).

Bias: a tendency to "read" one's own expectations into the analysis of data, thereby confirming one's prior beliefs.

Blackboard: "a suite of enterprise software products and services that power a total "e-education infrastructure" for schools, colleges, universities, etc." (South Central Regional Library Council Distance Learning Glossary, 2002, p. 1).

Blended learning: a blend of distance and direct contact. See hybrid learning.

Case studies: in an evaluation study, each course is a case or unit of analysis.

Checklists: a list of desirable attributes, for example, webpage evaluation and instructor competencies.

Consequential basis: the two lower boxes (underlying values and unintended consequences) of the unfolding model.

Consortia: an affiliation of organizations around a common purpose. Universities may form a consortia to pool their resources and expand their distance delivery.

Cost–benefit: with relevance, the upper right box of the unfolding model. A mathematical analysis in which the costs of a course are compared with benefits. Costs can include (1) costs to the university and (2) costs to learners. Benefits in an educational context can be quantified as outcomes (e.g., grade point average or percentage of learners who complete).

Course components: the various pieces or parts of a course, for example, instructor, textbook, online discussions, assessment tasks.

Course implementation: the day-to-day delivery of the course.

Credibility: the trustworthiness or persuasive power of your evaluation report. Can be enhanced by strategies such as an audit trail, random sampling, and triangulation.

Criterion–referenced tests: tests in which points are given for meeting specific performance criteria.

Data sources: any source of data, including documents, surveys and questionnaires, interviews, and focus groups.

Deductive: using categories from an evaluation framework to code qualitative data.

Degree or diploma mills: organizations that have not been accredited and that offer online degrees that have little credibility or public acceptance.

Delivery methods: options for delivering instruction (e.g., lecture, text, video, Internet).

Digital: in electronics and computing, a term meaning "coded as numbers." A digital system uses two-state, either on–off or high–low voltage pulses, to encode, receive, and transmit information (Helicon Publishing, 2008).

Digital set-top box: box containing decoding equipment for satellite or cable television broadcasts. Such boxes represent a means of linking television sets to a network such as the Internet, enabling people to browse the worldwide web using their televisions as the monitor or to view video on demand (Helicon Publishing, 2008).

Distance education: "a generic, all-inclusive term used to refer to the physical separation of teachers and learners" (Schlosser & Simonson, 2006, p. 65).

Distance learning: "the desired outcome of distance education" (Willis & University of Idaho Engineering Outreach Staff, 2006, p. 1).

Dynamic: the quality of evolving, changing, and adapting. A characteristic of both educational technologies and the unfolding model.

Educational programs: educational phenomenon including "curriculum materials and other replicable instructional sequences" (Popham, 1993, p. 8). By this definition, a postsecondary course is a kind of program and the principles of program evaluation apply.

E-learning: "any learning that uses a network (LAN, WAN, or Internet) for delivery, interaction, or facilitation."

Ethics: conducting evaluation and research practice in accordance with federal laws on the protection of human subjects of research, which are reflected in your university's policies for the protection of human subjects.

Evaluation: an attempt to judge the worth, value, or quality of something (Coldeway, 1988).

Evaluation model: a theoretical framework, with a diagram including boxes or arrows, intended to guide evaluation studies.

Evaluation practice: collecting and analyzing data and making evaluative conclusions.

Feedback: instructor comments on student assignments, tests, quizzes and exams.

Focus group: a group of individuals who discuss their perceptions of the course in a group lead by a facilitator. Can be face-to-face or online.

Formative evaluation: "appraisals of quality focused on instructional programs that are still capable of being modified" (Popham, 1993, p. 13).

Human–computer interaction: use of the web, podcasting, and other computer-based methods of work.

Hybrid delivery: combining a traditional face-to-face classroom setting with online components, such as the syllabus, grade book, exams, and supplemental documents. These components can be delivered via the Internet through a *learning management system*, such as Blackboard (South Central Regional Library Council Distance Learning Glossary, 2002).

Individualized learning: a method of learning that leads the learner to proceed at his or her own pace. The content may also be tailored to the individual learner's needs. Delivery methods include correspondence, computer-based training, independent learning, etc. (South Central Regional Library Council Distance Learning Glossary, 2002).

Inductive: instead of using coding categories from a framework, coding categories emerge from the analysis of qualitative data.

Institutional review board (IRB): university committees that review and exempt research and evaluation proposals in accordance with federal regulations for the protection of human subjects.

Instructional design: the systematic process of translating general principles of learning and instruction into plans for instructional materials and learning (South Central Regional Library Council Distance Learning Glossary, 2002).

Interactive media: new technology such as CD-ROM and online systems that allow users to interact with other users or to choose their own path through the material (Helicon Publishing, 2008).

Interactive television (iTV): a combination of video and computer technology in which the user's actions, choices, and decisions affect the way in which the program unfolds.

Interview protocols: a set of interview questions.

Joint Standards on Evaluation: standards or applied ethics of professional conduct for evaluators developed by the Joint Committee on Standards for Educational Evaluation (1994).

Learning Environment 1.0: a focus on content presentation, access and download, fixed or static design, instructor-shaped design, and other characteristics of Web 1.0 (Sinclair, McClaren, & Griffin, 2006).

Learning Environment 2.0: a focus on communication and interactions, dynamic subject matter, designs codeveloped with learners, and other characteristics of Web 2.0. (Sinclair, McClaren, & Griffin, 2006).

Learning management systems (LMS): integrated software products that track learner progress, beginning with an inventory of learning preferences and goals and tracking progress both within and among courses (South Central Regional Library Council Distance Learning Glossary, 2002).

Learning objects: an item to facilitate learning that is created on a web page and housed in a frame that can be moved independently from the other objects on the page (Helicon Publishing, 2008).

Messick's (1989) framework: a model of test validity based on scientific evidence, values, and unintended consequences and used to guide comprehensive studies of the merit and worth of tests.

Mixed methods: quantitative and qualitative data are blended to provide an analysis of both course outcomes and processes.

Model: beliefs about "the concepts and structure of evaluation work . . . which provide guidelines for arriving at defensible descriptions, judgements and recommendations" (Madaus & Kellaghan, 2000, pp. 19–20). Sometimes used interchangeably with "framework" and "approach" (e.g., Moss, 1998a; Messick, 1998; Markus, 1998).

Multimedia: "any document which uses multiple forms of communication, such as text, audio, and/or video" (Willis & University of Idaho Engineering Outreach Staff, 2006).

Nomadicity: portability, for example, laptops or wireless Internet access.

Norm-referenced tests: tests in which total points earned are converted into a placement on the normal curve of all students' total scores.

Online courses: courses that can be accessed anytime, anywhere via the world wide web. Learners need a computer, Internet access, and basic skills in using the Internet (South Central Regional Library Council Distance Learning Glossary, 2002).

Online learning: a learning environment that uses the Internet as the delivery vehicle, synonymous with e-learning (South Central Regional Library Council Distance Learning Glossary, 2002).

Online training: same as *online learning*, but it implies the professional or corporate level.

Outcomes: the final "product" of a course, usually grades or completion rates.

Personal digital assistants (PDAs): handheld computer designed to store names, addresses, and diary information and to send and receive faxes and e-mail (Helicon Publishing, 2008).

Podcasting: a method of distributing *multimedia* files, such as audio or video programs, over the Internet using syndication feeds, for playback on mobile devices and personal computers. The term **podcast**, like "radio," can mean both the content and the method of delivery. The host or author of a podcast is often called a podcaster. (Wikipedia)

Portals: customized, adaptive webpages that are personalized in appearance and content and contain information about the user in a database (Sheehan & Jafari, 2003).

Program: "a set of resources and activities directed toward one or more common goals, typically under the direction of a single manager or a management team" (Wholey, 1987, p. 78). By this definition, a university course is a program, just as a set of courses leading to a degree such as a master's of educational technology is also a program.

Program evaluation: an investigation of the merit and worth of a set of activities.

Qualitative: data summarized by textual patterns or themes and sourced from interviews or focus groups.

Quality assurance: evaluation procedures to maintain high standards of quality.

Quantitative: data summarized by numbers or statistics and sourced from surveys, outcomes, and completion rates.

Relevance: with cost–benefit, the upper right box of the unfolding model. Alignment between the course and the needs of society, the meaningfulness of the course, and the transfer of learning to authentic contexts, that is, the "real world."

Research: in contrast to evaluation, the practice of collecting, analyzing, and presenting data in support of a theory or model.

Sampling: systematic ways of selecting interview or survey respondents. Can be random, convenience, or stratified.

Scientific approach: the rigorous and credible use of data, whether quantitative, qualitative, or mixed methods, to support evaluative claims or theories.

Scientific basis: the two upper boxes (scientific evidence, relevance, and cost–benefit) of the unfolding model.

Scientific evidence: the results or findings from surveys, interviews, outcomes, checklists, and course management data.

Seamless: in an online course, technology is said to be seamless (or transparent) when it is easy to use, intuitive in nature, and not the focus of the learning experience (South Central Regional Library Council Distance Learning Glossary, 2002).

Self-paced learning: Learners may move through and complete a course alone without a cohort group or fixed schedule.

Stakeholder: a person associated with or affected by a program, whether or not they have a say in its future (e.g. school administrators, teachers, parents, students, community groups; Weiss, 1986).

Standards: Specific goals for distance and e-learning courses.

Summative evaluation: "appraisals of quality focused on completed instructional programs" (Popham, 1993, p. 13).

Surveys: Questionnaires designed to ascertain opinions, knowledge, attitudes, or behaviors.

Synchronous: "communication in which interaction between participants is simultaneous" (Willis & University of Idaho Engineering Outreach Staff, 2006).

Teleconferencing: synchronous exchange of audio, video, or text (or a combination) between two or more remote sites using telecommunication technology such as telephone or cable lines, satellite transmission, etc. (South Central Regional Library Council Distance Learning Glossary, 2002).

Triangulation: comparing your findings across different respondents, different respondent groups, or different sources such as documents, course outlines, webpages, interviews, and open-ended survey items.

Underlying values: the lower left box of the unfolding model. Encompasses course goals and objectives, rhetoric, ideology, and theory.

Unfolding model: a dynamic framework based on Messick's (1989) four-faceted framework of validity for the evaluation of distance courses and e-learning that provides a comprehensive assessment of merit and worth and that can be adapted for the next wave of technological development.

Unintended consequences: the lower right box of the unfolding model. Can be either instructional or social and positive or negative.

Validity: "an integrated evaluative judgment of the degree to which empirical evidence and theoretical rationales support the *adequacy* and *appropriateness* of *inferences* and *actions* based on test scores or other modes of assessment" (Messick, 1989, p. 13).

Videoteleconferencing: "a teleconference including two way video" (Willis & University of Idaho Engineering Outreach Staff, 2006, p. 1).

Virtual schools: schools which deliver courses and instruction online.

Web 1.0: learners find information on the web and download it without changing anything at the website. Characterized by an architecture of presentation (Sinclair, McClaren, & Griffin, 2006).

Web 2.0: users contribute to growing pools of information, becoming codevelopers of websites and citizen-producers and publishers, working in a range of media. Some examples of these very popular sites and massively distributed online applications are eBay, Amazon, and Wikipedia, MySpace, You Tube, along with a rapidly growing number of personal weblogs, or blogs, as well as downloadable video and audio podcasts. Characterized by an architecture of participation (Sinclair, McClaren, & Griffin, 2006).

Web accessibility initiative (WAI): international standards for web accessibility. You can find international standards for web accessibility, strategies, guidelines, and resources on evaluating webpages for conformance to various accessibility guidelines at *www.w3.org/WAI*.

Webcasting: using technology to simultaneously broadcast live video and/or audio via the Internet to multiple computers (South Central Regional Library Council Distance Learning Glossary, 2002).

Wikipedia: a free, online encyclopedia that "allows registered users to add, edit or delete content" (Sinclair, McClaren, & Griffin, 2006). Website: *www.wikipedia. org*.

Worldwide web (WWW): "a graphical hypertext-based Internet tool that provides access to homepages created by individuals, businesses, and other organizations" (Willis & University of Idaho Engineering Outreach Staff, 2006).

Bibliography

The reader should note that there are often disagreements and inconsistencies across definitions in both distance education (Tallent-Runnels et al., 2006) and in program evaluation (King, 2003). In preparing this glossary, the sources listed below were reviewed. Other sources of definitions in this glossary can be found in the Reference List.

DiStefano, A., Rudestam, K. E., & Silverman, R. J. (Eds.). (2004). *Encyclopedia of distributed learning.* Thousand Oaks, CA: Sage.

E-learners.com Distance Learning Glossary. Retrieved September 16, 2006, from *www. elearners.com/resources/glossary.asp*.

Helicon Publishing. (2008). *The Hutchinson dictionary of computers, multimedia, and the Internet: The Hutchinson encyclopedia.* Retrieved September 29, 2008, from *www.tiscali. co.uk/reference/dictionaries/computers/*.

Joint PE Standards. Retrieved April 5, 2008, from *www.wmich.edu/evalctr/jc/*.

Schlosser, L. A., & Simonson, M. R. (2006). *Distance education: Definition and glossary of terms.* Charlotte, NC: Information Age Publishing.

South Central Regional Library Council Distance Learning Glossary. (2002). Retrieved April 15, 2008, from *www.lakenet.org/training/dlglossary.html*.

Wikipedia, The Free Encyclopedia. Retrieved September 16, 2006, from *www.wikipedia. org/*.

Willis, B., & the University of Idaho Engineering Outreach Staff. (2006). *Distance education at a glance: Guide 13: Glossary of distance education terminology.* Retrieved September 10, 2006, from *www.uidaho.edu/eo/dist13.html*.

APPENDIX C

■ ■ ■ ■ ■ ■ ■ ■ ■

List of Associations

Advanced Distributed Learning (ADL): established in late 1997 in cooperation with the Department of Defense, the White House Office of Science and Technology, and others to facilitate the cooperation of government, academia, and industry in the development of e-learning standards to enhance the reusability and quality of and reduce the associated costs of learning systems.

American Association for Higher Education and Accreditation (AAHEA): AAHEA's primary function is to ensure and strengthen academic quality and ongoing quality improvement in academic courses, programs, and degrees. Website: *www.aahea.org/welcome.htm*.

American Association of University Professors (AAUP): an organization to advance academic freedom and shared governance, to define fundamental professional values and standards for higher education, and to ensure higher education's contribution to the common good. Resources on distance education and intellectual property are available at *www.aaup.org/AAUP/issuesed/distance-ed/DE-IP-resources.htm*.

American Council on Education (ACE): Founded in 1918, ACE seeks to influence public policy in higher education through advocacy, research, and program initiatives. Their members and associates include approximately 1,800 accredited, degree-granting colleges and universities and higher education–related associations, organizations, and corporations. Source: ACE website: *www.acenet.edu/AM/Template.cfm?Section=About1*.

American Disability Association (ADA): a national organization with a mission to meet the informational needs of Americans with diverse disabilities, to promote awareness of disability culture, and to enhance the quality of life and access to freedom. Manages ADAnet, an international distributed computer network for people with disabilities, has created many disability newsgroups that are still in use, and uses the Internet as a unifying technology. Website: *www.adanet. org/contact_us.html.*

American Distance Education Consortium (ADEC): a nonprofit distance education consortium of approximately 65 state universities and land-grant colleges. The consortium promotes the creation and provision of high-quality, economical distance education programs and services to diverse audiences through information technologies. Website: *www.adec.edu/admin/adec-background.html.*

American Evaluation Association (AEA): an international professional association of evaluators devoted to the application and exploration of program evaluation, personnel evaluation, technology, and many other forms of evaluation. Evaluation involves assessing the strengths and weaknesses of programs, policies, personnel, products, and organizations to improve their effectiveness. AEA has approximately 4,000 members representing the entire United States as well as more than 60 foreign countries. Website: *www.eval.org/aboutus.asp.*

Center for Applied Research in Educational Technology (CARET): a project of the International Society for Technology in Education, Education Support Systems, and the Sacramento County Office of Education. Funded with a grant from the Bill & Melinda Gates Foundation, CARET provides a wealth of information on research in technology-based environments. See *caret.iste.org/ index.cfm?fuseaction=partners.*

Council for Higher Education Accreditation (CHEA): an association of 3,000 degree-granting colleges and universities advocating for self-regulation of academic quality through accreditation. The CHEA database has information for over 7,000 educational institutions and over 17,000 accredited programs by recognized U.S. accrediting organizations. Website: *www.chea.org/.*

International Society for Technology in Education (ISTE): "a nonprofit professional organization with a worldwide membership of leaders and potential leaders in educational technology. ISTE is dedicated to promoting appropriate uses of information technology to support and improve learning, teaching, and administration in K–12 education and teacher education." See *caret.iste.org/index. cfm?fuseaction=partners.*

National Center for Higher Education Management Systems: provides the higher education community with access to national data collected about higher education with data files dating back over 30 years. Website: *www.nchems. org/InfoServices/infoserv.htm.*

National Education Telecommunications Organization and EDSAT Institute (NETO/EDSAT): A global organization for the development and support of distance learning. Founded in 1988 as a not-for-profit, nongovernmental organization to bring together United States and other countries to strengthen instructional and educational opportunities and telecommunication systems dedicated to education. Website: *www.netoedsat.org/About.htm#Description.*

North American Council for Online Learning (NACOL): a Washington, DC-based nonprofit organization made up of K–12 online programs; it provides a variety of resources to members and nonmembers and hosts the annual Virtual School Symposium, the main K–12 online learning conference (Watson, 2007). Website: *www.ncol.org.*

Partnership for 21st Century Skills: an advocacy organization of business community, education leaders, and policymakers to bring 21st-century skills into education. The Partnership encourages schools, districts, and states to advocate for the infusion of 21st-century skills into education and provides tools and resources to help facilitate and drive change. Website: *www.21stcenturyskills.org/index.php.*

Rural Broadband Coalition: An organization that advocates to bring cost-effective broadband and high-speed access to the Internet across rural America and to dismantle barriers to competitive broadband availability. Website: *www. ruralbroadbandcoalition.net/about.html.*

Sloan Consortium: helps learning organizations continually improve the quality, scale, and breadth of their online programs, according to their own distinctive missions, so that education will become a part of everyday life, accessible and affordable for anyone, anywhere, at any time, in a wide variety of disciplines. Website: *www.sloan-c.org.*

Southern Regional Education Board (SREB): the nation's first interstate compact for education, SREB was created in 1948 by southern states. SREB helps government and education leaders work cooperatively to advance education and has had a significant focus on online learning. Website: *www.sreb.org.*

Teleconferencing: Video networks connecting remote sites or locations.

United States Distance Learning Association (USDLA): to provide national leadership in the field of distance learning, to advocate and promote the use of distance learning, to provide current information on distance learning, to represent the distance learning community before government policy and regulatory bodies, and to serve and support the state, consortium, and individual organizations that belong to USDLA. Provides annual recognition and awards of outstanding achievements in distance learning; promotes partnerships among education, business, health care, and government and liaisons with international organizations. Website: *www.usdla.org/html/aboutUs/goals.htm.*

Virtual High School: a pioneer online learning for high school students and online course design for teachers. Website: *www.govhs.org.*

Western Cooperative for Educational Communications (WCET): a membership-supported organization open to providers and users of educational technologies. Their mission is to promote and advance the effective use of technology in higher education through the cooperative efforts of their member network. Website: *www.wcet.info/about/.*

World Wide Web Consortium (W3C): made up of organizations around the world to develop specifications, guidelines, software, and tools to maximize the potential of the worldwide web. International standards for web accessibility, strategies, guidelines and resources, and support materials are available at *www. w3.org/WAI.*

References

Abma, T. A., & Stake, R. E. (2001). Stake's responsive evaluation: Core ideas and evolution. In J. C. Greene & T. A. Abma (Eds.), *New directions for Evaluation: No. 92. Responsive evaluation* (pp. 7–21). San Francisco: Jossey-Bass.

Abt Associates, Inc. (2006). *Evaluation of the initial impacts of the National Science Foundation's Integrative Graduate Education and Research Traineeship Program: Final report.* Retrieved December 5, 2007, from *www.nsf.gov/pubs/2006/nsf0617/nsf0617.pdf.*

Academic Committee for the Creative Use of Learning Technologies. (2000). *The creative use of learning technologies.* Unpublished manuscript, University of British Columbia.

Agar, M. H. (1996). *The professional stranger: An informal introduction to ethnography.* San Diego, CA: Academic Press.

Aggarwal, A. K. (Ed.). (2003). *Web-based education: Learning from experience.* Hershey, PA: Information Sciences.

Alkin, M. C., & Christie, C. A. (2004a). An evaluation theory tree. In M. C. Alkin (Ed.), *Evaluation roots: Tracing theorists' views and influences* (pp. 12–65). Thousand Oaks, CA: Sage.

Alkin, M. C., & Christie, C. A. (2004b). Evaluation theory tree revised. In M. C. Alkin (Ed.), *Evaluation roots: Tracing theorists' views and influences* (pp. 381–392). Thousand Oaks, CA: Sage.

Allen, I. E., & Seaman, J. (2006). *Making the grade: Online education in the United States, 2006.* Retrieved January 2, 2007, from *www.sloan-c.org/publications/survey/pdf/making_the_grade.pdf.*

American Psychological Association. (1954). Technical recommendations for psychological tests and diagnostic techniques. *Psychological Bulletin, 51,* 1–38.

American Psychological Association. (1966). *Standards for educational and psychological tests and manuals.* Washington, DC: Author.

American Psychological Association, American Educational Research Association, and National Council on Measurement in Education. (1974). *Standards for educational and psychological tests.* Washington, DC: American Psychological Association.

American Psychological Association, American Educational Research Association, and National Council on Measurement in Education. (1985). *Standards for educational and psychological testing.* Washington, DC: American Psychological Association.

Andrusyszyn, M., & Davie, L. (1997). Facilitating reflection through interactive journal writing in an online graduate course: A qualitative study. *Journal of Distance Education, 12*(1/2), 103–126.

Angoff, W. H. (1988). Validity: An evolving concept. In H. Wainer & H. I. Braun (Eds.), *Test validity* (pp. 19–31). Hillsdale, NJ: Erlbaum.

Athabasca University. (2007). *Athabasca University: Canada's open university.* Retrieved February 8, 2007, from *www.athabascau.ca/.*

Awalt, C. (2007). Speaking personally—with Tony Bates. *The American Journal of Distance Education, 21*(2), 105–109.

Baker, E. L., & Niemi, D. (1996). School and program evaluation. In D. C. Berliner & R. C. Calfee (Eds.), *Handbook of program evaluation* (pp. 926–944). New York: Macmillan.

Baker, E. L., & O'Neil, H. F. (Eds.). (1994). *Technology assessment in education and training.* Hillsdale, NJ: Erlbaum.

Baker, E. L., & O'Neil, H. F. (2006). Evaluating web-based learning environments, In H. F. O'Neil & R. S. Perez (Eds.), *Web-based learning: Theory, research, and practice* (pp. 1–20). Mahwah, NJ: Erlbaum.

Banathy, B. H. (1999). *Systems design of education: Concepts and principles for effective practice.* Englewood Cliffs, NJ: Educational Technology.

Bartolic-Zlomislic, S., & Bates, A. W. (1999). Investing in on-line learning: Potential benefits and limitations. *Canadian Journal of Communication, 24*(3), 349–366.

Bassey, M. (1999). *Case study research in educational settings.* Philadelphia: Open University Press.

Bates, A. W. (1995). *Technology, open learning and distance education.* London: Routledge.

Bates, A. W. (2000). *Managing technological change: Strategies for college and university leaders.* Windsor, Ontario: Jossey-Bass.

Bejar, I. (2007, January 11). *Psychometrics as a learning science.* Paper presented at a meeting of the College of Education and Human Development, University of Minnesota.

Belanger, F., & Jordan, D. H. (2000). *Evaluation and implementation of distance learning: Technologies, tools and techniques.* Hershey, PA: Idea Group.

Benbunan-Fich, R., Hiltz, S. R., & Harasim, L. (2004). The online interaction learning model: An integrated theoretical framework for learning networks. In S. R. Hiltz & R. Goldman (Eds.), *Learning together online: Research on asynchronous learning networks.* Mahwah, NJ: Erlbaum.

Bendus, O. (2005). Evaluation of online courses: Integrating principles of effective online teaching into the practice of evaluation. In G. Richards (Ed.), *Proceedings of the World Conference on E-Learning in Corporate, Government, Healthcare, and Higher Education 2005* (pp. 231–233). Chesapeake, VA: AACE. Retrieved September 8, 2007, from *www.editlib.org/index.cfm?fuseaction=Reader.ViewAbstract&paper_id=21174&from=NEWDL*.

Berg, B. L. (2007). *Qualitative research methods for the social sciences* (6th ed.). New York: Pearson.

Bett, S., French, D., Farr, G., & Hooks, L. (1999). Augmenting traditional teaching with Internet-based options. In D. Harris (Ed.), *Internet-based learning: An introduction and framework for higher education and business* (pp. 47–62). Sterling, VA: Stylus.

Bickman, L. (1987). The functions of program theory. In L. Bickman (Ed.), *New directions for program evaluation: No. 33. Using program theory in evaluation* (pp. 5–18). San Francisco: Jossey-Bass.

Black, E. W., Ferdig, R. E., & DiPietro, M. (2008). An overview of evaluative instrumentation for virtual high schools. *American Journal of Distance Education, 22*(1), 24–45.

Blackboard. (2007). Retrieved October 5, 2007, from *www.blackboard.com/us/index.Bb*.

Blustein, H., Goldstein, P., & Lozier, G. (1999). Assessing the new competitive landscape. In R. N. Katz & Associates (Eds.), *Dancing with the devil: Information technology and the new competition in higher education* (pp. 51–72). San Francisco: Jossey-Bass.

Bourdeau, J., & Bates, A. (1997). Instructional design for distance learning. In S. N. Dijkstra, N. M. Seel, F. Shott, & R. D. Tennyson (Eds.), *Instructional design: International perspectives: Vol. 2. Solving instructional design problems* (pp. 369–397). Mahwah, NJ: Erlbaum.

Bourne, J. R., & Moore, J. C. (Eds.). (2004). *Elements of quality online education: Into the mainstream.* Needham, MA: Sloan Center for Online Education.

Brabazon, T. (2003). *Digital hemlock: Internet education and the poisoning of teaching.* Sydney: University of New South Wales Press.

Bransford, J. D., Sherwood, R., Hasselbring, T., Kinzer, C., & Williams, S. (1990). Anchored instruction: Why we need it and how technology can help. In D. Nix & R. Spiro (Eds.), *Cognition, education, and multimedia: Exploring ideas in high technology* (pp. 115–141). Hillsdale, NJ: Erlbaum.

Braun, H. (1994). Assessing technology in assessment. In E. L. Baker & M. F. O'Neil, Jr. (Eds.), *Technology assessment in education and training* (pp. 231–246). Hillsdale, NJ: Erlbaum.

Breuch, L. K. (2004). *Virtual peer review: Teaching and learning about writing in online environments.* New York: State University of New York Press.

Brown, J. S., Collins, A., & Duguid, P. (1996). Situated cognition and the culture of learning. In D. P. Ely & T. Plomp (Eds.), *Classic writings on instructional technology.* Englewood, CO: Libraries Unlimited.

Buchner, A., Faul, F., & Erdfelder, E. (2007). *G*Power 3.* Retrieved December 5, 2007, from *www.psycho.uni-duesseldorf.de/abteilungen/aap/gpower3/*.

Bunderson, C. V. (2003). Four frameworks for viewing blended learning cases: Comments and critiques. *Quarterly Review of Distance Education, 4*(3), 279–288.

Buros Institute of Mental Measurements. (2008). *Test reviews online: Test reviews when you need them.* Retrieved January 16, 2005, from *buros.unl.edu/buros/jsp/search.jsp.*

Campbell, D., & Stanley, J. (1963). *Experimental and quasi-experimental designs for research.* Chicago: Rand McNally.

Caracelli, V. J. (2000). Evaluation use at the threshold of the 21st century. In V. J. Caracelli & H. Preskill (Eds.), *New directions for evaluation: No. 88. The expanding scope of evaluation use* (pp. 99–111). San Francisco: Jossey-Bass.

Center for the Virtual University (CVU), The Office of Distance Education and Lifelong Learning, University of Maryland University College. (2007). Accessibility in distance education: A resource for faculty in online teaching. Retrieved April 8, 2008, from *www.umuc.edu/ade/.*

Chaney, B., Hensleigh, E., Dorman, J. M., Glessner, S. M., Green, L. M., Lee, B., et al. (2007). Development of an instrument to assess student opinions of the quality of distance education courses. *American Journal of Distance Education, 21*(3), 145–164.

Chapelle, C. A., Jamieson, J., & Hegelheimer, V. (2003). Validation of a web-based ESL test. *Language Testing, 20*(4), 409–439.

Chapman, D. D. (2006). Building an evaluation plan for fully online degree programs. *Online Journal of Distance Learning Administration, 9*(1), 1–16.

Chatterji, M. (2005). Evidence on "what works": An argument for extended-term mixed-method (ETMM) evaluation design. *Educational Researcher, 34*(5), 14–24.

Chelimsky, E. (1998). The role of experience in formulating theories of evaluation practice. *American Journal of Evaluation, 19*(1), 35–55.

Chen, H. T. (1990). *Theory-driven evaluation.* Newbury Park, CA: Sage.

Chen, H. T. (2005). *Practical program evaluation: Assessing and improving planning, implementation, and effectiveness.* Thousand Oaks, CA: Sage.

Chen, L., & Iris, C. (2004). ITV: An emerging tool in education. *Educational Technology, 64*(6), 61–62.

Cheung, D. (1998). Developing a student evaluation instrument for distance teaching. *Distance Education, 9*(1), 23–42.

Chico State University. (2003). *Rubric for online instruction.* Retrieved July 30, 2004, from *www.csuchico.edu/celt/roi/.*

Chioncel, N. E., van der Veen, R. G. W., Wildemeersch, D., & Jarvis, P. (2003). The validity and reliability of focus groups as a research method in adult education. *International Journal of Lifelong Education, 22*(5), 495–517.

Chou, C. (2003). Interactivity and interactive functions in web-based learning systems: A technical framework for designers. *British Journal of Educational Technology, 34*(3), 265–280.

Christensen, T. K. (2003). Finding the balance: Constructivist pedagogy in a blended course. *Quarterly Review of Distance Education, 4*(3), 235–243.

Christie, C. A. (2001). What guides evaluation? A study of how evaluation practice maps on to evaluation theory. *Dissertation Abstracts*, AAT 3040164.

Cizek, G. J. (2001). More unintended consequences of high-stakes testing. *Educational Measurement, Issues and Practice, 20*(4), 19–27.

Cizek, G. J., & Bunch, M. B. (2007). *Standard setting: A guide to establishing and evaluating performance standards on tests.* Thousand Oaks, CA: Sage.

Claeys, C. (1999). Assessing cost-effectiveness for virtual learning and instruction: Why and how? In C. M. Feyten & J. W. Nutten (Eds.), *Virtual instruction: Issues and insights from an international perspective* (pp. 7–34). Englewood Cliffs, NJ: Libraries Unlimited.

Clark, R. C., & Mayer, R. E. (2003). *E-learning and the science of instruction: Proven guidelines for consumers and designers of multimedia learning.* San Francisco: Jossey-Bass/Pfeiffer.

Clark, R. E. (1994a). Assessment of distance learning technology. In E. L. Baker & H. F. O'Neil, Jr. (Eds.), *Technology assessment in education and training* (pp. 63–78). Hillsdale, NJ: Erlbaum.

Clark, R. E. (1994b). Media will never influence learning. *Educational Technology Research and Development, 42,* 21–29.

Clark, T. (2001). *Virtual schools: Trends and issues. A study of virtual schools in the United States.* Retrieved September 16, 2006, from *www.wested.org/online_ pubs/virtualschools.pdf.*

Cobb, P., & Bowers, J. (1999). Cognitive and situated learning perspectives in theory and practices. *Educational Researcher, 28*(2), 4–15.

Cobb, T. (1997). Cognitive efficiency: Toward a revised theory of media. *Educational Technology Research and Development, 45*(4), 21–35.

Cognition and Technology Group at Vanderbilt. (1993). Anchored instruction and situated cognition revisited. *Educational Technology, 33*(3), 52–70.

Cohen, J. (1992). A power primer. *Psychological Bulletin, 112,* 155–159.

Coldeway, D. O. (1988). Methodological issues in distance education research. *The American Journal of Distance Education, 2*(3), 45–54.

Collis, B. A. (1993). Evaluating instructional applications of telecommunications in distance education. *Educational and Training Technology International, 30*(3), 266–274.

Collis, B. (1996). *Tele-learning in a digital world: The future of distance learning.* London: International Thomson Publications.

Conlon, T. (2006). Formative assessment of classroom concept maps: The reasonable fallible analyzer. *Journal of Interactive Learning Research, 17*(1), 15–36.

Comeaux, P. (2005). Assessment and learning. In P. Comeaux (Ed.), *Assessing online learning* (pp. xix–xxvii). Bolton, MA: Anker Publishing.

Council for Higher Education Accreditation. (2006). *Degree mills: An old problem and a new threat.* Retrieved September 16, 2006, from www.chea.org/ degreemills/frmpaper.htm.

Creeve, J. C., & Caracelli, V. J. (Eds.). (1997). *Advances in mixed-method evaluation: The challenges and benefits of integrating diverse paradigms.* San Francisco: Jossey-Bass.

Cremer, D. J. (2001). Education as commodity: The ideology of online education and distance learning. *Journal of the Association for History and Computing,
4*, 1–5.

Crocker, L., & Algina, J. (1986). *Introduction to classical and modern test theory.*
Toronto: Holt, Rinehart & Winston.

Cronbach, L. J. (1980). *Toward reform of program evaluation.* San Francisco: Jossey-
Bass.

Cronbach, L. J. (1982). *Designing evaluations of educational and social programs.* San
Francisco: Jossey-Bass.

Cronbach, L. J., & Meehl, P. E. (1955). Construct validity in psychological tests.
Psychological Bulletin, 52, 232–281.

Cureton, E. E. (1951). Validity. In E. R. Lindquist (Ed.), *Educational measurement*
(pp. 621–694). Washington, DC: American Council on Education.

Davidson, E. J. (2000). Ascertaining causality in theory-based evaluations. In P.
J. Rogers, T. A. Hacsi, A. Petrosino, & T. A. Huebner (Eds.), *New directions
for evaluation: No. 87. Program theory in evaluation: Challenges and opportunities*
(pp. 17–26). San Francisco: Jossey-Bass.

Davidson, E. J. (2005). *Evaluation methodology basics: The nuts and bolts of sound
evaluation.* Thousand Oaks, CA: Sage.

Davis, B. (2002, February 26). *Complexity science and schooling.* Presentation to the
Faculty of Education, University of British Columbia.

Deane, S. (2005). *Online education: Is it for you?* Bloomington, IN: Authorhouse.

Dede, C. (2005). Speaking personally. *American Journal of Distance Education,
19*(2), 119–123.

Dede, C., Honan, J. P., & Peters, L. C. (Eds.). (2005). *Scaling up success: Lessons learned
from technology-based educational improvement.* San Francisco: Jossey-Bass.

de Kerckhove, D. (1995). *The skin of culture: Investigating the new electronic reality.*
Toronto: Somerville House.

Denzin, N. K., & Lincoln, Y. S. (2005). *The Sage handbook of qualitative research.*
Thousand Oaks, CA: Sage.

Derntl, M., & Motschnig-Pitrik, M. (2004). Patterns for blended, person-
centered learning: Strategy, concepts, experiences, and evaluation. In
*Proceedings of the 2004 ACM Symposium on Applied Computing, Nicosia,
Cyprus.* New York: ACM Press. Retrieved April 8, 2008, from *delivery.
acm.org/10.1145/970000/968087/p916-derntl.pdf?key1=968087&key2=4
500497021&coll=GUIDE&dl=GUIDE&CFID=63437030&CFTOKE
N=60680882.*

Design-Based Research Collective. (2003). Design-based research: An emerging
paradigm for educational inquiry. *Educational Researcher, 32*(1), 5–8.

Dijkstra, S. (1997). Educational technology and media. In S. Dijkstra, N. Seel, F.
Shott, & R. D. Tennyson (Ed.), *Instructional design: International perspectives:
Volume 2. Solving instructional design problems* (pp. 137–143). Mahwah, NJ:
Erlbaum.

Dodds, P. (Ed.). (2004). *SCORM 2004 overview.* Available at *www.adlnet.org.*

Dodds, P., & Fletcher, J. D. (2004). Opportunities for new "smart" learning environments enabled by next-generation Web capabilities. *Journal of Education Multimedia and Hypermedia, 13*(4), 391–404.

Donaldson, J. L. (2007). *Itineraries for success: Plans for priority programs. University of Tennessee Extension.* Retrieved September 3, 2007, from *agweb.ag.utk.edu:8090/ eesd/eesd.nsf/August%/2022%20930%20am.ppt#276,12,Inputs:Whatweinvest.*

Dorr, G., & Seel, N. (1997). Instructional delivery system and multimedia environments in instructional design. In R. D. Tennyson, F. Schott, N. M. Seel, & S. Dijkstra (Eds.), *Instructional design, international perspectives: Vol. 2. Solving instructional design problems.* Mahawah, NJ: Erlbaum.

Duderstat, J. J. (1999). Can colleges and universities survive in the information age? In R. N. Katz & Associates (Eds.), *Dancing with the devil: Information technology and the new competition in higher education* (pp. 1–26). San Francisco: Jossey-Bass.

Duffy, T. M., & Jonassen, D. H. (Eds.). (1992). *Constructivism and the technology of instruction: A conversation.* Hillsdale, NJ: Erlbaum.

Duncan, S. (2005). The U.S. Army's impact on the history of distance education. *Quarterly Review of Distance Education, 6*(4), 397–404.

Educause Evolving Technologies Committee. (2004). Surveying the digital landscape: Evolving technologies 2004. *Educause, 39*(6), 78–92.

Eisenhardt, K. M. (1989). Building theories from case study research. *Academy of Management Review, 14*(4), 532–550.

Evans, T., & Nation, D. (1993). *Reforming open and distance education.* London: Kogan Page.

Ezell, A., & Bear, J. (2005). *Degree mills: The billion-dollar industry that has sold over a million fake diplomas.* New York: Prometheus Books.

Fabos, B., & Young, M. D. (1999). Telecommunication in the classroom: Rhetoric versus reality. *Review of Educational Research, 69*(3), 217–259.

Fahy, P. J. (1999). Reflections on the productivity paradox and distance education technology. *Journal of Distance Education, 13*(2), 66–73.

Farrington, G. C. (1999). The new technologies and the future of residential undergraduate education. In R. N. Katz & Associates (Eds.), *Dancing with the devil: Information technology and the new competition in higher education* (pp. 73–94). San Francisco: Jossey-Bass.

Fetterman, D. M. (1997). Ethnography. In L. Bickman & D. J. Rog (Eds.), *Handbook of applied social research methods* (pp. 473–504). Thousand Oaks, CA: Sage.

Finkelstein, M. J., Frances, C., Jewett, F. I., & Scholz, B. W. (Eds.). (2000). *Dollars, distance, and online education: The new economics of college teaching and learning.* Phoenix, AZ: American Council on Education/Oryx Press Series on Higher Education.

Fisher, F., Esche, S., Ubell, R., & Chassapis, C. (2007). *Feasibility of a fully online undergraduate mechanical engineering degree for non-traditional learners.* Retrieved September 19, 2007, from *http://www.icee.usm.edu/ICEE/conferences/asee2007/papers/2828_FEASIBILITY_OF_A_FULLY_ONLINE_ UNDERGRADU.pdf*

Fitzpatrick, J. L., Sanders, J. R., & Worthen, B. R. (2004). *Program evaluation: Alternative approaches and practical guidelines* (3rd ed.). New York: Pearson.

Fleitas, J. (1999). *Nursing-pediatric, band-aides at Columbia University*. Retrieved April 16, 2008, from *lehman.cuny.edu/faculty/jfleitas/bandaides/sitemap.html*.

Fletcher, J. D., Tobias, S., & Wisher, R. A. (2007). Learning anytime, learning anywhere: Advanced distributed learning and the changing face of education. *Educational Researcher, 36*(2), 96–102.

Flick, U. (1992). Triangulation revisited: Strategy of validation or alternative? *Journal for Theory of Social Behaviour, 22*(2), 175–198.

Flyvberg, B. (2006). Five misunderstandings about case study research. *Qualitative Inquiry, 12*(2), 219–245.

Forsyth, I., Jolliffe, A., & Stevens, D. (1995). *Evaluating a course: Practical strategies for teachers, lecturers and trainers*. London: Kogan Page.

Foucault, M. (1980). Two lectures. In C. Gordon (Ed.), *Power/knowledge: Selected interviews and other writings by Michel Foucault* (pp. 78–108). New York: Pantheon Books.

Fowler, F. J., Jr. (2001). *Survey research methods* (3rd ed.). Thousand Oaks, CA: Sage.

French, D. (1999). Preparing for Internet-based learning. In D. French, C. Hale, C. Johnson, & G. Farr (Eds.), *Internet-based learning: An introduction and framework for higher education and business* (pp. 9–24). Stirling, VA: Stylus.

Galston, W. A. (1999). Value pluralism and liberal political theory. *American Political Science Review, 93*(4), 769–778.

Gardner, H. (1999). *The disciplined mind: What all students should understand*. New York: Simon & Schuster.

Garrison, D. R., & Anderson, T. D. (1999). Avoiding the industrialization of research universities: Big and little distance education. *American Journal of Distance Education, 13*(2), 48–63.

Gilliani, B. (2003). *Learning theories and the design of e-learning environments*. Lanham, MD: University Press of America.

Goldman-Segall, R. (1995). Configurational validity: A proposal for analyzing ethnographic multimedia narratives. *Journal of Educational Multimedia and Hypermedia, 4*(2–3), 163–182.

Goldman-Segall, R. (2006). *Introduction to Constellations 2.6*. Retrieved February 8, 2007, from *orion.njit.edu/merlin/tools/C25/index.html*.

Gooler, D. (1979). Evaluating distance education programmes. *Canadian Journal of University Continuing Education, 6*(1), 43–55.

Gouli, E., Gogoulou, A., Papanikolaou, K., & Grigoriadou, M. (2005). Evaluating learner's knowledge level on concept mapping tasks. In P. Goodyear, D. G. Sampson, D. Yang, O. T. Kinshuk, R. Hartley, & N. S. Chen (Eds.), *Proceedings of the 5th IEEE International Conference on Advanced Learning Technologies* (pp. 424–428). Los Alamitos: IEEE Computer Society.

Grabe, M., & Grabe, C. (1998). *Technology for meaningful learning* (2nd ed.). Toronto: Houghton Mifflin.

Graf, D., & Caines, M. (2003). *WebCT exemplary course project: 2003 rubric.* Retrieved August 1, 2004, from *www.webct.com/service/ViewContent?contentID=13423678.*

Graham, C. R. (2006). Blended learning systems: Definition, current trends, and future directions. In C. J. Bonk & C. R. Graham (Eds.), *The handbook of blended learning: Global perspectives, local designs* (pp. 3–21). San Francisco: Wiley.

Granello, D. H., & Wheaton, J. E. (2004). Online data collection: Strategies for research (practice & theory). *Journal of Counseling and Development, 82*(4), 387.

Gray, A., & O'Grady, G. (1993). Interactive television: Expanding established skills or new experiences for old? In M. Ryan (Ed.), *Proceedings of APITITE 94* (pp. 665–670). Murray Hill, NSW: Australian Computer Society.

Green, D. R. (1998). Consequential aspects of the validity of achievement tests: A publisher's point of view. *Educational Measurement: Issues and Practice, 17*(2), 16–19.

Greenbaum, T. L. (2002). *Moderating focus groups: A practical guide for group facilitation.* Thousand Oaks, CA: Sage.

Greene, J. C. (2007). *Mixed methods in social inquiry: Research methods for the social sciences.* San Francisco: Jossey-Bass.

Greene, J. C., & Caracelli, V. J. (1997). Editors' notes. In J. C. Greene & V. J. Caracelli (Eds.), *New directions for education: No. 74* (pp. 1–3). San Francisco: Jossey-Bass.

Greeno, J. G. (1997). On claims that answer the wrong questions. *Educational Researcher, 26*(1), 5–17.

Groves, R. M., Fowler, F. J., Jr., Couper, M. P., Lepkowski, J. M., Singer, E., & Tourangeau, R. (2004). *Survey methodology.* Hoboken, NJ: Wiley.

Guba, E. G., & Lincoln, Y. S. (1985). *Naturalistic inquiry.* Beverly Hills, CA: Sage.

Guion, R. M. (1980). On trinitarian doctrines of validity. *Professional Psychology, 11,* 385–398.

Hamilton, D. (1977). Making sense of curriculum evaluation: Continuities and discontinuities in an educational idea. In L. Shulman (Ed.), *Review of research in education* (pp. 318–347). Itasca, IL: Peacock.

Hammond, R. L. (1973). Evaluation at the local level. In B. R. Worthen & J. R. Sanders (Eds.), *Educational evaluation: Theory and practice* (pp. 157–169). Worthington, OH: Charles A. Jones.

Hannafin, M. J., Hall, C., Land, S., & Hill, J. (1994). Learning in open environments: Assumptions, methods and implications. *Educational Technology, 34*(8), 48–55.

Hannafin, M. J., Hannafin, K. M., Land, S. M., & Oliver, K. (1997). Grounded practice and the design of constructivist learning environments. *Educational Technology Research and Development, 45*(3), 101–117.

Hannafin, M., Land, S. & Oliver, K. (1999). Open learning environments: Foundations, methods and models In C. M. Reigeluth (Eds.), *Instructional design: Theories and models: Vol. 2. A new paradigm of instructional theory* (pp. 115–140). Mahwah, NJ: Erlbaum.

Harasim, L., Hiltz, S. R., Teles, L., & Turoff, M. (1996). *Learning networks: A field guide to teaching and learning online.* Cambridge, MA: MIT.

Harrison, P. J., Saba, F., Seeman, B. J., Molise, G., Behm, R., & Williams, M. D. (1991). Development of a distance education assessment instrument. *Educational Technology Research and Development, 39*(4), 65–77.

Hartley, K., & Robson, L. (1998a). *Teaching teams that work: A faculty guide.* Victoria, BC: Province of British Columbia, Ministry of Advanced Education, Training and Technology.

Hartley, K., & Robson, L. (1998b). *Teams that work: A team skills handbook for students.* Burnaby, BC: BCIT.

Harun, M. H. (2002). Integrating e-learning into the workplace. *Internet and Higher Education, 4*, 301–310.

Hazari, S. (2002). *BlackBoard @ R. H. Smith student/faculty evaluation report.* Retrieved September 29, 2008, from *http://www.sunilhazari.com/education/webct/bbeval.pdf*

Helicon Publishing. (2008). *The Hutchinson dictionary of computers, multimedia and the Internet: The Hutchinson encyclopedia.* Retrieved September 29, 2008, from *http://www.tiscali.co.uk/reference/dictionaries/computers/*

Henderson, L., & Putt, I. (1999). Evaluating audio-conferencing as an effective learning tool in cross-cultural contexts. *Open Learning, 14*(1), 25–37.

Hendricks, M. (1994). Making a splash: Reporting evaluation results effectively. In J. S. Wholey, H. P. Hatry, & K. E. Newcomer (Eds.), *Handbook of practical program evaluation* (pp. 549–575). San Francisco: Jossey-Bass.

Henri, F. (1992). Computer conferencing and content analysis. In A. Kaye (Ed.), *Collaborative learning through computer conferencing: The Najaden papers* (pp. 117–136). Berlin Heidelberg: Springer Verlag.

Henry, G. T. (2000). Why not use? In V. J. Caracelli & H. Preskill (Eds.), *New directions for evaluation: No. 88. The expanding scope of evaluation use* (pp. 85–98). San Francisco: Jossey-Bass.

Henry, G. T., & Julnes, G. (1998). Values and realist evaluation. In G. T. Henry, G. Julnes, & M. M. Mark (Eds.), *New directions for evaluation: No. 78. Realist evaluation: An emerging theory in support of practice* (pp. 53–71). San Francisco: Jossey-Bass.

Herrmann, A., Fox, R., & Boyd, A. (1999). Benign educational technology? *Open Learning, 14*(1), 3–7.

Hiltz, S. R., & Goldman, R. (Eds.). (2005). *Learning together online: Research on asynchronous learning networks.* Mahwah, NJ: Erlbaum.

Honebein, P. C. (1996). Seven goals for the design of constructivist learning environments. In B. G. Wilson (Ed.), *Constructivist learning environments: Case studies in instructional design* (pp. 11–24). Englewood Cliffs, NJ: Educational Technology.

Horton, W. (2001). *Evaluating e-learning.* Alexandria, VA: American Society for Training and Development.

House, E. R. (2003). Introduction. In T. Kellaghan, D. L. Stufflebeam, & L. A. Wingate (Eds.), *International handbook of educational evaluation, Part 1* (pp. 9–14). Boston: Kluwer Academic.

House, E. R., & Howe, K. R. (2000). Deliberative democratic evaluation. In K. E. Ryan & L. deStefano (Eds.), *New directions for evaluation: No. 85. Evaluation as a democratic process: Promoting inclusion, dialogue, and deliberation* (pp. 3–12). San Francisco: Jossey-Bass.

Hubley, A. M., & Zumbo, B. D. (1996). A dialectic on validity: Where we have been and where we are going. *Journal of General Psychology, 123*(3), 207–215.

Hughes, J., & Attwell, G. (2002). A framework for the evaluation of e-learning. *Proceedings of European seminars—exploring models and partnerships for e-learning in SMEs.* Retrieved April 8, 2008, from *www.theknownet.com/ict_smes_seminars/papers/Hughes_Attwell.html.*

Institute for Higher Education Policy. (1999). *What's the difference? A review of contemporary research on the effectiveness of distance learning in higher education.* Washington, DC: ERIC ED 429 524, The Institute for Higher Education Policy. Retrieved April 8, 2008, from *www.eric.ed.gov/ERICDocs/data/ericdocs2sql/content_storage_010000019b/80/17/87/09.pdf.*

Interactive TV Alliance. (2002). *Interactive TV: A short history.* Retrieved April 9, 2008, from *www.itvalliance.org/index2.html.*

Jacobson, M. J. (2006). From non-adaptive to adaptive educational hypermedia: Theory, research and methodological issues. In G. D. Magonlas & S. Y. Chan (Eds.), *Advances in web-based education* (pp. 302–330). Hershey, PA: Idea Group.

Johnstone, S. M., & Krauth, B. (1996). Balancing quality and access: Some principles of good practice for the virtual university. *Change, 28*(2), 38–41.

Joint Committee on Standards for Education. (1994). *Program evaluation standards: How to assess evaluation of educational programs* (2nd ed.). Thousand Oaks, CA: Sage.

Jonassen, D. (1991). Objectivism versus constructivism: Do we need a new philosophical paradigm? *Educational Technology Research and Development, 39*(3), 5–14.

Jonassen, D. H., Myers, J. M., & McKillop, A. M. (1996). From constructivism to constructionism: Learning *with* hypermedia/multimedia rather than *from* it. In B. G. Wilson (Ed.), *Constructivist learning environments: Case studies in instructional design* (pp. 93–106). Englewood Cliffs, NJ: Educational Technology.

Jones, A., & Petre, M. (1994). Computer-based practical work at a distance: A case study. *Computers in Education, 22*(1–2), 27–37.

Jones, A., Scanlon, E., Butcher, P., Greenberg, J., Ross, S., Murphy, P., et al. (1998). Learning with computers: Experiences of evaluation. *Computers and Education, 30*(1/2), 1–9.

Jones, A., Scanlon, E., Tosunoglu, C., Ross, S., Butcher, P., Murphy, P., et al. (1996). Evaluation of computer assisted learning at the Open University—15 years on. *Computers and Education, 26,* 5–15.

Jones, M. G., Jones, B. D., & Hargrove, T. Y. (2003). *The unintended consequences of high-stakes testing.* New York: Rowman & Littlefield.

Kane, M. T. (2001). Current concerns in validity theory. *Journal of Educational Measurement, 38*(4), 319–342.

Kane, M. T. (2006). Validation. In R. L. Brennan (Ed.), *Educational measurement* (4th ed., pp. 17–64). Westport, CT: Praeger.

Kane, M. T. (2008). Terminology, emphasis and utility in validation. *Educational Researcher, 37*(2), 76–82.

Kanuka, H., & Anderson, T. (1998). Online social interchange, discord and knowledge construction. *Journal of Distance Education, 13*(1), 57–74.

Kee, J. E. (1994). Benefit-cost analysis in program evaluation. In J. S. Wholey, H. P. Hatry, & K. E. Newcomer (Ed.), *Handbook of practical program evaluation* (pp. 456–488). San Francisco: Jossey-Bass.

Keegan, D. (1986). *Foundations of distance education.* New York: Croom Helm.

Keegan, D. (1993). Reintegration of the teaching acts. In D. Keegan (Ed.), *The theoretical principles of distance education* (2nd ed., pp. 113–134). New York: Routledge.

Kellaghan, T., Stufflebeam, D. L., & Wingate, L. A. (2003). Introduction. In T. Kellaghan, D. L. Stufflebeam, & L. A. Wingate (Eds.), *International handbook of educational evaluation: Part 1* (pp. 1–8). Boston: Kluwer Academic.

Kent, T. W., & McNergney, R. F. (1999). *Will technology really change education? From blackboard to web.* Thousand Oaks, CA: Sage.

King, J. (2003). The challenge of studying evaluation theory. In C. A. Christie (Eds.), *New directions for evaluation: No. 97. The practice-theory relationship in evaluation* (pp. 57–68). San Francisco: Jossey-Bass.

King, K., Pealer, L., & Bernard, A. (2001). Increasing response rates to mail questionnaires: A review of inducement strategies. *American Journal of Health Education, 32,* 4–15.

Kirkpatrick, D. L. (1998). *Evaluating training programs: The four levels* (2nd ed.). San Francisco: Berrett-Koehler.

Kirkpatrick, D. L., & Kirkpatrick, J. D. (2006). *Evaluating training programs. The four levels* (3rd ed.). San Francisco: Berrett-Koehler.

Kish, L. (1995). *Survey sampling.* New York: Wiley.

Klein, J. D., Spector, J. M., Grabowski, B., & de la Teja, I. (2004). *Instructor competencies: Standards for face-to-face, online and blended settings* (3rd ed.). Greenwich, CT: Information Age.

Klinger, S. (2002). *"Are they talking yet?" Online discourse as political action in an education policy forum.* Vancouver: Unpublished doctoral dissertation, University of British Columbia.

Knapper, C. K. (1980). *Evaluating instructional technology.* New York: Wiley.

Kozinets, R. V. (2002). The field behind the screen: Using netnography for marketing research in online communications. *Journal of Marketing Research, 39,* 61–72,

Krueger, R. A. (n.d.). *Logic models: Getting started with logic models. A guide for preparing logic models for educational programs.* Retrieved April 5, 2008, from *www.tc.umn.edu/~rkrueger/evaluation_lm.html.*

Krueger, R. A., & Casey, M. A. (2004). *Focus groups: A practical guide for applied research* (3rd ed.). Beverly Hills, CA: Sage.

Kuhn, T. S. (1987). What are scientific revolutions? In L. Kruger, L. J. Daston, & M. Heidelberger (Eds.), *The probabilistic revolution: Vol. 1. Ideas in history* (pp. 7–22). Cambridge, MA: MIT Press.

Lam, P., & McNaught, C. (2005). Building an evaluation culture and evidence base for e-learning in three Hong Kong universities. *British Journal of Educational Technology, 36*(4), 599–614.

"Learn while you drive!" (2006, October 1). *The New York Times Book Review,* p. 29.

Lecompte, M. D., & Preissle, J. (1993). *Ethnography and qualitative design in educational research* (2nd ed.). Toronto: Academic Press.

Lentz, B. E., Imm, C. S., Yost, J. B., Johnson, N. P., Barron, C., Lindberg, M. S., et al. (2004). Empowerment evaluation and organizational learning: A case study of a community coalition designed to prevent child abuse and neglect. In D. M. Fetterman & A. Wandersman (Eds.), *Empowerment evaluation: Principles in practice* (pp. 155–183). New York: Guilford Press.

Levin, H. M. (1983). *Cost-effectiveness: A primer.* Beverly Hills, CA: Sage.

Levin, H. M. (1993). *Raising educational productivity.* Retrieved September 30, 2008, from *http://www.csus.edu/indiv/l/langd/Levin.pdf*

Levin, H. M. (2001). Waiting for Godot: Cost-effectiveness analysis in education. In R. J. Light (Ed.), *New directions for evaluation: No. 90. Evaluation findings that surprise* (pp. 55–68). San Francisco: Jossey-Bass.

Lewins, A., & Silver, C. (2007). *Using software in qualitative research: A step-by-step guide.* Thousand Oaks, CA: Sage.

Lincoln, Y. S., & Guba, E. G. (1985). *Naturalistic inquiry.* Beverly Hills, CA: Sage.

Linn, R. L., Baker, E. L., & Dunbar, S. B. (1997). Complex performance-based assessment: Expectations and validation criteria. *Educational Researcher, 20*(8), 5–21.

Ljosa, E. (1993). Understanding distance education. In D. Keegan (Ed.), *Theoretical principles of distance education* (pp. 175–188). New York: Routledge.

Loevinger, J. (1957). Objective tests as instruments of psychological theory. *Psychological Reports, 3,* 635–694.

Lookatch, R. (1997). Multimedia improves learning—Apples, oranges and the type I error. *Contemporary Education, 68*(2), 110–113.

Lorenzo, G., & Moore J. C. (2002). *Report to the nation: Five pillars of quality online education.* Needham, MA: The Sloan Consortium.

Mabry, L. (2001). Responsive evaluation is to personalized assessment as. . . . In J. C. Greene & T. A. Abma (Eds.), *New directions for evaluation: No. 92. Responsive evaluation* (pp. 89–102). San Francisco: Jossey-Bass.

MacDonald, C. J., Breithaupt, K., Stodel, E. J., Farres, L. G., & Gabriel, M. A. (2002). Evaluation of web-based educational programs. *International Journal of Testing, 2*(1), 35–61.

MacPhail, F. (1998). Moving beyond statistical validity in economics. *Social Indicators Research, 45*(1), 119–149.

Madaus, G. F., & Kellaghan, T. (2000). Models, metaphors and definitions in evaluation. In D. L. Stufflebeam, G. F. Madaus, & T. Kellaghan (Eds.), *Evaluation models: Viewpoints on educational and human services evaluation* (2nd ed., pp. 19–32). Boston: Kluwer Academic.

Mahmood, A. K., & Ferneley, E. (2006). Embodied agents in e-learning environments: An exploratory case study. *Journal of Interactive Learning Research, 17*(2), 143–162.

Maki, R. H., Maki, W. S., Patterson, M., & Whittaker, P.D. (2000). Evaluation of a web-based introductory psychology course. *Behavior, Research Methods, Instruments and Computers, 32*, 212–216.

Malikowski, S. R., Thompson, M. E., & Theis, J. G. (2007). A model for research into course management systems: Bridging technology and learning theory. *Journal of Educational Computing Research, 36*, 149–173.

Mann, C. C. (1998). Quality assurance in distance education: The Surrey MA (TESOL) experience. *Distance Education, 19*(1), 7–22.

Markus, K. (1998). Science, measurement and validity: Is completion of Messick's synthesis possible? *Social Indicators Research, 45*(1), 7–34.

Martinez, R., Liu, S., Watson, W., & Bichelmeyer, B. (2006). Evaluation of a web-based master's degree program: Lessons learned from an online instructional design and technology program. *The Quarterly Review of Distance Education, 7*(3), 228–267.

Mayadas, F. A., Alfred P. Sloan Foundation, & Picciano, A. G. (2007). Blended learning and localness: The means and the end. *Journal of Asynchronous Learning Networks, 11*(1). Retrieved August 12, 2007, from *www.sloan-c.org/publications/jaln/v11n1/index.asp*.

Mayer, R. E. (1999). *The promise of educational psychology: Learning in the content areas*. Upper Saddle River, NJ: Prentice Hall.

Mayer, R. E., Heiser, J., & Lonn, S. (2001). Cognitive constraints on multimedia learning: When presenting more material results in less understanding. *Journal of Educational Psychology, 93*(1), 187–198.

McAlister, S. (1998). Credible or tentative? A model of Open University students with "low" educational qualifications. *Open Learning, 13*(3), 33–42.

McCulloch, K. H. (1997). Participatory evaluation in distance learning. *Open Learning, 12*(1), 24–30.

Mehrens, W. A. (1997). The consequences of consequential validity. *Educational Measurement: Issues and Practice, 16*(2), 16–18.

Meier, S. T., & Davis, S. R. (1990). Trends in reporting psychometric properties of scales used in counseling psychology research. *Journal of Counseling Psychology, 37*, 113–115.

Melton, R. F. (1995). Developing a formative evaluation system for distance teaching. *Open Learning, 10*(2), 53–57.

Menzies, H. (1996). *Whose brave new world? The information highway and the new economy.* Toronto: Between the Lines.

Merriam, S. B. (2002). *Qualitative research in practice: Examples for discussion and analysis.* San Francisco: Jossey-Bass.

Merrill, M. D. (2002). A pebble-in-the-pond model for instructional design. *Performance Improvement, 417,* 39–44.

Merrill, M. D. (2007). A task-centered instructional strategy. *Journal of Research on Technology in Education, 40*(1), 33–50.

Mertens, D. (2004). *Research and evaluation in education and psychology: Integrating diversity with quantitative, qualitative and mixed methods* (2nd ed.). Thousand Oaks, CA: Sage.

Messick, S. (1988). The once and future issues of validity: Assessing the meaning and consequences of measurement. In H. Wainer & H. I. Braun (Eds.), *Test validity* (pp. 33–45). Hillsdale, NJ: Erlbaum.

Messick, S. (1989). Validity. In R. L. Linn (Ed.), *Educational measurement* (3rd ed., pp. 13–103). New York: MacMillan.

Messick, S. (1994). The interplay of evidence and consequences in the validation of performance assessments. *Educational Researcher, 23*(2), 13–23.

Messick, S. (1995a). Standards of validity and the validity of standards in performance assessment. *Educational Measurement: Issues and Practices, 14*(4), 5–8.

Messick, S. (1995b). Validity of psychological assessment. Validation of inferences from persons' responses and performances as scientific inquiry into score meaning. *American Psychologist, 50*(9), 741–749.

Messick, S. (1996). Validity and washback in language testing. *Language Testing, 13*(3), 241–256.

Messick, S. (1998). Test validity: A matter of consequence. *Social Indicators Research, 45*(1), 35–44.

Miles, M. B., & Huberman, A. M. (1994). *Qualitative data analysis: An expanded sourcebook* (2nd ed.). Thousand Oaks, CA: Sage.

Miller, R. L., & Campbell, R. (2006). Taking stock of empowerment evaluation: An empirical review. *American Journal of Evaluation, 27,* 296–319.

Ministry of Advanced Education, Training and Technology, Government of British Columbia. (2000). *Charting a new course. Part 1: The context.* Retrieved April 16, 2008, from *www.aved.gov.bc.ca/serviceplans/annualreports/98_99/ar9899.pdf.*

Moisey, S. D., Ally, M., & Spencer, B. (2006). Factors affecting the development and use of learning objects. *American Journal of Distance Education, 20,* 143–161.

Molenda, M. (1997). Historical and philosophical foundations of instructional design: A North American view. In R. D. Tennyson, F. Shott, N. Seel, & S. Dijkstra (Ed.), *Instructional design: International perspectives. Volume 1: Theory, research and models* (pp. 41–53). Mahwah, NJ: Erlbaum.

Moore, M., & Kearsley, G. (1996). *Distance education: A systems view.* Toronto: Wadsworth.

Moss, P. (1998a). Recovering a dialectical view of rationality. *Social Indicators Research, 45*(1), 55–67.

Moss, P. (1998b). The role of consequences in validity theory. *Educational Measurement: Issues and Practice, 17*(2), 6–12.

Nardi, P. M. (2006). *Doing survey research: A guide to quantitative methods* (2nd ed.). New York: Pearson.

NASA Dryden Learning Technologies Project. (2007). *Anchored instruction.* Retrieved February 12, 2007, from *www.ed.psu.edu/nasa/achrtxt.html.*

National Commission for the Protection of Human Subjects of Biomedical and Behavioral Research. (1979, April 18). *The Belmont report: Ethical principles and guidelines for the protection of human subjects of research.* Retrieved April 18, 2008, from *ohsr.od.nih.gov/guidelines/belmont.html.*

National Science Foundation, Division of Research, Evaluation and Communication, Directorate for Education and Human Resources. (2007). *OERL: Online evaluation resource library.* Retrieved December 10, 2007, from *oerl.sri.com/home.html.*

Nielsen, J. (2000). *Designing web usability: The practice of simplicity.* Indianapolis, IN: New Riders Publishing.

Noble, D. F. (1998). Digital diploma mills: The automation of higher education. Retrieved October 23 2008, from *http://www.firstmonday.org/issues/issue3_1/index.html*

Noble, D. F. (2003). *Digital diploma mills: The automation of higher education.* Toronto: Between the Lines.

North American Council for Online Learning. (2007). *National standards of quality for online courses.* Retrieved September 22, 2007, from *www.nacol.org/nationalstandards/.*

North American Council for Online Learning and the Partnership for 21st century skills. (2006, November). *Virtual schools and 21st century skills. Retrieved April 16, 2008, from www.21stcenturyskills.org/documents/Vsand21stCenturySkillsFINALPaper.pdf.*

Oakes, J. M. (2002). Risks and wrongs in social science research: An evaluator's guide to the IRB. *Evaluation Review, 26*(5), 443–479.

Offerman, M., & Tassava, C. (2006). A different perspective on blended learning: Asserting the efficacy of online learning at Capella University. In C. J. Bonk & C. R. Graham (Eds.), *The handbook of blended learning: Global perspectives local designs* (pp. 235–244). San Francisco: Wiley.

Office of the Under Secretary of Defense for Personnel and Readiness. (2007). *Advanced Distributed Learning. Retrieved April 16, 2008, from www.adlnet.gov/about/index.aspx.*

O'Graw, K. D., & Williams, J. E. (2006). Psychology experiments: A web-based resource for enhancing science training through simulations. In S. Glen, K. E. Partney, D. Relberger, & C. Thorsen (Eds.), *Virtual decisions* (pp. 67–87). Mahwah, NJ: Erlbaum.

Ongbuwezie, A. (2006, April). *A taxonomy of mixed methods*. Paper presented at the annual conference of the American Educational Research Association. San Francisco, CA.

Organization for Economic Co-operation and Development. (1999). *No significant difference*. Paris: Author.

Parlett, M., & Hamilton, D. (1977). Evaluation as illumination: A new approach to the study of innovatory programmes. In D. Hamilton, D. Jenkins, C. King, B. McDonald, & M. Parlett (Eds.), *Beyond the numbers game: A reader in educational evaluation* (pp. 6–22). Basingstoke, UK: Macmillan.

Patrick, S., & Levin, D. (2007). *Virtual schools and 21st century skills, NECC presentation*. Retrieved October 15, 2007, from *www.nacol.org/resources/*.

Patton, M. Q. (1990). *Qualitative evaluation and research methods*. Newbury Park, CA: Sage.

Patton, M. Q. (1997). *Utilization-focussed evaluation: The new century text* (3rd ed.). Newbury Park, CA: Sage.

Patton, M. Q. (2000). Overview: Language matters. In R. K. Hopson (Ed.), *New directions for evaluation: No. 86. How and why language matters in evaluation* (pp. 5–16). San Francisco: Jossey-Bass.

Pesl Murphrey, T., & Dooley, K. E. (2006). Determining e-learning competencies: Using Centra to collect focus group data. *Quarterly Review of Distance Education, 7*(1), 75–82.

Peters, O. (1993). Distance education in a postindustrial society. In D. Keegan (Ed.), *Theoretical principles of distance education* (pp. 39–60). New York: Routledge.

Phipps, R. A., & Merisotas, J. (2000). *Quality on the line: Benchmarks for success in Internet-based distance education*. Washington, DC: Institute for Higher Education Policy.

Piaget, J. (1967). *Biology and knowledge: An essay on the relations between organic regulations and cognitive processes*. Chicago: University of Chicago Press.

Picciano, A. (2002). Beyond student perceptions: Issues of interaction, presence, and performance in an online course. *Journal of Asynchronous Learning Networks, 6*(1), 21–40. Retrieved October 5, 2007, from *www.aln.org/publications/jaln/v6n1/v6n1_picciano.asp*.

Plake, B. S., & Impare, J. C. (2001). *Fourteenth mental measurements yearbook*. Lincoln: Buros Institute of Mental Measurements, University of Nebraska-Lincoln.

Popham, W. J. (1993). *Educational evaluation*. Toronto: Allyn & Bacon.

Popham, W. J. (1995). *Classroom assessment: What teachers need to know*. Boston: Allyn & Bacon.

Popham, W. J. (1997). Consequential validity: Right concern—wrong concept. *Educational Measurement: Issues and Practice, 16*(2), 9–13.

Popham, W. J. (2004). *America's failing schools*. New York: Routledge Falmer.

Qayyum, A., & Bates, A. W. (1999). Case #7. Learning through new technologies: The response of adult learners to Microsoft Certified Engineer Program at Burnaby Community Skills Centre. Retrieved February 10, 2001, from *http://det.cstudies.ubc.ca/detsite/framewhat-index.html*

Read, B. (2006, September 1). "Wikimania" participants give the online encyclopedia mixed reviews. *The Chronicle of Higher Education.* Retrieved September 10, 2006, from *chronicle.com/weekly/v53/i02/02a06201.htm.*

Reckase, M. D. (1998a). Consequential validity from the test developer's perspective. *Educational Measurement: Issues and Practice, 17*(2), 13–16.

Reckase, M. D. (1998b). The interaction of values and validity assessment: Does a test's level of validity depend on a researcher's values? *Social Indicators Research, 45*(1), 45–54.

Reigeluth, C. M. (1999). *Instructional design theories and models: A new paradigm of instructional theory: Volume 2.* Mahwah, NJ: Erlbaum.

Reigeluth, C. M., & Frick, T. (1999). Formative research: A methodology for creating and improving design theories. In C. M. Reigeluth (Ed.), *Instructional-design theories and models: A new paradigm of instructional theory* (Vol. 2, pp. 633–651). Mahwah, NJ: Erlbaum.

Richards, L. (2005). *Handling qualitative data: A practical guide.* Thousand Oaks, CA: Sage.

Ritchie, D., & Earnest, J. (1999). The future of instructional design: Results of a Delphi study. *Educational Technology, 39,* 35–42.

Roberts, T. (Ed.). (2006). *Self, peer and group assessment in e-learning.* Hershey, PA: Information Science.

Roberts, T. G., Drani, T. A., Telg, W., & Lundy, L. L. (2005). The development of an instrument to evaluate distance education courses using student attitudes. *American Journal of Distance Education, 19*(1), 51–64.

Robson, J. (2000). Evaluating on-line teaching. *Open Learning, 15*(2), 151–171.

Rogers, P. J., Petrosino, A., Huebner, T. A., & Hacsi, T. A. (2000). Program theory evaluation: Practice, promise and problems. In D. J. Rog & D. Fournier (Eds.), *New directions for evaluation: No. 76. Progress and Future directions in evaluation: Perspectives on theory, practice and methods* (pp. 5–14). San Francisco: Jossey-Bass.

Ross, S. M., & Morrison, G. R. (1997). Measurement and evaluation approaches in instructional design: Historical roots and current perspectives. In R. D. Tennyson, F. Schott, N. Seel, & S. Dijkstra (Eds.), *Instructional design: International perspectives: Vol. 1. Theory, research and models* (pp. 327–351). Mahwah, NJ: Erlbaum.

Rossi, P., Freeman, H., & Lipsey, M. (1999). *Evaluation: A systematic approach* (6th ed.). Thousand Oaks, CA: Sage.

Rossman, P. (1992). *The emerging worldwide electronic university.* Westport, CT: Greenwood Press.

Rowley, D., Lujan, H., & Dolence, M. (1998). *Strategic choices for the academy: How demand for lifelong learning will re-create higher education.* San Francisco: Jossey-Bass.

Rubin, H. J., & Rubin, I. S. (2005). *Qualitative interviewing: The art of hearing data* (2nd ed.). Thousand Oaks, CA: Sage.

Ruhe, V. (1998). E-mail exchanges: Teaching language, culture and technology for the 21st century. *TESL Canada Journal, 16*(1), 88–95.

Ruhe, V. (2002a). *A course in writing effectively for UNHCR: Evaluation report.* Unpublished manuscript, Commonwealth of Learning.

Ruhe, V. (2002b). Issues in the validation of assessment in technology-based distance and distributed learning: What can we learn from Messick's framework? *International Journal of Testing, 2*(2), 143–159.

Ruhe, V. (2003). Applying Messick's framework to the evaluation data of distance/distributed instructional programs. (Doctoral dissertation, University of British Columbia).

Ruhe, V., & Bates, T. (1999a). Case #5. Learning through new technologies: The response of adult learners to German 430. Unpublished manuscript, University of British Columbia.

Ruhe, V., & Bates, T. (1999b). Case #12. Learning through new technologies: The response of adult learners to Psychology 101. Unpublished manuscript, University of British Columbia.

Ruhe, V., Qayyum, A., & Bates, T. (1999). A cross-case comparison of the "Learning Through New Technologies: The Response of Adult Learners" Project. Unpublished manuscript, University of British Columbia.

Ruhe, V., & Zumbo, B. D. (2006). Using Messick's framework to validate assessment tasks in online environments: A course in writing effectively for UNHCR. In D. Williams, S. L. Howell, & M. Hricko (Eds.), *Online assessment, measurement and evaluation: Emerging practices* (pp. 203–226). Hershey, PA: Idea Group.

Rumberger, R. W. (2003). The advantages of longitudinal design In G. D. Haertl & B. Means (Eds.), *Evaluating educational technology: Effective research designs for improving learning* (pp. 205–229). New York: Teachers College Press.

Rumble, G. (1981). Evaluating autonomous multimedia distance education systems: A practical approach. *Distance Education, 21,* 64–90.

Salomon, G. (Ed.). (1993). *Distributed cognitions: Psychological and educational considerations.* New York: Cambridge University Press.

Sandholtz, J. H., Ringstaff, C., & Dwyer, D. C. (1997). *Teaching with technology: Creating student-centered classrooms.* New York: Teachers College, Columbia University.

Saris, W. E., & Gallhofer, I. N. (2007). *Design, evaluation, and analysis of questionnaires for survey research.* Hoboken, NJ: Wiley.

Sauve, L. (1993). What's behind the development of a course on the concept of distance education? In D. Keegan (Ed.), *Theoretical principles of distance education* (pp. 93–112). New York: Routledge.

Scanlon, E., Jones, A., Barnard, J., Thompson, J., & Calder, J. (2000). Evaluating information and communication technologies for learning. *Educational Technology and Society, 3*(4), 1–10. Retrieved February 14, 2004, from *ifets. ieee.org/periodical/vol_4_2000/ scanlon.html.*

Schaik, P. V., & Ling, J. (2005). The psychometric evaluation of educational intranets. *Journal of Educational Computing Research, 33*(1), 81–100.

Schiffman, S., Vignare, K., & Geith, C. (2007). Why do higher-education institutions pursue online education? *Journal of Asynchronous Learning Networks,*

11(2). Retrieved August 12, 2007, from *www.sloan-c.org/publications/jaln/v11n2/index.asp.*

Schlosser, L. A., & Simonson, M. R. (2006). *Distance education: Definition and glossary of terms.* Charlotte, NC: Information Age.

Schwartz, D. L., Bransford, J. D., & Sears, D. (2005). Efficiency and innovation in transfer. In J. P. Mestre (Ed.), *Transfer of learning from a modern multidisciplinary perspective* (pp. 1–51). Charlotte, NC: Information Age.

Schwartz D., Lin, X., Brophy, S., & Bransford, J.D. (1999). Toward the development of flexibly adaptive instructional designs. In C. M. Reigeluth (Ed.), *Instructional design theories and models: A new paradigm of instructional theory* (Vol. 2, pp. 183–213). Mahwah, NJ: Erlbaum.

Scriven, M. (1972). Pros and cons about goal-free evaluation. *Evaluation Comment, 3*(4), 1–8.

Scriven, M. (1993). The nature of evaluation. In M. Scriven (Ed.), New directions in evaluation: No. 58. Special issue: Hard-won lessons in program evaluation (pp. 5–48). San Francisco: Jossey-Bass.

Scriven, M. (2003). Evaluation theory and metatheory. In T. Kellagan, D. L. Stufflebeam, & L. A. Wingate (Eds.), *International handbook of educational evaluation: part 1* (pp. 15–30). Boston: Kluwer Academic.

Scriven, M. (2004, October). Key evaluation checklist. Retrieved April 4, 2008, from *www.wmich/edu/evalctr/checklists/kec.htm.*

Scriven, M. (n.d.). *Evaluation: The sleeper discipline awakes: Evaluation in its own right.* Retrieved April 5, 2008, from *64.233.167.104/search?q=cache:pbz7ANc nKOIJ:homepages.wmich.edu/~mscriven/THE%2520SLEEPER%2520DISCI PLINE%2520AWAKES.doc+%22program+evaluation+is+a+profession%22& hl=en&ct=clnk&cd=2&gl=us.*

Seel, N. (1997). Models of instructional design: Introduction and overview. In R. D. Tennyson, F. Shott, N. Seel, & S. Dijkstra (Ed.), *Instructional design: International perspectives: Vol. 1. Theory, research and models* (pp. 355–360). Mahwah, NJ: Erlbaum.

Seel, N. & Winn, W. D. (1997). Research on media and learning: Distributed cognition and semiotics. In R. B. Tennyson, F. Schott, S. Dijkstra, & N. Seel (Eds.), *Instructional design, international perspectives* (Vol. 1, pp. 293–326). Mahwah, NJ: Erlbaum.

Seely Brown, J. S., & Duguid, P. (2000). *The social life of information.* Boston: Harvard Business School Press.

Selwyn, E. (1997). The continuing weakness of educational computing research. *British Journal of Educational Technology, 28*(4), 305–307.

Sener, J., & Humbert, J. (2002). *Student satisfaction with online learning: An expanding universe.* Available at *sln.suny.edu/sln/public/original.nsf/dd93a8da0b7ccce08 52567b00054e2b6/755285ffb5847a4385256c3c006246ea/$FILE/Student%20 Satisfaction%20-%20John%20Sener%20and%20Joeann%20Humbert.doc.*

Sener, J., & J. Humbert, J. (2003). Student satisfaction with online learning: An expanding universe. In J. Bourne & J. Moore (Eds.), *Elements of quality online education: Practice and direction* (Vol. 4, pp. 245–259). Needham, MA: The Sloan Consortium.

Seok, S. (2007). Standards, accreditation, benchmarks and guidelines in distance education. *Quarterly Review of Distance Education, 8*(4), 387–398.

Shalinsky, A. (1998). *Microsoft certified systems engineer orientation guide for Burnaby Community Skills Centre.* Burnaby, BC: Open Learning Agency, Workplace Training Systems.

Shannon, D, M., & Bradshaw, C. C. (2002). A comparison of response rate, response time, and costs of mail and electronic surveys, *Journal of Experimental Education, 70*(2), 179–192.

Shea, P. (2007). Bridges and barriers to teaching online college courses: A study of experienced online faculty in thirty-six colleges. *Journal of Asynchronous Learning Networks, 11*(2). Retrieved August 12, 2007, from *www.sloan-c.org/publications/jaln/v11n2/index.asp.*

Sheehan, M., & Jafari, A. (2003). *Designing portals: Opportunities and challenges.* Hershey, PA: Idea Group.

Shen, J., Hiltz, S. R., & Bieber, M. (2006). Collaborative online examinations: Impacts on interaction, learning, and student satisfaction. *IEEE Transactions on Systems, Man, and Cybernetics, Part A: Systems and Humans, 36,* 1045–1053.

Shepard, L. A. (1997). The centrality of test use and consequences for test validity. *Educational Measurement: Issues and Practice, 16*(2), 5–8.

Sidani, S., & Sechrest, L. (1999). Putting program theory into operation. *American Journal of Evaluation, 20*(2), 227–238.

Simonson, M. (2006). Growing by degrees. *Quarterly Review of Distance Education, 7*(2), 1–2.

Simonson, M., Schlosser, C., & Hanson, D. (1999). Theory and distance education: A new discussion. *American Journal of Distance Education, 13*(1), 60–75.

Simonson, M., Smaldino, S. E., Albright, M., & Zvacek, S. (2008). *Teaching and learning at a distance: Foundations of distance education* (4th ed.). Upper Saddle River, NJ: Prentice-Hall.

Simpson, W. B. (1991). *Cost containment for higher education: Strategies for public policy and institutional administration.* New York: Praeger.

Sinclair, G., McClaren, M., & Griffin, M. J. (2006). *E-learning and beyond.* Victoria, BC: British Columbia Ministry of Advanced Education.

Singer, E. A., Jr. (1959). In C. W. Churchman (Ed.), *Experience and reflection.* Philadelphia: University of Pennsylvania Press.

Skinner, B. F. (1965). *Science and human behavior.* New York: The Free Press.

Smith, A., Armstrong, M., & Brown, S. (1999). *Benchmark and threshold standards in higher education.* London: Kogan Page.

Snow, R. E. (1997). Individual differences. In R. D. Tennyson, F. Schott, N. Seel, & S. Dijkstra (Eds.), *Instructional design: International perspectives: Vol. 1. Theory, research and models* (pp. 215–242). Mahwah, NJ: Erlbaum.

South Central Regional Library Council Distance Learning Glossary (2002). Retrieved April 5, 2008, from *www.lakenet.org/training/dlglossary.html.*

Southern Regional Educational Board, Educational Technology Cooperative. (2006). Online teaching evaluation for state virtual schools. Retrieved October 15, 2007, from *www.sreb.org/programs/EdTech/pubs/2006Pubs/06T04_Online_teaching_evaluation_checklist.pdf.*

Southern Regional Educational Board, Educational Technology Cooperative. (2007a). *Checklist for evaluating SREB-SCORE learning objects.* Retrieved October 15, 2007, from *www.sreb.org/programs/EdTech/pubs/pubsindex.asp.*

Southern Regional Educational Board, Educational Technology Cooperative. (2007b). Evaluation criteria for SREB-SCORE learning objects. Retrieved October 15, 2007, from *www.sreb.org/programs/EdTech/pubs/2007pubs/07T04_Eval_Crit_SCORE_Lrn.pdf.*

Southern Regional Educational Board. (2007c). *State virtual schools—Successes and growing pains.* Retrieved October 15, 2007, from *www.sreb.org/programs/EdTech/pubs/2007pubs/07T06_Summary_Report_state_virtual.pdf.*

Stake, R. E. (1967). The countenance of educational evaluation. *Teachers College Record, 68,* 523–540.

Stake, R. E. (1995). *The art of case study research.* London: Sage.

Stoesz, P. R. (2005). *Exploring the intersection of ethics and method in evaluation practice: An MDS study of compatibility and conflict within the program evaluation standards* (2nd ed.). Unpublished master's thesis, University of British Columbia, Vancouver.

Stoesz, P. R., & Zumbo, B. D. (2003, June). *Ascertaining the dimensions of compatibility, conflict and compromise among the program evaluation standards.* Paper presented at the annual meeting of the Canadian Evaluation Society, Vancouver, BC.

Stoll, C. (1999). *High-tech heretic: Why computers don't belong in the classroom and other reflections by a computer contrarian.* New York: Random House.

Strijker, A. (2004). *Reuse of learning objects in context: Human and technical issues.* Enschede, the Netherlands: PrintPartners.

Strober, E. (2005). Is power sharing possible?: Using empowerment evaluation with parents and nurses in a pediatric hospital transplantation setting. *Human Organization, 64*(2), 201–210.

Stroupe, C. (2007). *COMP 5250, New media writing, University of Minnesota at Duluth. Gathering.* Retrieved October 15, 2007, from *www.d.umn.edu/~cstroupe/f06/5250/gathering.html.*

Stufflebeam, D. L. (2001). *Evaluation models.* In D. L. Stufflebeam, *New directions for evaluation: No. 89* (pp. 7–98). San Francisco: Jossey-Bass.

Stufflebeam, D. L. (2004). The 21st-century CIPP model: Origins, development, and use. In M. C. Alkin (Ed.), *Evaluation roots* (pp. 245–266). Thousand Oaks: Sage.

Stufflebeam, D. L., Foley, W. J., Gephart, W. J., Guba, E. G., Hammond, R. I., Merriam, H. O., et al. (1971). *Educational evaluation and decision-making.* Bloomington, IN: Phi Delta Kappa.

Stufflebeam, D. L., & Shinkfield, A. J. (2007). *Evaluation theory, models, and applications.* San Francisco: Jossey-Bass/Pfeiffer.

Suen, H., & Stevens, R. (1993). Analytic considerations in distance education research. *American Journal of Distance Education, 7*(3), 61–69.

Tallent-Runnels, M. K., Thomas, J. A., Lan, W. Y., Cooper, S., Ahern, T. C., Shaw, S. M., et al. (2006). Teaching courses online: A review of the research. *Review of Educational Research, 76*(1), 93–135.

Tashakkori, A., & Teddlie, C. (1998). *Mixed methodology: Combining qualitative and quantitative approaches.* Thousand Oaks, CA: Sage.

Tashakkori, A., & Teddlie, C. (Eds.). (2003). *Handbook of mixed methods in social and behavioural research.* Thousand Oaks, CA: Sage.

Taylor-Powell, E., & Henert, E. (2008, February). *Developing a logic model: Teaching and training guide.* Madison, WI: Board of Regents of the University of Wisconsin System. Retrieved April 8, 2008, from *www.uwex.edu/ces.pdande/evaluation/pdf/lmguidecomplete.pdf.*

Tenner, A. R. (1996). *Why things bite back: Technology and the revenge of unintended consequences.* New York: Knopf.

Tennyson, R. D. (1997). A system dynamics approach to instructional systems development. In R. D. Tennyson, F. Shott, N. Seel, & S. Dijkstra (Eds.), *Instructional design: International perspectives: Vol. 1. Theory, research and models* (pp. 413–426). Mahwah, NJ: Erlbaum.

Tennyson, R. D., & Elmore, R. L. (1997). Learning theory foundations for instructional development. In R. D. Tennyson, F. Shott, N. Seel, & S. Dijkstra (Eds.), *Instructional design: International perspectives: Vol. 1. Theory, research and models* (pp. 55–78). Mahwah, NJ: Erlbaum.

Thorndike, E. L. (1913). *Education psychology.* New York: Routledge.

TLT Group. (2008a). The flashlight program. Retrieved April 9, 2008, from *www.tltgroup.org/flashlightp.htm.*

TLT Group. (2008b). Flashlight templates. Retrieved April 5, 2008, from *www.tltgroup.org/Flashlight/FLO/Templates.htm.*

Tobias, S. (2006). The importance of motivation, metacognition, and help seeking in web-based learning. In H. F. O'Neil, Jr. & R. S. Perez (Eds.), *Web-based learning: Theory, research and practice* (pp. 203–220). Hillsdale, NJ: Erlbaum.

Tyler, R. W. (1942). General statement on evaluation. *Journal of Educational Research, 35,* 492–501.

Universitas 21. (2008). About Universitas 21. Retrieved September 19, 2008, from *http://www.universitas21.com/about.html*

U.S. Department of Education, Office of Innovation and Improvement. (2007). *Star schools program.* Retrieved October 15, 2007, from *www.ed.gov/programs/starschools/eval.html.*

U.S. General Accounting Office, Program Evaluation and Methodology Division. (1990). *Case study evaluations.* Washington, DC: U.S. Government Printing Office.

Van Dusen, G. C. (2000). *Digital dilemma: Issues of access, cost, and quality in media-enhanced and distance education.* San Francisco: Jossey-Bass.

van Dijk, T. A. (1998). *Ideology: A multi-disciplinary approach.* Thousand Oaks, CA: Sage.

Van Horn, R. (1998). Power tools: Tomorrow's high-performance courseware: A rough sketch. *Phi Delta Kappa, 79*(7), 556–558.

Van Maanen, J. (1988). *Tales of the field: On writing ethnography.* Chicago: University of Chicago Press.

Van Slyke, C., Kittner, M., & Belanger, F. (1998). *Distance education: A telecommuting perspective. In Proceedings of the fourth America's conference on information systems* (pp. 666–668). Retrieved April 18, 2008, from *aisel.isworld.org/article_by_author.asp?Author_ID=479.*

Virvou, M., & Kabassi, K. (2002). Reasoning about users' actions in a graphical user interface. *Human-Computer Interaction, 17*(4), 369–398.

Visscher-Voerman, I., & Gustafson, K. L. (2004). Paradigms in the theory and practice of education and training design. *Educational Technology: Research and Development, 52*(2), 69–89.

Watson, J. F. (2007). *A national primer on K–12 online learning.* Vienna, VA: North American Council for Online Learning.

Weiss, C. H. (1986). The stakeholder approach to evaluation. In E. R. House (Ed.), *New directions for program evaluation: No. 19* (pp. 145–157). San Francisco: Jossey-Bass.

Weiss, C. H. (1998). *Evaluation: Methods for studying programs and policies* (2nd ed.). Upper Saddle River, NJ: Prentice Hall.

Wellburn, E. (1999). Educational vision, theory, and technology for virtual learning in K–12: Perils, possibilities, and pedagogical decisions. In C. Feyten & J. Nutta (Eds.), *Virtual instruction: Issues and insights from an international perspective* (pp. 35–64). Englewood, CO: Libraries Unlimited.

West, R. E., Waddoups, G., & Graham, C. R. (2007). Understanding the experiences of instructors as they adopt a course management system. *Educational Technology, Research and Development, 55*, 1–26.

Wholey, J. S. (1987). Evaluability assessment: Developing program theory. In L. Bickman (Ed.), *New directions for evaluation: No. 33. Using program theory in evaluation* (pp. 77–92). San Francisco: Jossey-Bass.

Wihoit, G. (2007, November 9). Why online learning is important to states. Presentation at The Virtual School Changing the Course of Education Symposium. Retrieved October 15, 2007, from *www.nacol.org/events/vss/speakers.php.*

Willis, B. (1993). *Distance education: A practical guide.* Englewood Cliffs, NJ: Educational Technology.

Willis, B. (1994). Distance education: Obstacles and opportunities. *Educational Technology, 34*, 34–36.

Willis, B., & University of Idaho Engineering Outreach Staff. (2006). *Distance education at a glance. Guide 13: Glossary of distance education terminology.* Retrieved September 10, 2006, from *www.uidaho.edu/eo/dist13.html.*

Willis, J. (2000). The maturing of constructivist instructional design: Some basic principles that can guide practice. *Educational Technology, 40*(1), 5–16.

Wilson, M., Qayyum, A., & Boshier, R. (1998). Worldwide America: Think globally, click locally. *Distance Education, 19*(1), 109–123.

Wolf, R. M. (1987). The nature of education evaluation. *International Journal of Educational Research, 1*, 7–20.

Woodley, A., & McIntosh, N. (1980). *The door stood open: An evaluation of the Open University younger learners' pilot scheme.* Barcome, UK: Falmer Press.

Worthen, B., Sanders, J., & Fitzpatrick, J. (1997). *Program evaluation: Alternative approaches and practical guidelines.* New York: Longman.

Yorke, M., & Longden, B. (2004). *Retention and student success in higher education.* Berkshire, UK: McGraw-Hill Education.

Zaharias, P. (2005). E-learning design quality: A holistic conceptual framework. In C. Howard, J. Boettcher, L. Justice, P. Rogers, & G. A. Berg (Eds.), *Encyclopedia of distance learning* (pp. 763–771). New York: Idea Group.

Zaharias, P. V. (2004). *Developing a usability evaluation method for e-learning applications: From functional usability to motivation to learn.* Retrieved September 8, 2007, from *www.eltrun.gr/eltrun/phd-studies/completed-phds/a-usability-evaluation-method-for-e-learning-courses-1/paper-of-phd-thesis-dr-zaharias.doc/file.*

Zhang, J., Sun, Y., Wang, X., & Wu, G. (2003). An analysis of learners' interactions with course package and learning support services in distance learning. In G. Richards (Ed.), *Proceedings of World Conference on E-Learning in Corporate, Government, Healthcare, and Higher Education 2003* (pp. 361–368). Chesapeake, VA: AACE. Retrieved September 8, 2007, from *www.editlib. org/index.cfm?fuseaction=Reader.ViewAbstract&paper_id=14954.*

Zigrell, J. (1991). *The uses of television in American higher education.* New York: Praeger.

Zumbo, B. D. (Ed.). (1998). Opening remarks to the special issue on validity theory and the methods used in validation: Perspectives from the social and behavioral sciences. *Social Indicators Research: An International and Interdisciplinary Journal for Quality-of-Life Measurement, 45*, 1–3.

Zumbo, B. D. (2007). Validity: Foundational issues and statistical methodology. In C. R. Rao & S. Sinharay (Eds.), *Handbook of statistics, 26, Psychometrics* (pp. 45–79). Amsterdam, The Netherlands: Elsevier Science B.V.

Author Index

Abma, T. A., 83
Agar, M. H., 138
Aggarwal, A. K., 186
Albright, M., 59
Algina, J., 77
Alkin, M. C., 11, 25–27, 27–39, 74
Allen, I. E., 4
Ally, M., 150
Anderson, T., 61, 140, 161, 200
Andrusyszyn, M., 60
Angoff, W. H., 75, 76
Armstrong, M., 170
Attwell, G., 43, 47–48, 57
Awalt, C., 2, 163, 175, 244

Baker, E. L., 9, 25, 50, 54, 56, 57, 94, 147, 209
Banathy, B. H., 194
Barnard, J., 45–46
Bartolic-Zlomislic, S., 65, 160, 162
Bassey, M., 115
Bates, A. W., 2, 42, 43, 45, 56, 57, 65, 66, 70, 71, 154, 158, 159, 160, 162, 168, 175, 179, 181, 187, 190, 197, 213, 220
Bates, T., 127, 134, 141, 160, 196
Bejar, I., 77
Belanger, F., 42, 43–45, 57, 58, 65, 197
Benbunan-Fich, R., 178
Bendus, O., 109, 121, 244
Berg, B. L., 97, 98, 104, 106, 108, 136, 139, 141

Bernard, A., 131
Bett, S., 197
Bichelmeyer, B., 62
Bickman, L., 34
Bieber, M., 177
Black, E. W., 121
Blustein, H., 169, 198
Boshier, R., 69
Bourdeau, J., 159, 168, 179, 190, 197
Bourne, J. R., 191
Bowers, J., 176, 179, 181
Boyd, A., 68
Brabazon, T., 69, 72, 174, 189, 190
Bradshaw, C. C., 131
Bransford, J. D., 180, 182, 199
Breithaupt, K., 31
Breuch, L. K., 178
Brophy, S., 199
Brown, J. S., 176, 181
Brown, S., 170
Buchner, A., 114
Bunch, M. B., 245
Bunderson, C. V., 42, 50, 55–56, 57, 71, 72, 238

Caines, M., 94
Calder, J., 45–46
Campbell, D., 28
Campbell, R., 37, 38
Caracelli, V. J., 24, 37, 39, 60, 83, 108
Casey, M. A., 138, 139

290

Subject Index

"f" following a page number indicates a figure;
"t" following a page number indicates a table

About the Authors

Valerie Ruhe, PhD, has worked extensively in the field of evaluation and assessment. She has 10 years of professional program evaluation experience in distance education, K–12, and higher education. Most recently she was an Assessment and Evaluation Consultant at the Center for Teaching and Learning at the University of Minnesota, where she advised faculty and departments on program evaluation and student assessment. In 2008 she returned to her alma mater, the University of British Columbia, where she is an Evaluation Studies Specialist. Dr. Ruhe has published articles on the validity of online assessments in the *International Journal of Testing*; two statewide, record linkage evaluation studies of a national reading program in *Spectrum: A Journal for School Administrators*; and a chapter on online assessment in *Online Assessment, Measurement and Evaluation: Emerging Practices*.

Bruno D. Zumbo, PhD, is Professor of Measurement, Evaluation, and Research Methodology, and of Statistics at the University of British Columbia. He is widely published in research methodology, validity and validation processes, as well as in statistical science and program evaluation methodology. Dr. Zumbo's work has had wide-ranging influence across many fields in the social, educational, and health sciences. His many accomplishments include, most notably, serving as the editor of the *International Journal of Testing* from 2001 to 2004 and as guest editor of the special issue on Messick's validity framework in *Social Indicators Research: An International and Interdisciplinary Journal for Quality-of-Life Measurement*. He is also the recipient of the 2005 Samuel J. Messick Memorial Award in recognition of his many contributions to foundational and methodological issues in validity and psychometrics.